GETTING YOUR BOSS'S NUMBER

Getting Your Boss's Number

AND MANY OTHER WAYS TO
USE THE ENNEAGRAM AT WORK

Michael J. Goldberg

HarperSanFrancisco
An Imprint of HarperCollins*Publishers*

GETTING YOUR BOSS'S NUMBER: *And Many Other Ways to Use the Enneagram at Work*. Copyright © 1996 by Michael J. Goldberg. All rights reserved. Printed in the United States of America. No part of this book may be used or reproduced in any manner whatsoever without written permission except in the case of brief quotations embodied in critical articles and reviews. For information address HarperCollins Publishers, 10 East 53rd Street, New York, NY 10022.

HarperCollins Web Site: http://www.harpercollins.com

HarperCollins®, ⬛ ®, HarperSanFrancisco™, and A TREE CLAUSE BOOK® are trademarks of HarperCollins Publishers Inc.

FIRST EDITION

Library of Congress Cataloging-in-Publication Data
Goldberg, Michael J.
    Getting your boss's number : and many other ways to use the enneagram at work / Michael J. Goldberg.
    Includes bibliographical references.
    ISBN 0–06–251298–6 (cloth)
    ISBN 0–06–251325–7 (pbk.)
    ISBN 0–06–251468–7 (intl. pbk.)
    1. Enneagram.   2. Typology (Psychology).   3. Managing your boss.   I. Title.
BF698.35.E54G65   1996
158.7—dc20   96–20586

96 97 98 99 00 RRD(H) 10 9 8 7 6 5 4 3 2 1

CONTENTS

INTRODUCTION

Harry, an ardent, young (but already senior) marketing executive for a major software developer, was on the phone with a question. A real go-getter and an accomplished deal-maker, he was a Three—a can-do, workaholic, get-it-done type. Harry's company had been bought out by a large traditional firm, and now Harry had to report to his "warden," as he put it, "who doesn't understand the business."

Quickly, we typed the new boss: his knee-jerk tendency to say no, his paranoia, the tendency to blame and assume the worst: he was a Six. The problem crystallized: a go-go Three is a cautious, prudent Six's worst nightmare.

"Tell him," I said, "what you can't do. Why things won't work. Explain where your projects are vulnerable."

"What?" asked Harry incredulously.

"Look, you've been barreling ahead like you always do. But Sixes are Cassandras. They need to know that the downside is being handled."

Two days later Harry called, relief apparent in his voice. "I'm astonished," he said. "As I listed the problems, he paid attention. He visibly relaxed. Then he gave me a couple of green lights. It was the most rapport I've ever felt with him. The more negative I was, the happier he was!"

Harry added some months later, "The Enneagram reveals the basic game you are playing, what is important to you, and what is not. To know someone's Enneagram style makes real communication possible. But to know your own style is completely transforming."

Based on ancient philosophic traditions, the Enneagram is a profound, elegant, and compassionate approach to people and their relationships. It describes nine basic worldviews, nine different ways of doing business in the world. Each of the nine personality types is something of a pathway through life, with likely obstacles and pitfalls along the way. Each style has its own natural gifts, limitations, and blind spots, its own distinctive ways of thinking, acting, and being. Each relishes particular information—facts, feelings, and understandings—while ignoring other information, especially anything that doesn't fit preconceived notions or inclinations.

"Every man, wherever he goes, is encompassed by a cloud of comforting convictions," said Bertrand Russell, "which move with him like flies on a summer's day." When you know your Enneagram number, your game is called. The Enneagram exposes the unconscious assumptions that drive the way you see yourself, do your work, relate to your colleagues, and make decisions. Instead of operating from the myths of "comforting convictions," you can, with clear intent, invoke your true reservoir of talents and skills.

Along with clarifying the strengths and limitations of your own worldview, the Enneagram reveals what lies behind the behavior of your boss, your co-workers, your clients, and your employees. With the Enneagram you're in a position to understand why others act in the bizarre, inconsiderate, intrusive, self-interested, seductive, or charming ways they do. Once you know how people see things from the inside out, you can see their behavior as growing out of a consistent philosophy of life that makes perfect sense to them, whether you agree with it or not.

You can then tailor your message to the deeply held concerns of the listener, even if these concerns are not clearly expressed or even conscious. The Enneagram proposes, for example, that instead of throwing up your hands in frustration at your Connoisseur Four boss's profound emotionality (or perhaps learning some flavor-of-the-month technique to try to "manage" him), you *feel* the world from his perspective. Fours, as we shall see, are masters at exploring their deep passions and creativity, even though they may seem moody or depressed to you. If you understand the Enneagram Four, you'll know not to try to cheer him up (the worst!) but to give him space and even how to meet him in his tempestuous, creative inner office.

"To see ourselves as others see us is a most salutary gift," wrote Aldous Huxley. "Hardly less important is the capacity to see others as they see themselves." Many of us, like Harry, yield to the temptation to think of the other types as a defective version of our own. But the Enneagram teaches that we are different in important ways:

- Ones want to get things right.
- Twos want to help others.
- Threes want to work hard and succeed.
- Fours want to explore their true feelings.
- Fives want objective information.
- Sixes worry about problems and want to know what's happening under the table.
- Sevens want the exciting, positive possibilities and a dizzying array of experiences.

- Eights want to exercise full dominion.
- Nines want to empathize with all the players and get the whole picture.

This is the Enneagram's whole "method" in brief: to know your own worldview intimately and then to consider other people from the only point of view that they are used to—their own. The latest management fashion, however practicable in certain situations, carries all the advantages and limitations of its writer's Enneagram bias, made into gospel for all. You can manage by objectives (like the Three Peter Drucker) or thrive on chaos (like the Seven Tom Peters). The Enneagram, by contrast, is the elusive "big tent": it embraces the various approaches of your boss, your colleagues, your workers, your consultants, and yourself; it shows not only how they interact but how they are dependent upon one another; it demonstrates their value and necessity in various situations; and it allows you to mesh with them consciously, creatively, and effectively.

The beauty of the Enneagram is how well it works *at work*. I've worked with managers at the Central Intelligence Agency using the Enneagram to analyze leadership and management behavior. This work can be enlightening as well as humbling as we learn to put our own personality biases aside and see the world from the point of view of those we seek to understand. I have found the Enneagram attractive to organizations that want to develop their leaders, whether prominent multinationals or small nonprofits. The Enneagram teaches how to marshal your style's powers and skills and to consciously draw up those that are not so familiar. If nothing else, the Enneagram is about how to have an impact. I work with an automobile manufacturer using the system to conceptualize marketing and sales. I've been to a good number of hospitals where administrators work with the Enneagram for professional development, planning, and conflict resolution. And even at several consulting firms, we use the Enneagram to facilitate client decision making and problem solving. The possible applications of the Enneagram are myriad.

Managers and workers from all these organizations as well as other clients of mine—lawyers, doctors, psychologists, headhunters, manufacturers, scientists, advertising executives, accountants, retailers, and managers and employees of government agencies, nonprofits, and public interest groups—appear in these pages, sometimes disguised to preserve confidentiality.

Enneagram Styles at Work

At work, each Enneagram type has a characteristic agenda and operates within a particular decision-making frame. Twos tend to see difficulties as people problems ("We need a better employee assistance program in this organization"). Sixes ask questions that test congruence and authority ("We need to make sure the boss knows what he's doing").

- Ones measure against an objective ideal standard and want to do the right thing.
- Twos focus on interpersonal and emotional issues and want to be helpful and depended upon.
- Threes focus on hard work and achievement so that they can be successful and admired.
- Fours center on their own creativity and soulful feelings and want to be quality producers, providers, or purveyors.
- Fives seek information and understanding, with as few entanglements as possible, and want to be the wisdom keeper or master of the game.
- Sixes worry about the hidden agendas and any possible downside risks so that they can prepare.
- Sevens want to keep their options open and focus on exciting upside ideas, possibilities, and experiences.
- Eights want to make sure they take and keep power and control.
- Nines want to bring all sides together so that the workplace is intermeshed and free of conflict.

Sometimes your characteristic style may mean you are solving the wrong problem because of your tendency to invoke particular frames of reference and ignore others. Chuck, an ebullient Seven owner of a company that manufactured swimwear and sunglasses (with a loose, fun Seven company culture), thought that he had a morale problem when his company was failing. Sevens like things upbeat, so Chuck increased the perks to his senior executives. But Chuck's real problem was not morale but quality control—too much product was being returned for defects in manufacture—and a total lack of financial controls, and Chuck began to understand these problems only in long discussions with his trustee in bankruptcy. As Abraham Maslow pointed out, "When all that you have is a hammer, everything starts to look like a nail."

Though none of the types is bad in itself, being unconsciously wedded to an Enneagram style limits flexibility, imagination, and choices. Caught up in habitual ways of perceiving, you miss important pieces of the whole. Knowing your vantage point and that of the people you work with does more than build perspective; it clears the mind so that discernment is possible. It loosens the heart to the experience of others. It focuses the will so that you can get out of your own way and act with concentrated intention, power, and effectiveness.

The Enneagram of Organizations

The Enneagram was originally applied to groups and larger systems. As we shall see, organizations, like individuals, have their characteristic blind spots as well as strengths.

Everyone, of whatever type, must relate to the Enneagram style of his or her workplace or team. The Enneagram is the most cogent and precise approach to organizational culture that I know. It focuses employees and managers alike on asking important questions about their own work team: What is valued and what is not? What are this company's goals? What happens on this team when someone fails? How are decisions and plans made? Knowing your company's Enneagram style means that you won't be fighting a fight you didn't know you were fighting.

- One organizations have strong norms and operating controls to maintain high quality (Motorola).
- Two organizations are people oriented, focused on meeting the emotional needs of employees and clients (Mary Kay Cosmetics).
- Three organizations are fast-tracked achievers, through super-efficient, image-conscious marketing, sales, and production (McDonald's, Federal Express).
- Four organizations deliver distinctive products and services that show panache, elegance, and good taste (Ritz-Carlton, Henri Bendel).
- Five organizations are focused on closely managing information and ideas (C-SPAN, M&M/Mars).
- Six organizations focus on parrying threats from the competition through superior intelligence and employee loyalty (the CIA).
- Seven organizations generate lots of imaginative ideas through interdisciplinary networking to survive in an ever-changing marketplace (3M).
- Eight organizations stay on top by exercising power and control and by setting standards with their muscle in a rough-and-tumble marketplace (Microsoft).
- Nine organizations manage overwhelming input through routine in a dependable, predictable, and orderly manner with patience and equanimity (U.S. Postal Service).

The way an organization treats individuals whose Enneagram points diverge from its own offers a crystal-clear take on what is valued and not valued in the system. No organization can ignore or disenfranchise any of the Enneagram perspectives without consequences. *The Enneagram's "prime directive" is to value what you are not.*

Learning the Enneagram's Nine Personality Types

The best way to learn the Enneagram is to see the types in action. When I teach classes, I call on an array of live representatives of each type, who reveal their strategies and perspectives in life's situations. While much can be said about the customary behaviors, idiosyncrasies, and predispositions of the types, you really know the types only when you meet them. That is the purpose of this book.

Here is the briefest description of each of the nine Enneagram types.

One: The Perfectionist. Ones want to get things right. Critical, idealistic, judgmental Ones make decisions with an internalized "single correct way" in mind. They want their work to reflect their extremely high standards. Though their continual sermonizing, teaching, and monitoring of others may make people feel nitpicked and rejected, their fiercest anger is turned inward on themselves. At their best, these upright, fastidious, high-energy paragons are honest and idealistic, with superb powers of criticism and a clear vision of what should be.

Two: The Helper. Twos want to be appreciated for all they do for you. Sweet, emotionally seductive, and manipulative, relationship-oriented Twos make themselves indispensable to and adored by important others as a path to power and influence. Twos are the powers behind the throne, with exquisite radar for the feelings, appetites, and preferences of others. They excel at customer service, whether the customers are outside or inside the company. The Jewish Mother, the Italian Mother, the Queen Bee, and the Boss's Secretary Who Really Runs the Company are archetypes. Others may see Twos as prideful and power-hungry apple polishers. However, at their best Twos can be genuinely sensitive, helpful, and humble "servant leaders," who inspire and bring out the best in others.

Three: The Producer. Threes want to be lauded for getting the job done. Enthusiastic, efficient, high-performing, competitive Type A's, Threes keep their eyes on the prize (the bottom line) and seek to be loved for their achievements. Others may see Threes, concerned as they are with image and approval, as expedient, artificial, superficial, and insensitive, and Threes do run the risk of becoming their résumé or their long list of accomplishments. But at their best Threes are charismatic leaders, eager, efficient, practical problem solvers, and accomplished team players and motivators. Threes know how the world works and what to do about it.

Four: The Connoisseur. Fours gravitate to the authentic, the beautiful, the true (which is always just out of reach), or the unusual and outré. Melancholic, romantic, elitist Fours look under the surface for the deeper meaning, and they manifest impeccable taste within their concerns. They make decisions based on the vicissitudes of feeling. As they see it, they're easily satisfied with the best. Others may see them as intense and flamboyant tragedians or snooty, acerbic critics. At their best, Fours are doyens of the creative and the beautiful who live the passionate life with panache, elegance, and good taste.

Five: The Sage. Fives want mastery over their personal domain. Emotionally detached, penurious Fives seek to observe the world from a safe and protected vantage point while stockpiling facts, theories, and information. They camouflage themselves and minimize needs, preferring not to rely on their relationships. Others may see Fives as emotionally detached, scientific observers of life who hide in their office or behind a wall of data or expertise. The best Fives are sensitive and respectful of boundaries and can be wizards in their field, brilliant, intense, committed, but somewhat remote leaders and entrepreneurs, and perspicacious analysts, theorists, and advisers.

Six: The Troubleshooter. Sixes are preoccupied with worst-case scenarios. They stew over who can be trusted, whether the boss is on the level, and what could possibly go wrong. Others may be frustrated by Sixes' overpreparedness, procrastination, and paranoia. At their best, Sixes can be original thinkers, imaginative, faithful, sensitive, intuitive, committed, and ultimately courageous partisans, especially in defense of their team, the boss, or themselves. They are terrific at ferreting out the hidden motives and concerns of others and especially the pitfalls along the way.

Seven: The Visionary. Sevens want to keep all positive options open and active. Engaging, high-energy romancers, innovative and upbeat planners, Sevens are also the classic superficial Peter Pans who won't grow up. So wedded are they to the glorious possibilities of the vision they are spinning that they have a hard time perceiving the downside and the pitfalls and so avoid closure, pain, conflict, ordinary commitments, and routine work. Enthusiastic initiators of projects, they may fail to follow through. Others may experience them as narcissistic, quixotic, and irresponsible. The best Sevens are gifted visionaries, perceptive and witty idealists, inspirational and charming amalgamators of ideas, and enthusiastic networkers of people.

Eight: The Top Dog. Eights want power and control. Expansive, blunt, and domineering, Eights lack restraint and express and feel feelings (whether positive or negative) easily and loudly. Contentious, they seek out confrontations (often without realizing it), believing the truth comes out in a fight, and focus on their own powers and the other's shortcomings. Others may be repelled by their bullying, excess, and lack of scruples. At their best, Eights can be excellent, bold kingpins, entrepreneurs, and empire builders, untroubled

by obstacles or propriety. Natural paladins, top-dog Eights are often genuinely protective and nurturing of the underdogs in their charge.

Nine: The Mediator. Nines want to include all people and points of view
and to avoid discord. Nines are calming and compromise easily; they see
clearly and identify so strongly with the needs, enthusiasms, and points of view
of their fellows that others' wants seem like their own desires. Others may see
Nines as spacey and neglectful, as pluggers and plodders, as bureaucrats no
matter where they are found, and colleagues may be put off by Nines' obsessive being of two minds, their tendency to embrace ambiguity, and their deliberate pursuit of seeming irrelevancies. At their best, warm, openhearted Nines
lead by inspiring others: they crystallize others' positions and desires without
their own agenda intruding. The best Nines are naturally in touch with the
flow of group and organizational events. They therefore can be excellent team
builders, boundary spanners, and diplomats (whatever the work).

A Cautionary Note

Although the Enneagram describes nine types, there is really only one type
that is guaranteed to be dangerous: that is "the Enneagrammer" who seeks to
explain all things in terms of type. Like certain college sophomores who have
discovered psychology, this person now understands Everything. What the Enneagrammer usually fails to understand is that superficial, shoot-from-the-hip
typing—based on behavior and not intent—can be more harmful than helpful. Rating the types as better or worse is similarly silly. None of the nine types
has a monopoly on integrity, commitment, intelligence, vision, heart, and values. As we shall see, each type is a continuum of sophistication, expertise, and
effectiveness on the one end and discombobulation and insecurity on the
other.

Working the Enneagram

Generally people become fascinated with the nine Enneagram types, which
are subtle and rich and revealing. They recognize the types easily in their colleagues and friends, in their spouses especially, and in one another at Enneagram workshops. The process is generally moving, surprising, and a whole lot
of fun. But some years ago, at a retreat outside Austin, Texas, a human resources manager said to me, "So you have these very interesting types. So
what? Where does it go?"

The Enneagram was designed long ago as a *process tool*, not as a labeling
device. The personality types are just the beginning. *The Enneagram is a tool*

for clarifying, balancing, and mastering the various pulls on your type. By understanding them you can loosen your type's monopoly on your behavior. You can then gain access to all of the Enneagram styles yourself, for enhanced effectiveness, connectedness, and change and transformation. In this way the Enneagram is eminently functional in the real world of business, in disputes and misunderstandings, for planning and training, for influencing with integrity so that you can make yourself heard plainly and surely.

Regardless of the particular aspects of your type, like any place that you call home, what really matters is *location.* The location of each of the types on the Enneagram in relation to the others is crucial; each Enneagram type is something of a force field, with specific pulls—in the form of the other Enneagram points—acting upon it. Some forces hound you or hold you back. Some inspire and empower you. This array of forces makes the Enneagram more than a collection of interesting boxes for pigeonholing your colleagues and yourself. The Enneagram is about movement.

Besides our home-base point, four other points primarily influence the way we feel and behave. These are the High Performance and Stress Points and the points on either side of our home base, the two "wings."

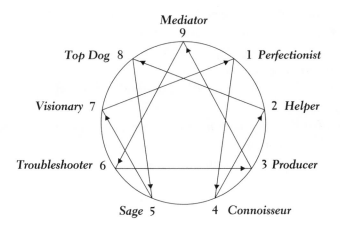

High Performance and Stress Points

On the Enneagram symbol, each point is connected to two others by arrows. Movement *in* the direction of the arrow is to the Stress Point. Movement *against* the direction of the arrow is to the High Performance Point (sometimes referred to as the "heart" or "security" point, because when we shift here we feel assured). High Performance Points and Stress Points are important Enneagram lodestars. The Stress Point describes how you hunker down when you're overwhelmed. The High Performance Point describes what happens when you loosen up and enter a "flow state."

The Stress Point

The Stress Point kicks in during crunch time. We begin to behave like our Stress Point when we are overwhelmed, fed up, or alienated. Our world shrinks. We are more resistant and brittle than usual, more discombobulated. The easygoing Nine, for example, begins to think like a Six. She feels uncharacteristically self-doubting and paranoid. Other people no longer seem trustworthy. She gets suspicious of their motives. Even her colleagues may become suspicious as they get sucked into her Stress Point.

The Stress Point is the place where we feel like a victim: of the system, of other people, of our boss, of our own failings. We feel frustrated, defended, filled with blame for ourselves and/or for others.

- One (at Four) is swept away by feelings like melancholy and envy instead of being guided by values.
- Two (at Eight) becomes a bossy steamroller instead of a helper and supporter of others.
- Three (at Nine) blows a fuse and is indecisive, overwhelmed, and passive instead of quick thinking, proactive, and fast-tracked.
- Four (at Two) becomes codependent and excitable instead of self-contained and self-possessed.
- Five (at Seven) spews ideas and theories instead of considering and valuing each one.
- Six (at Three) charges ahead and maniacally produces instead of thinking through the implications.
- Seven (at One) rigidly and critically holds to one alternative instead of playfully and open-mindedly considering many.
- Eight (at Five) becomes oversensitive and withdrawn instead of bold and engaged.
- Nine (at Six) becomes suspicious, accusatory, and isolated rather than easygoing, trusting, and connected.

But the Stress Point also genuinely helps people get through stress. You can implode, or you can consolidate and learn about focus and rigor. A Six, paralyzed with fear, can go to Stress Point Three and kick out a project anyway. A Seven who is all over the map can get things in order pretty quickly at Stress Point One. "When I go to One," says Carl, a breezy Seven management consultant, "I am in diligence mode. I wouldn't say it's fun. But usually it's what's called for under the circumstances."

The High Performance Point

The High Performance Point is where we put it all together, where we can see what's essential. We know what our real needs are and how to meet them. This is the expansive flow state: we go with the flow, we overflow with creativity and inspiration, and we shower our gifts on others. A flow state is where you enjoy using your skills, powers, and abilities. It is the place of *virtuosity*. "I like to do my thinking in a group of smart people at Seven," says Carl, the Seven consultant, "but when it's time for closure I need to be alone. I go to Five."

Our High Performance Point mobilizes our true potential. When the Nine moves to High Performance at Three, she sees clearly and aims for specific goals. Action comes naturally. Those around her seem to share her sharp, task-oriented focus. Things get done.

- One (at Seven) opens to imaginative possibilities and alternative frameworks rather than rigidly demanding one right way.
- Two (at Four) turns to look inside, to find his or her own pathway rather than hiding out by taking care of others.
- Three (at Six) becomes thoughtful, introspective, and prudent rather than being on a fast-tracked ego trip.
- Four (at One) connects with solid, eternal verities rather than tempestuous, evanescent emotions.
- Five (at Eight) willingly engages to make an impact and a difference rather than just detaching and observing.
- Six (at Nine) trusts the process and the organization, feeling aligned with the team rather than suspicious and alone.
- Seven (at Five) treasures select ideas, thoughtfulness, and wisdom rather than prodigally creating and discarding whatever comes to mind.
- Eight (at Two) activates the protector and nurturer rather than single-mindedly pursuing personal power and revenge on enemies.
- Nine (at Three) becomes efficient and effective, acting on Nine's own position rather than being immobilized by taking every position.

The Wings

Each point has beside it two wings, a counterclockwise wing (One in the case of Two) and a clockwise wing (Three in the case of Two). I call the counterclockwise wing the Shadow Point and the clockwise wing the Ally Point. Once you know the wings of the people you work with, you have a sense of what they are running from and where they long to go.

The Shadow Point

The counterclockwise wing is the rejected part of the self, what Jung called the shadow. Each of the Enneagram types casts a particular shadow behind it.

The shadow is the part of ourselves of which we say, "Good Heavens, I am not that!" The shadow may appear as comical or contemptible. These are our dangerous or distasteful feelings and desires, our snotty judgments, our guilty secrets. But the shadow can also hold excellent parts of ourselves that we have disowned. Frequently we project our shadow material onto others; an ambitious Four disdains Threes for their tacky materialism. When you know people's shadows, you know a lot about them (usually more than they know).

We try to run from the Shadow Point, which literally pursues us from behind on the outer circle of the Enneagram diagram. How empowering to know that your prissy, overcontrolled, overorganized One colleague is fighting a constant battle against chaos (at Nine) or that a happy-go-lucky Seven is fleeing rampant fear and paranoia (at Six).

Owning the shadow as a part of ourselves allows us to gain access to and channel the enormous power and energy that we might spend running from it. For example, Sevens keep constantly upbeat and on the move, worried that their fears (at Six) will catch up with them. The beginning of wisdom for Sevens is to know that they keep their fear in their Shadow Point; once conscious of it, they need not flee from it.

The Ally Point

The clockwise wing, the Ally Point, is something of an antidote to one's Enneagram style, a practical source of leverage. Look ahead to the Ally Point to see what draws you, what excites you, what will get you out of your morass. It's what each point really wants, the catalyst for transformation. Such knowledge is enormously useful. How good to know, for example, that your colleague, a workaholic Three, wants and needs to reconnect with his heart's desire (Four). Or that your overheated Four boss chills out when she has the space and emotional distance of the Five perspective, which you can provide.

The Enneagram teaches that we work best when the wings are in balance. Sometimes people tilt more to their Ally or Shadow, preferring to explore the issues of one over the other. Neither is better. But either way, such folks have the work of balancing (integrating) the overlooked wing.

The Triads

The Enneagram divides the nine types into three groups:

- the Feeling Group (Two, Three, and Four)
- the Mental Group (Five, Six, and Seven)
- the Sensing Group (Eight, Nine, and One).

All of us have access to all three perceptual pathways, just as we all have access to the other Enneagram points, but each of us is primarily comfortable with one.

The Feeling Group

Points Two, Three, and Four are concerned with *people*. They focus on motion and *emotion*. Twos focus outward to the feelings of others (empathy). Fours explore their own psyche, down and inward. Threes avoid their own and others' feelings so they can get the job done.

Two, Three, and Four are sometimes called the image or vanity points. To them, how they appear to others matters a lot. Twos want to be admired as indispensable helpmates, Threes bask in the glory others see in their accomplishments, and Fours want others to know they are deep and authentic. Such pride makes each of these points competitive ("I am better than you") within its respective area of concern.

In order to make a decision, Two, Three, and Four *compare and contrast*. Which do I like better? Which is more important or has the bigger payoff? They know right away, and therefore their decisions—within their expertise— usually come pretty quickly.

The Mental Group

Points Five, Six, and Seven put their trust in *ideas*. Concepts and information are the coin of their realm. These are visual people (the word *idea* is from the Greek "to see"); fear is their central concern.

Fives take their fear inward, and it petrifies them. Sevens bounce up and out from their fear instead of dealing with it, using it to catapult them into exciting new possibilities. Sixes struggle directly with intrepidity, either running from fear or compulsively confronting it (fight or flight). People in this group search for legitimate, trustworthy authority; it is their own inner authority they are unwittingly looking for.

The Mental triad likes to *analyze*, to take a problem apart and look at its component parts to see how they fit together, particularly in the context of a system or a theory. These three points solve problems by trying to *understand* them.

The Sensing Group

For points Eight, Nine, and One issues of *will* are central. "Whose will is more powerful, yours or mine?" Righteous Ones try to impose the "correct way." Eights want their own way. Nines try to avoid expressing their will. When their will is thwarted, each of these types has a characteristic anger. Eights explode their anger outward toward others. Ones turn the anger in on themselves. Apparently placid Nines, ambivalent about their will, are simultaneously the most easygoing (at first) and the most willful (later) on the Enneagram.

Eight, Nine, and One decide by *comparing with precedent*: How have we done it before? What category does this fit into? An Eight either outrageously explodes convention or, as with Saddam Hussein, justifies himself by comparisons to a predecessor (Nebuchadnezzar). Either way, the referent is what has happened before. Nines are creatures of habit ("Why do we sort the mail this way? Because we've done it this way since the Truman administration, that's why"). Ones decide by referring to the established rules.

Type and Countertype

Although it may be tempting to pigeonhole your colleagues into Ennea-boxes based on their behavior alone, this can lead you astray. As we've seen, each Enneagram type organizes around a basic issue, such as fear for Sixes or a sense of loss for Fours. But a person's orientation can be toward or against this basic issue, so that Sixes can run from their fear in the phobic version or, in the counterphobic version, run compulsively toward what they are afraid of while seeming quite bold and fearless. But the counterphobe is still "run by" fear. Similarly, while the typical Four is filled with melancholy or longing, the countertype is manic, still organized around sadness but marshaled against it. The key to understanding the Enneagram types is uncovering the organizing issues.

Ways to Use This Book

Since the Enneagram is a circle, you can enter it anywhere. You might want to begin by reading about the point you suspect is your own. Or you may prefer to read about the person you work with who is currently giving you the most trouble. Wherever you choose to enter the system, you'll find energetic pathways to every point. You can always get to there from here.

The Enneagram is a marvelous tool for getting the best from people—and for knowing when to steer clear of them, too. Each Enneagram type does well or struggles under particular conditions.

- What is being avoided? Is my co-worker running from a shadow issue? Fives do well when they acknowledge the strong emotions that they avoid (at Shadow Four).
- What can be changed? How to claim the Ally's powers? Obsessive, intractable Nines stuck in a morass are instantly helped by ordering priorities (at Ally One).
- What circumstances and environment allow High Performance? Sevens recharge best when they have time alone (High Performance Five).
- Is it crunch time? What puts my colleague in Stress? Sixes on deadline stop fretting and grind it out (Stress Point Three).

The Enneagram is particularly helpful if you find yourself clashing with others. The more you can adjust to see the world from a problem person's point of view, the more effective you'll be when you encounter her. When you know the Enneagram, you can respond to a colleague's best *intentions*, regardless of her *behavior*.

The Enneagram is also handy for helping members of a work team coalesce, and this is how I find it most useful. You can see how people at different Enneagram points relate to or miss one another. Indeed, you can predict the likely misconceptions and difficulties from each Enneagram point's preconceptions.

In the chapters that follow you'll find detailed descriptions of each type, along with true stories, adventures, and examples. You can start working the Enneagram right away to real effect. And the more you use it, the more you make the system your own. Enjoy.

ONE   The Perfectionist

AKA	The Paragon, the Reformer, the Purist, the Judge
Worldview	There's a right way; let me teach you.
High Side	Visionary, principled, committed, stable, earnest, meticulous, disciplined, objective, scrupulous, noble
Low Side	Self-righteous, ruthless, coldhearted, arrogant, rigid, judgmental of self and others
Leadership Style	By the book, by example, up to standard, total quality management
Credo	Zero defects
Appeal to	Duty, ethics, standard operating procedures, the Golden Rule
Don't Appeal to	The quick-and-dirty fix; "Because I say so"
Talk/Communication Style	Preaching, teaching, lecturing; "I ought to"; "You should"
Makes You Feel	That you have a clear and higher purpose, dealt with fairly; and—sometimes—nitpicked, flawed, judged
Appearance	Well scrubbed, neat, proper; rigid posture, tightly muscled jaw, and a stiff upper lip
Good Work Setting	Ordered, planned, committed, everybody on the same page, clear objectives, work to standards is respected
Difficult Work Setting	Chaotic, where the basic premises and rules change, or where feelings rather than standard operating procedures are central in judgment

Books	*Principle Centered Leadership* by Steven Covey *Poor Richard's Almanac* by Benjamin Franklin *The Analects* by Confucius
Sayings	"Tsk, Tsk!" "Nothing valuable ever came easy." "The reasonable man adapts himself to the world. The unreasonable one persists in trying to adapt the world to himself. Therefore all progress depends on the unreasonable man." —George Bernard Shaw, a One "I'd rather be right than President." —John C. Calhoun "There, but for the grace of God, goes God." —Winston Churchill, of Stafford Cripps, a One
Of the One Persuasion	Ross Perot, Felix Unger, Confucius, Miss Manners, Nelson Mandela, Martha Stewart, author and moralist Dennis Prager, Dudley Do-Right, Margaret Thatcher, Jeane Kirkpatrick, Lucy van Pelt, Thomas More, Mary Poppins, the Amish, the Puritans, Singapore, Utopia
High Performance	7 Pleasure in ambiguity, spontaneity, imagination and innovation; considers alternative possibilities instead of one right way
Stress	4 Emotional, melancholic, self-examining, self-pitying, but a wake-up call to feelings and intrapsychic complexity
Ally	2 *Energized* by feeling feelings of and for others, by compassion and equity instead of law; by helping a particular individual
Shadow	9 *Grounded* by "going with the flow," by respecting organic processes, and empathy for the positions of others
Virtue	Serenity
Vice	Anger

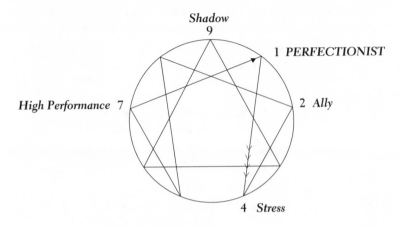

Shadow
9

1 PERFECTIONIST

High Performance 7

2 *Ally*

4 *Stress*

Getting to Know a One

John's Story

John is highly successful and popular senior manager at one of the national security agencies. He is nicknamed "The Perfectionist," even by people who have never heard of the Enneagram.

John is courtly and extremely civilized. He welcomes visitors to his office with a slight bow. Some who don't know him consider him fussy and arrogant, a bit cold. He speaks firmly and enunciates clearly. Every Monday he writes a mission statement for himself for the week ahead, consciously trying to frame his work in terms of his values. And, indeed, he takes pride in his reputation as an honorable guide through the moral quagmire of the agency's work. On his wall hangs a sign that reads: "Tenets, anyone?"

John sees his greatest strength as "clearly communicating to the analyst what must be done." His analysts agree: "The best thing about John is that he lets you know what the agency requires, what the rules are, how to get ahead." For many young people who see his agency as a dysfunctional morass, John is a godsend, a terrific guide and mentor.

John keeps in his desk legal-sized files for each of his employees. A page is stapled to the left side of the file, headed with the name of the analyst—Andrea, for example. Here John lists Andrea's accomplishments and what she does well. On the right side of the file is a list headed "The Ideal Andrea." Here John lists the requirements for each employee to improve. For Andrea the paper reads: "She needs to host a working conference in [her field]. She needs to brush up on [a foreign language]. She needs to do a stint on an overseas assignment." John shares both lists with the employee and checks off the "ideal" items as they are accomplished. Each employee's professional life is planned about three years in advance. To my initial surprise, this kind of guidance was almost universally appreciated.

John is well known as a fine editor and reviewer of analysts' work. "I would call him brutal but fair," says one of his employees who would have preferred a boss with warmer people skills. Some find his concern with details overdone. "John is a fellow who takes great pains," said a colleague, "and gives them to others."

In response to that kind of criticism John says, "The bottom line is, it's important to do a good job, manage your resources well, and get out a quality product. If that involves criticizing people, even if they get hurt, the criticism happens. We don't make widgets here. Of course I try to be nice, but the bottom line is 'Let's get it right,' not 'Let's all be friends.' I don't have much of an I-hope-you-really-like-me part when it comes to work, and you can double-underline that."

Do you recognize John? John is a One.

The Basic Premise

Ones are people of *principle*. They believe in the right way, the honorable way, and they want the work done impeccably no matter how much time or effort it takes. They want to teach you to do the same.

Ones are the people at work who are good scouts. They are conscientious, well behaved, well organized, punctual, and hardworking. They are detail oriented and meticulous. They follow the rules.

But at the same time Ones are also vexed: they look around and see everything that isn't right—the incompetence, the lack of commitment, the disorganization, the self-pity and dissembling, the lack of courtesy, the bad grammar and spelling, and, perhaps most of all, the lack of values. This they resent.

But they rarely collapse in self-pity like a Four or hole up like a Five. The wrongheadedness all around spurs them to remedial action. Ones are compulsive do-gooders. They not only practice goodness, they preach goodness, and they have lots of energy to set you right.

Ones are intense, fire-breathing dragons with very good manners. Their dragon fire can be a sanctifying, purifying fire—something to test your mettle and make you the best you can be—or it can be a punishing hellfire that will burn you to a crisp. Since they strain mightily to be proper and polite, their fire leaks out in angry spurts, like a corked volcano. Most Perfectionists won't even know that they have cauterized their colleagues.

Ones are looking for, and rely on, the simple but eternal verities. This is the uncomplicated, optimistic, *applied* morality of Benjamin Franklin, a One. Franklin stressed temperance, order, frugality, industry, and moderation. Later, at the urging of a mentor, he added humility to his original list. "I cannot boast of much success in acquiring the reality of this virtue," he wrote, "but I had a good deal with regard to the appearance of it."[1]

Stephen Covey writes in *The Seven Habits of Highly Effective People*:

> Our security comes from knowing that, unlike other centers based on people or things which are subject to frequent and immediate change, correct principles do not change. We can depend on them.
>
> Principles don't react to anything. They don't get mad and treat us differently. They won't divorce us or run away with our best friend. They aren't out to get us. . . . Principles are deep, fundamental truths, classic truths, generic common denominators. They are tightly interwoven threads running with exactness, consistency, beauty, and strength through the fabric of life.[2]

This is the One worldview, succinctly stated.

People of the Book

In order to fashion their vision of perfection, Ones take the official standards—of whatever higher authority they identify with—and make them their own. These can be ethics, the company's standard operating procedures, professional obligations, what their parents said, the company bible, or the Bible itself.

Ones are people of the book, literally. Many Ones, if they find no rulebook in their department, will write one. Lucy, a nurse in a critical care facility, arrived on the job to discover that there was no medication policy. She insisted on writing one, but the process took nine months. Meanwhile the unit was without a policy. Ones understand the need to create formalized systems and regulations, but they are rarely quick to act and can get caught in minutiae.

"My work does not require spontaneity," says Jim, a One internist. "It's not creative. It's more a diligent algorithm, a set of rules for arriving at a conclusion based on clues."

Ones are great believers in preventive maintenance. They have backup procedures ready in case of a breakdown or a crisis. Robert, a One who owns a custom furniture business, has created detailed checklists for common situations such as making a sales call on a new client or supervising the manufacture of a piece, and he makes these protocols available to all concerned. Also on his computer are similar personal protocols for packing for a skiing or camping trip and for coaching his son's football team.

Psychology

Ones had an early baptism by fire: typically a parent or an important adult was demanding or highly critical. Unlike Twos and Threes, who were praised (Twos for being helpful and Threes for accomplishment), Ones were kept on a tight leash and sharply told when they violated the rules. Many Ones can remember the moment they vowed never to make a particular mistake—or any mistake—again.

Ones were usually serious, well-scrubbed, good children who learned to control (control was always the issue) their own anger and to put their own messy needs aside. They chose to identify with a set of guidelines rather than with their feelings; sometimes they simply identified with the oppressor. "If only I just try harder at keeping the rules, at being orderly and disciplined," thinks the One, "surely the proper authorities will notice and reward me."

But as they get older, Ones can't help but notice that the official rules haven't paid off as expected. Ones are left humiliated, having sold themselves out for a false promise that a just universe would reward their impeccable behavior. This leads to a bad case of resentment and bitterness. Ones are mad at the world and madder at themselves, though they frequently don't know it because they are still pretending to be good. Moral martyrs, they are frequently obsessed with honor in others precisely because they sense they have sold their own, and for a poor price.

The Good News

Ones are *pragmatic.* They are hard workers who accomplish a lot. Like John, they make terrific mentors.

John's boss at the agency, a Three, says, "He is simply the best coach you could imagine. If I had an employee who needed to hone his skills, I'd send him to John first. The people who work for him always improve. But if I needed something quick and dirty, and sometimes I do, I'd definitely go somewhere else."

Ones want you to do your best. They want the project to be the best. They add meaning to ordinary activity and make you feel you are part of an honorable and noble undertaking. They pay attention to implications, to the significance and consequences of actions. They can see your potential, your *virtue.* They want you to see it, too.

This makes them bona fide *visionaries.* They see with precision and clarity an idealized version of whatever is at hand—a person, a project, a relationship, or the resolution of a predicament. As a result, Ones can help you get clear about your work plan and goals. Touching base with a One before beginning a project or leading an important meeting can reconnect you with a deep sense of purpose.

Ones at their best are *principled rather than rule bound.* They're more interested in helping people preserve self-respect and work from their best selves than they are in doling out criticism and retribution. They'll work to make the company a good corporate citizen. They're interested in issues like employee health and safety, product quality, dealing fairly with the consumer, corporate philanthropy, and community involvement.

Ones are the conscience of the Enneagram (and everyone in it). As *deeply moral idealists,* they believe they do what they do because it is right, not for money or passing fame. When you are sure of what's right, when you naturally reference guiding principles, it's easy to be a self-reliant majority of One.

Ones *care about quality.* W. Edwards Deming, a curmudgeonly statistician who was the father of the quality movement, was a One. For Deming, the pathway to quality is to "reduce variations" by maintaining strong statistical controls, a solid One approach. Deming said that quality needs to be built in to a product; eliminating defects by (Six-like) inspection after the fact misses the point. Deming argued against the practice of awarding contracts to the lowest bidder; quality, not just low cost, needs to be required from contractors, too. Indeed, anything that detracts from pride in quality was suspect to Deming, even management by objectives, a goal-oriented Three approach. And he urged the necessity of "improving constantly and forever," which are the One's words to live by.

Value Driven

All Ones want to help, and they devote lots of energy and enthusiasm to the greater good. My friend Deke, who holds a high-powered and demanding position as a research scientist in industry, spends enormous amounts of time on the Internet without remuneration, discussing ethical questions in his field of inquiry. He hosts two discussion groups, one for scientists and one for ethicists. He posts long, thoughtful messages. Ones work tirelessly for whatever they believe in.

Unlike Fives and Nines, Ones cannot be bystanders. Like Threes, they have a bias to action. Their gears are engaged. They are bound to share their values and their views, even if they are not solicited and even if they might not be in the chain of command. Ann is a high school English teacher with no real computer experience. But when her school district set out to hire a director of technology to supervise computer learning, Ann felt that they had incorrectly designed the job for a technical expert. She had strong views: that such a person should not hide out in his office but should be an "instructional leader," as she put it, visiting classrooms, and be easily accessible for teacher consulting and training. Making her views known became her crusade. She wrote the hiring committee, who revised the job description. She met with her principal, the president of the teacher's association, and even the superintendent of the district to make sure they understood. Ones must apply their substantial vision: they take responsibility to make it happen.

While each Enneagram type fixates on certain personal values, Perfectionist Ones are the most self-consciously attuned to questions of *values and ethics*. They want to do the right thing. "I don't mind firing people. But I don't like to lay people off," says Rusty, a One who is a supervisor at a construction firm. "When you fire someone, you have a performance-related reason. If they don't show up or do their job, you say, 'I'm sorry, you don't get to work here.' That doesn't feel uncomfortable at all. That feels like I'm doing my job.

"But when you lay someone off, it has nothing to do with the person's performance. It's a financial decision imposed from the outside. I don't think that's right—and I don't think it's good for the company in the long run."

Perfectionists

Ones have all the workplace advantages of a compulsive. They're on time (for them, punctuality has a moral dimension). They are terrific schedulers and organizers. They are nearly always prepared. Ones keep control through a high-intensity focus on details: "Mind the pennies, and the dollars take care of themselves." Most Ones will keep superb work-related notes, journals, and paperwork. "My records pass whatever litmus test there is for records," says Ethan, a One who runs the quality program at a manufacturer. "Ninety percent of my records are as good as any records can possibly be. Ten percent are just very good."

Although others often perceive their attention to detail as perfectionism, most Ones do not see themselves that way. Rather, they are just trying to do the right thing or "make as few errors as possible."

Maggi, who owns a chain of bookstores, says, "The notion that Ones want to be perfect is a mistake that, as a One, is something I would notice anyway. I don't want to be perfect. That seems impossible. I always know, though, that I can be better. There's always a way to improve."

Emile Coué's "Every day in every way I am getting better and better" could be the One mantra.

The Bad News

One day when George Abbott, the great man of the Broadway theater, was playing golf, he fell on the fairway. Abbott was over one hundred years old at the time. When he didn't get up, his wife leaned over and started to shake him. "Get up, George, get up!" she pleaded. "Don't just lay there." After a moment, Abbott opened his eyes. "*Lie* there," he said.

Ones are the preachers and grammarians of the Enneagram; they're captivated by sin and syntax, sometimes at the expense of addressing what's really happening.

What Forest?

Many Ones can't see the forest for the trees. John's boss at the agency says, "I'd send my pitchers or my hitters to him. He could tell you what was wrong with each of them. But I don't think I'd let him manage the whole ball game. He's too detail oriented. He puts in too many hours. He works too hard and he's too intense. Everything is full blast. He has no rheostat."

Committed more to being right or appearing right than getting the job done, Ones will avoid tasks they think won't come out perfectly, and they take forever trying to do perfectly things that just need to get done. "I just can't work with Phoebe anymore," says Joan, a vice president for development at a large university. "Here we are on a crisis deadline for a proposal involving millions of dollars. We're not finished with large sections, and Phoebe is struggling to get all the tenses to agree."

Yet Ones think of themselves as efficient because they are so hardworking. But some Ones work hard, not smart. Low-side Ones are the great Pyrrhic victors, more interested in winning a moral victory and proving their case than in completing a practical task.

Righteous and Rule Bound

The low side of One is total quality management gone awry. *Business Week* reported on a Silicon Valley scientific equipment manufacturer that sent a thousand of its managers through quality programs in an effort to change the company's culture. They did. A unit that produced high-tech vacuums increased on-time delivery from 42 percent to 92 percent. One of its service departments shot to the top of the industry's ratings for timely repairs. But the vacuum production people were so focused on meeting the idealized timetable measuring "quality" production that they did not have time to return customers' queries. The business rapidly lost market share. The repair people were so pressed to meet their schedules that they did not take time to explain to customers what they were doing wrong or how to avoid repairs in the future. Even the company's quality manager said, "All of the quality-based charts went up and to the right, but everything else went down."[3] Ones need to remember that their precious standards—whether for cutting costs, for speeding up production, for continuous improvement, or for measuring performance—are not an end in themselves. There are the customers and the marketplace to consider (Ally Point Two), along with the big picture (High Performance Seven).

This is the One's common problem of being more concerned with form that substance or with law over equity. Low-side Ones stifle initiative with a mindless rigidity.

Serious trouble arises when these honorable moralists become moralistic, when teaching becomes preaching (or finger wagging), and when there is only "one right way." This is not so much My Way (as with an Eight) as The Way. They often impose themselves on others for the other's "own good."

The *Los Angeles Times* reported that a reader "attended a puppet show recently with daughter MacKenzie, 3, who became overly concerned with other children not adhering to the announced rules. When she was told that she should spend a little more time worrying about herself and a little less time worrying about others, she exclaimed, 'I can't do that. That would be selfish.'"[4]

Ones do not, cannot, suffer fools gladly. Their criticism can be brutal, demeaning, ruthless, and public. For example, Jim, the internist, feels no compunction about bawling out patients who smoke. "I don't care what they think of me," he says. "Smoking is idiotic."

Ones are ideal driven, not customer or market driven (like Twos and Threes). A "zero defects" policy may sound great, but in fact it's not if it produces no benefit for customers.

"One of my nurses gave a routine medication to a patient," said a nursing director, a Two, at a large hospital in Texas. "The label had expired four days before. The pharmacist—she's a One—heard about it and went nuts. 'Never, never, never use expired medicine!' She bit my head off.

"'Get real, Linda,' I said to her, 'You're not going to tell me that there was any difference in the medication four days earlier. These expiration dates are very conservative. The pills were there and the patient needed them. I just don't see the big deal.'

"Anyway, she wrote an event form and there was an inquiry. She explained her case very righteously.

"In front of everybody, I turned to her and said, 'If you're so upset, how come there was expired medicine in the pharmacy to begin with?' She turned all shades of green."

It was the perfect squelch for a One.

The Inner Inquisitor

Smile more. But not until you floss your teeth.
—A One talking to herself

You may feel blasted by a One at work, but that's nothing compared to the inquisition going on inside his head. Ones have an Inner Inquisitor who monitors their behavior and offers a running commentary. Art, a corporate trainer says, "When I'm giving a speech, while the words are coming out of my mouth, I simultaneously critique how I am doing. Am I connecting with the audience? Am I being clear? Am I talking down to them? Am I talking over their heads? At the end of the talk there's no need for me to do an evaluation. I know exactly where I stand."

The One conscience, which makes them so conscientious, does not speak with a still, small voice. He is Jiminy Cricket on steroids: "How could you be so stupid?" "You should be more productive, creative, neater!" "You should be having a better time."

Having an Inner Inquisitor would be bad enough, but Ones think everyone else has a comparable slave driver lurking inside. However, Ones think that unlike themselves, dutiful if beleaguered, other people seem not to be listening to theirs. The result is that when other people's work is not up to snuff the One charges them not merely with a problem of competence, but with a crime of moral turpitude. Tom, a One engineer, says about a young employee, "He *knows* better. He just doesn't want to do what it takes."

It's hard for some Ones to mesh gears with an employee whom they see as "sinful"—someone who makes too many mistakes or disregards the rules. The tendency is to obliterate the offender. Sinners are beyond the pale; better just to remove them from the scene. Ones can fire folks without regret and without empathy if their failure seems intentional. Ones' behavior is hyperintentional; they imagine others are making equally conscious—even moral—choices. Ones' justice is as swift as the hand of God and just as punitive. Jonathan, a buyer for a chain of department stores, had repeated problems with a company's product. When the company didn't fix it after repeated promises to do so, he refused to carry *any* of the company's products, even those that were not a problem. "If you had a cancer in your arm, you wouldn't cut it off an inch at a time, you'd cut the whole thing off right at the shoulder," said Jonathan.

Many auditors, accountants, and people who work with numbers are Ones. "I love being an accountant," said Cathy with a smile, "because you have the numbers and reports in black and white. You can prove to people that they are wrong."

The unevolved One is a moral accountant keeping track of every credit and debit. But, as Lao Tzu noted, "The polished accountant uses no tallies."

Compulsive and Excessively Responsible

The work identity of Ones is profoundly shaped by their relentless avoidance of mistakes.

When Art, the corporate trainer, goes on the road for a training, he never takes a slide box, which would easily fit into his briefcase; instead, he packs the whole carousel and the slide projector. He finishes putting the slides in the carousel about two days before the trip. Then, until it's time to leave for the airport, he checks and rechecks to make sure the slides are in the right order. Contrast this with his partner Mike, a Seven, who prepares the night before and, if he can't get his secretary to stay late and get the slides together on such short notice, does without them.

Ones are exceedingly responsible, sometimes too much so. Kay, a One and the new executive director of a foundation, was at the office until midnight most nights. She felt resentful about the work load but was unable or unwilling to say anything about it. Finally, after months on the job and at the end of her rope, she called the chairman of the board and angrily told him she needed an assistant, at least part-time. He said, "Of course you need help. Why haven't you come to me sooner?" As Kay told me this story, her eyes filled with tears. For a One to admit she is overworked or needs help (that is, is imperfect) can be a humiliating confession.

Naïve

Opposite to Sixes, who understand that work is politics and that people act out of self-interest, Ones deal in moral absolutes that others may not see.

Ron, a chief of accountants at a famous Hollywood television studio, a One in a One profession, wanted to reward his best employee, Sarah the bookkeeper, a Nine. Since there was no money for a raise, he enthusiastically offered her, with the noblest intentions, some increased responsibility and decision-making authority: a chance to better herself, as he saw it. Sarah didn't respond for a time, and when he pressed her, assuming she would be as excited as he, she declined. She saw the change in the job description as burdensome, "more work for free." She thought her good work deserved a raise; more responsibility was the booby prize. Ron was flabbergasted.

Working with a One

Influencing a One

The One relates best to arguments that something is *for the greater good* or for the good of the company or the team or the work itself. Or that it's fair. Or that it will help "spread the word." Or that you will learn something valuable and be a better person for it. Or that others will be helped.

Whatever you do, don't appeal to expediency or a quick profit. "Hey, everybody does it—we can really make out here" will raise red flags for most Ones. Unlike Threes, who understand the need to cut corners to stay well placed in the rat race, Ones see that sort of compromise as a cheap shot, manipulative and demeaning. "Even if you win the rat race," goes the old encomium, "you're still a rat."

The quickest way to drive a fixated One crazy is to ask him to make an exception or recognize a special case. This is the ancient battle of law versus equity. Law—the One's best friend—demands equal treatment for all. Equity demands making exceptions for the legitimate special case, an apparent lack of orderliness that makes Ones feel disoriented and hopeless, as if they've lost their familiar moral compass.

Only when a One remembers that she's dealing with people, not abstract principles, is she able to make individual allowances (at Ally Point Two). You may have to gently remind her.

How a One Makes Decisions

Enneagram Twos and Threes are comparison shoppers who easily decide on the better of two existing choices. Ones instead compare existing choices to the ideal possibility. Ones imagine an idealized version, a hard-wired standard of excellence, and they measure existing choices against that.

Japanese baseball managers keep a precise ideal outcome in mind; the way they strategize is pure One. "Managers in Japan are afraid to make quick decisions because they are afraid of making a mistake," according to Tokyo Giant Warren Cromartie. "They have to discuss everything to death with their coaches before they make a move. I played one half-inning in Osaka that took forty-five minutes."[5]

Though very judgmental, actual judging is stressful for Ones; in fact, they identify with authority or principles or standards because it makes personal judgment unnecessary. ("It's not me judging you, it's the rules!") Therefore, for you or the One to exercise an independent judgment might strike a One as presumptuous. As they hold fast to their own standards, Ones may be patronizing or downright scornful of your impertinent, intrusive, and irrelevant opinions and feelings. Who cares what *you* think? Why not just look to the right way to do it? Appealing to the One's judgment means showing how your proposals are in line with the way things are traditionally done or honorably done or consciously done and how your ideas measure favorably against the one best way.

Once decisions are made, Ones still obsess about them, even if the decisions are not open for reversal. "I keep evaluating my decisions so that I can make better decisions in the future. I've been reconsidering my minivan purchase for the last three years," says Art, the trainer.

Group decision making is not always easy for Ones. Some Ones may struggle with an open-ended planning process that involves give and take as part of a group. It's hard to join others in arriving at a decision when you know you're right to begin with.

But Ones can be great facilitators of consensus. Though we think of Ones more as judges than mediators, evolved Ones are exceedingly evenhanded and will be scrupulous about giving all sides or stakeholders due process and a fair hearing. (Nines, the most natural mediators, tend to be more easily pushed around by the squeaky wheel, like Judge Lance Ito was during the O. J. Simpson trial.)

The One Leadership Style

Govern the people by regulation, keep order among them by chastisements, and they will flee from you and lose all self-respect. Govern them by moral force, keep order among them by ritual, and they will keep their self-respect and come to you of their own accord.
—Confucius, a One, talking about low and high One leadership

Ones are rock-solid, conscientious leaders who begin with the end in mind. They hold a clear vision of the "correct" result and a principled way of getting there. They lead by compulsively sharing this vision: they *must* tell you what it is, and you *must* do something about it.

Ones are more than willing to correct others—they're likelier to dish out criticism than praise—but they would prefer that everyone just know what the right thing is, as they do. This may mean that they hold you to a moral standard you may not know existed. They are not shy about tackling performance appraisals or other evaluation mechanisms.

Ones lead by inculcating programs, systems, and procedures. Whether financial, human resources, or technical, each system has a right way in which it can be run. Ones will mandate and prescribe. They keep people between the lines, and when someone strays they herd the exception back in. Maurice Lippens, chair of Lippens AG, the European financial services conglomerate, calls his management style "applying the pressure of orthodoxy."

One leaders tend to have clear boundaries. They show this by clearly setting up tasks, responsibilities, and reporting relationships. They know who's supposed to do what and who reports to whom. (Compare this with the leadership style of Sevens, where functional boundaries and reporting relationships overlap and are ever shifting.) This leads to strong, directive control over the people who work for them or the tasks that they or their group are supposed to perform. For a One, delegating feels chancy; it opens the possibility that the work won't be up to snuff. Ones know that within their areas of concern they can do nearly everything better, or at least more dutifully, than anyone else.

Ones give precise, detailed instructions for exactly what is required, and they like to receive the same. A senior attorney in a Buffalo, New York, law firm sent a young associate to New York City to file a federal lawsuit. He dictated to the associate, a Harvard Law School alumnus, a long and detailed memo—down to instructions about how to hail a cab at Kennedy Airport, which way to turn once he entered the courthouse at Foley Square, and where to find a fax machine to send the filing papers back home.

Work teams reporting to a One often operate very smoothly on the surface. Under his strong influence, John's work team at the agency, for example, meshed with good humor and warmth. In fact, a series of group dynamics instruments showed this team was exceptionally cohesive, maybe even a little too stuck together. "This team just seems to bring in outlyers and fit them in," said John with pride. "The norms are pretty damn clear."

Perhaps too clear. John complained to me that his work team was doing merely competent but not exceptional work. There was extreme cordiality among team members but not the enthusiasm that John would have liked. Although the team was home to some potential standouts, no individual was considered a star, and many team members expressed an unwillingness to be that visible. In an Enneagram One group, no one wants to make the big mistake. (As the One-ish Japanese saying goes, "The tall blade of grass gets mowed down.") Said John, almost as an afterthought, "Getting people to voice an opinion around here is like pulling teeth." Part of the reason for this is One's unfettered, well-intentioned criticality, which can shut people up fast.

The best One leaders set a moral tone that is not only pervasive but also workable. This may appear as concern with product quality or worker safety, social responsibility of the company or community involvement. The driving force is an appreciation of the best intentions of the enterprise.

The One Work Style

At their best, Ones are meticulous and hardworking. They're not looking for shortcuts. They want the job done right. Ones are very orderly. They like schedules and lists. They have a relentless eye for details. All Ones experience themselves as driven by values.

The early-bird One completes assignments, projects, and reports well in advance for fear of being late and imperfect. The procrastinating One delays because the work is not yet perfect. Either way, the timing of Ones operates in response to their vision of perfection.

Ones are literal and relentless in pursuit of that vision, which for most Ones includes fairness and honor. Henry, a Two, is vice president of the Texas hospital mentioned earlier. He supervises Linda, the One pharmacist. "Last year, Linda did a good job, but she was over budget. That counts a lot around here. She felt she saved in ways related to the purchase of inventory, so I gave her an above-average raise, 3.5 percent. Four percent would have been the maximum conceivable.

"But Linda thought she had met the job description precisely and deserved the 4 percent. Most of my meetings about raises last about five minutes; Linda and I talked for two hours. She was furious that she didn't get the maximum 4 percent, but she tried not to show it. She talked very politely through clenched teeth. She took the missing half percent as an invalidation of all her work, which it was not.

"She made an appointment for a day later. She came back with two file boxes. Her records were truly amazing. She knew where every penny went. Who cares that every aspirin is accounted for? But she was ready to prove her case. She said, 'The way you have considered my raise is not according to the rules. You set the standards. I followed them to the letter.' She argued that I never told her *personally and explicitly* that not being on budget would cost her a half percent. We had always talked about meeting the pharmacy's priorities; she took that to mean that her job was to meet the certification standards for pharmacies, and indeed that's what she had done.

"I told her, 'You're a department head. Use your common sense. You have to know there's no way around fiscal responsibility. It was obvious to all the others.'

"She said, 'It wasn't obvious to me. You're grading me down for an expectation that was not in writing and that I didn't know you had.'

"Finally, I relented. She was excruciatingly literal. She was so annoying! I had to admit I was never that explicit about what the consequences would be for not meeting her budget, although I think anybody else would have figured it out. But at this point my main thought was that this problem just wasn't worth my time. I told her, 'Okay, you're right.' She beamed! I said, 'I'll give you the half percent because it's so important to you. I value our ability to work effectively together in the future more than the dollars associated with that half percent. But never, never come into my office again and ask for more money if you are over budget.'

"I realized with Ones you have to be 100 percent literal. In that sense, *they are so with the program they're not with the program at all.*"

The One Learning Style

Ones learn from the outside in. "What are the rules and standards?" asks the One. "I will make them my own." Make crystal clear what is expected. Improvisational, loosely organized presentations are hard for Ones to take in. Brainstorming and other structured exercises can work neatly as long as the rules are expressed. They learn by watching closely, taking extensive notes, and making actual or mental checklists. Then they work by checking off the checklists.

The One Organization

A One organization is directive, prescriptive, and corrective. It naturally generates a profusion of regulations and standard operating procedures, which precisely describe the way things need to be done, top down. These may include codes for ethical conduct or appropriate dress, protocols for making sales, and even specific directions for employee temperament. A huge Midwest furnishings manufacturer gives new hires a 114-page rulebook of employee regulations. Employees may not have friends call them during work hours, and they may not leave the parking area during breaks. Each possible offense, from lateness to assaulting a supervisor, carries precise penalties.

Similarly, at Ross Perot's Electronic Data Systems, the One culture prescribed rigorous dress and grooming codes and a merciless dedication to overwork. Right and wrong were clear. Employees often slept nights at the office and traveled around the country with astonishing workloads, often not seeing their families for months at a time, as if they were on some latter-day crusade.

This compulsive—sometimes exclusive—focus on the perfection of details means that One organizations, though hardworking, can become estranged from market realities and the bottom line. Dedication to the ideal takes One organizations out of the real and often makes them less effective and efficient. "Zero defects" can be maddening as well as ineffective.

One organizations think they know the "one true path." This rigidity leaves them unavailable for alternative procedures and processes—for example, where a slight, perhaps undetectable or unimportant decrease in a quality standard might lead to a substantial increase in efficiency or effectiveness.

One organizations at their best have planned ahead. Their actions are not haphazard. They do what they say they are going to do. They keep to schedules. They are *honorable*. They work toward constant improvement.

Motorola, with its extraordinary, relentless emphasis on company-wide quality, is a famous One benchmark. After a massive company-wide drive to improve quality, Motorola was the first winner of the Baldridge Prize, the Commerce Department's prestigious award for quality. But as a true One proselytizer, Motorola expects each of its ten thousand suppliers to provide a timetable for when they, too, will apply for the Baldrige Prize, or Motorola will take its business elsewhere. According to William Wiggenhorn, a senior Motorola personnel executive, people "must accept our definition of work and the workweek: the time it takes to ship perfect products to the customer."[6]

Ones do best in a marketplace that is relatively stable or with a product that is so innovative or standard setting that it has a strong growth curve. Finding new "truths" in the latest quickly changing fads or trends or in the midst of a turbulent market and abruptly adjusting to them is not One's style.

Getting the Best from a One

Unequivocal Ones are absolutists who repress their Nine shadow, the home of chaos, ambivalence, and paradox. Nines know how to trust the natural order. Unable to discern which situations may be left alone to run their course (at Shadow Nine) and lacking a compassionate feel for what others really need or want (at Ally Two), absolutist Ones rigidly impose what they consider to be objective standards and rules on everything. When Ones balance their wings, they respond to the subjective needs of the situation rather than imposing an idealized solution.

When Ones balance the pulls of their wings, "letting it be" (on the Nine side) and serving others (at Two), they can claim the virtue of One, serenity, as expressed in the famous Serenity Prayer: "God grant me the serenity to accept the things I cannot change, the courage to change the things I can, and the wisdom to know the difference."

Ones in the flow state, freed of the burden of fixing the world, take on the perspective of high-minded Seven: an exciting panorama of imagination, innovation, and optimism. Overwhelmed Ones sink to a chaotic sea of melancholic feelings, the perspective of their Stress Point Four. These feelings make what is happening to the normally impersonal One quite personal, and they can be of great assistance in getting through stress.

Stress Point: Four

Ones move to Four under stress. The basic psychodynamic of Ones is the suppression of rage, and under stress these normally super-controlled people can be profoundly emotional, a startling change for most Ones. Immersed in a chaotic sea of melancholic and soulful feelings, the righteous One now sounds whiney and full of blame. He feels like the victim of people who just don't understand the importance of order and precision, of values and virtue, who are too emotional, and who are either unconscious or not conscientious.

Normally optimistic about enhancing the greater good and the general welfare, the One under stress may despair of having any ability to effect change. His complaints change from detailed criticism of others to self-absorbed hopelessness about his own prospects. "It's tainted. It's no good. Throw the whole thing out," says the One in Four.

But One in Four is also a wake-up call. Normally so sure he has the answer for others in objective principles, One now looks with uncertainty inside himself. At Four he is reminded of the nature and complexity of human feelings, most especially his own.

High Performance Point: Seven

In High Performance, Ones move from compulsiveness to impulsiveness, from "one right way" to pleasure in ambiguity, spontaneity, and innovation, the hallmark of Seven. They don't care so much if plans fall through or a schedule goes awry. They "let up." They don't take themselves so seriously. They fly lightly.

Not surprisingly, Ones do very well outside their normal routine, on overseas assignments where they are not the responsible official. Then it's easier for them to go to Seven, "although it's sometimes necessary to cross two states," says a One's spouse.

Seven inspires One to share the vision, to network with the right people, to get others on board. When One expands to Seven, the preacher/teacher becomes a collaborator and experimenter willing to take a flyer and make a mistake.

Asking a One "what if?" questions or encouraging a group to brainstorm is an effective way to create a Seven environment. We set up a once-a-week brainstorming session for John's uptight group at the CIA in an effort to foster more creativity, independence, risk taking, and fun. Since Ones feel safe with free-form creativity as long as they know what the rules are, we had clear rules for the sessions. Ideas would be generated without criticism or judgment. Any idea was potentially okay. The target was quantity over quality. In this scenario, it was impossible to make a mistake, the One bugaboo. Everybody loved it; John loosened up, and some stars emerged from the group.

Wings

Shadow Point: Nine

Ones find their Shadow Point at Nine: a chaotic, disorderly, and undifferentiated world where opposing, even incompatible, positions are true. Ones normally live in a black-and-white world, which may be without mercy, but at least justice is sure and swift and makes sense on its own terms. Nine is all about shades of gray; there, everything is negotiable and everything is connected.

But Shadow Point Nine grounds One in the real world of people. At Nine, One begins to see that her strongly held opinions have a legitimate flip side. "Nines used to drive me crazy. I hated their indecision," says John. "But now I seek them out precisely for their opinions, plural. I make it a conscious exercise. I ask, 'What do you think?' and then, 'What else do you think?' This widens my framework. Ones separate themselves. Nines stay connected. It's very useful." Ones are the most compulsive about changing others on the Enneagram; Nines are the least. At Nine, One learns to let go.

Ally Point: Two

At Two, the realm of attentiveness to others, Ones remember that they are not merely administering procedures, rules, and dogma, but that they work with people who have feelings. At Two, Ones learn to appreciate others. At Two, John learned to focus on the person in front of him instead of the idealized model inside his head.

"Two changes me in two ways," says John. "As far as the analysts who work for me, I still think I am damn good at seeing what their careers should be. But rather than just laying out an ideal plan, I listen more for their enthusiasms and heart's desires to help them make choices. It's more about them." A *Business Week* editorial reminds us that "[Total Quality Management] only works when a company finds out what its customers care about."[7]

Two creates compassion and is the way out for One. There is no true morality (One) without compassion (Two).

Cardinal Rules

If You Work with a One

- Neatness counts. The medium is the message. News or advice needs to be neatly packaged and categorized.
- Be polite and considerate. Ones believe in etiquette. Use the magic words: *please, thank you,* and *you're welcome.* Most Ones prefer that you be well groomed within the local rules.
- Be on time. Ones are devoted to staying on schedule, and if your lateness makes them late, they won't soon forgive you.
- Gentle teasing and humor go a long way. If you're going to suggest that a One "trust the process" or "go with the flow," smile when you say that.
- Go through proper channels. The administrative structure exists to serve order, a One priority. Ones hate for you to go above their heads.
- Admit your mistakes and mean it. Find the place where it's true that you have gone astray. Ones are usually right (in a narrow context) about what's wrong. Most Ones will forgive mistakes of judgment that are acknowledged. But mistakes arising from your bad habits, like your insensitivity or disorganization or your bad motives, like cover-ups or manipulations, are much harder for them to forgive.
- Play by the rules. Ones like lots of structure and definition in their assignments and reports. If you're the boss, explain how you want something done. If your boss is a One, find the way she wants to do it and do it exactly that way.
- Instead of disagreeing with a One, ask "what if" questions. This can create a Seven environment. (Disagreeing with Ones hardens their position because it seems as if you are calling their values into question.)
- When feeling nitpicked, remember the One is only trying to help.
- Ask permission before you take a One employee to task. "Is this a good time to discuss a problem I'm having with your work?" Ones don't take criticism well, but they are good at giving permission.
- Be accountable. Do what you say you're going to do. Some of the Enneagram types don't come to closure on details (Seven and Nine, for example). Ones need the *i*'s dotted and the *t*'s crossed.

If You Are a One

- Be a model, not a critic.
- Remember that much of what you say will be understood as critical even though you may not think it is.

- Check the context. Your criticism of others is probably correct (you are, after all, the expert on "what's wrong"), but you overfocus on it. Your context is probably skewed. This is a mistake. (Sorry!) What information (particularly the feelings of others or alternative routes or procedures) are you overlooking? It's not what's wrong but how you are run by what's wrong that matters.

- Use your vision of what's perfect and your understanding of what's wrong as a guide, not as a ball and chain.

- Pop the cork. All those repressed feelings, judgments, resentments are being stuffed down because you think they are unacceptable. Instead, they're in your way. When they are repressed they make you seem much angrier than you realize.

- Keep your agreements with yourself. All fixated Ones are serious self-torturers who make promises to themselves and break them. They change the rules after the game is played, raising the hurdle after they've taken the jump.

- Learn what "good enough" means.

- Forgive yourself.

- Mind your own business. Take a vacation from being superresponsible for the moral well-being of others.

- Do you want to be right or present? Judge away, if you want, but if your boss thinks you're judging him, don't plan on being at meetings of the inner circle. Work is not the Inquisition; people don't want irritating moralists or judges around.

- Encourage mistakes. Your severe, judging manner may invite employees or colleagues to hide their mistakes and thereby keep you from the information, feedback, or wisdom that you need.

1. Benjamin Franklin, *Autobiography* (New York: Appleton, 1900), 98.
2. Steven Covey, *The Seven Habits of Highly Effective People* (New York: Fireside, 1989), 122.
3. David Greising, "Quality: How to Make It Pay," *Business Week* (August 8, 1994).
4. *Los Angeles Times*, September 25, 1995, E2.
5. Cited in Robert Whiting, *You Gotta Have Wa* (New York: Vintage, 1989), 50.
6. William Wiggenhorn, "When Training Becomes an Education," *Harvard Business Review* (July/August 1990), 71.
7. *Business Week*, "Quality: From Buzzword to Payoff," August 8, 1994.

 # The Helper

AKA	The Guardian Angel, the Power Behind the Throne, the Needy Giver
Worldview	I support and empower others. They couldn't do it without me.
High Side	Generous helpers who bring out the best in others; assiduous, friendly, openhearted, full of enthusiasm and praise; kind, determined, loving
Low Side	Seductive flatterers; behind-the-scenes manipulators who meet other people's needs for their own purposes; martyrs; chameleons who change to please others
Leadership Style	Cheerleaders and appreciators of *people*; management by enthusiastic encouragement
Credo	I am needed.
Appeal to	Personal relationship; their desire to help; their special understanding of and talent with people
Don't Appeal to	Scientific evidence, theories, surveys, economic trends
Talk/Communication Style	Compliments, cajoling, personal questions, seductive charm
Makes You Feel	Appreciated, fully heard and taken care of; and—sometimes—manipulated, trapped, guilty
Appearance	Sweetly seductive; highly adjustable to audience
Good Work Setting	Work with people: therapy, sales, health care, service
Difficult Work Setting	Work without people: accountant, forest ranger, scientific research

Books	*Mary Kay on People Management* by Mary Kay Ash
	Leadership Is an Art by Max De Pree
	Servant Leadership by Robert Greenleaf
Sayings	"Whither thou goest, I will go; and where thou lodgest, I will lodge; thy people shall be my people, and thy God, my God."
	—The biblical Ruth of Moab, a Two, to her mother-in-law, Naomi
	"You can have everything you want in life, if you will just help others get what they want."
	—Zig Ziglar
	"Applause and the recognition it represents are among the world's most powerful forces."
	—Mary Kay Ash
	"I have always wanted a neighbor just like you."
	—Fred McFeely Rogers
Of the Two Persuasion	Mary Kay Ash, Max De Pree, Mister Rogers, Leo Buscaglia, Sally Jessy Raphael, Desmond Tutu, Mary Tyler Moore's Mary Richards, pediatrician T. Berry Brazelton, fashion designer Isaac Mizrahi
High Performance	4 Claim and act on own aspirations and passions
Stress	8 Bossy bully; ruthless powermonger
Ally	3 *Energized* by staying on task, by accomplishment, by being respected for competence and efficiency
Shadow	1 *Grounded* by acknowledging and adhering to standards, policies, and procedures (which they tend to bend)
Virtue	Humility
Vice	Pride

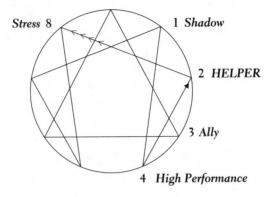

Stress 8

1 *Shadow*

2 HELPER

3 *Ally*

4 *High Performance*

Getting to Know a Two

Rhonda's Story

Rhonda is vice president for student services at a branch of a state university on the East Coast. Although she is hugely busy with lots of campus, community, and family activities ("I'm basically a mom—it just depends which family you're talking about," she says), she always makes time for me. I love to walk around campus with her. "This is my office," she says. "I could never sit at a desk all day. I manage by schmoozing around."

Everyone knows her and she knows most people by name; she gives each student or faculty member genuine individual attention. She frequently touches people with her hand and looks right into their eyes. When the comments are complaints, she doesn't bat an eye. "Problems are opportunities to get people what they want," she says. "I'm happy to wave my magic wand and do that."

On her desk is a sign given to her by her staff. It reads: "Supreme Goddess of the Universe." Underneath that: "Take a number."

Rhonda had been a nurse and while raising three young children became a part-time teacher at the university's School of Health Sciences. "When the vice president's job came open," she says, "I just decided I wanted it, even though I had no real experience or qualifications in educational administration.

"I found out who was on the hiring committee. I learned as much as I could about them, who they were, what they liked, and who they knew. I had some connections, and I saw no reason not to use them. They were doing an expensive national search and were reluctant to even grant me an interview. But once I got in the room, the job was mine. I tailored my answers to each person on the search committee. I knew I could make each of them feel like I was talking only to him. When I try, I can get most people to like me.

"I remember there was one older fellow who was concerned about keeping university traditions; there was also a younger board member who wanted a lot of innovations. Later, I found out they each thought I would be their best ally."

Now Rhonda has proven herself and no one regrets the decision. When she got her five-year pin many people were shocked she had been on the job only five years; she was such a part of the institution. "I work with my department heads. I resolve conflict. I serve on many committees. I supervise the personnel and development functions very closely. What keeps me going is that I realize I am having an impact on the students. Otherwise it would be meaningless."

She moves easily between worlds. "I have completely different wardrobes—and personalities—for campus, for going down to the state capital, for meeting with alumni and wealthy donors."

Carter, the university's president, who is a Six, relies on her substantially. "Many people think Rhonda runs the university. I give her a lot of credit. Of all the people who have worked for me, she manages me best. She brings in her issues. She proposes a solution and she says, 'Think about it.' And I do."

"What do you get criticized for?" I asked her. After a long pause: "Not much."

"Well, she's very manipulative," comments a social sciences dean. "She's very important around here, but you are not allowed to call her on her power game. She appears to do everything for others. But she's very ambitious, and she just won't cop to it."

I tell her the criticism. "Oh please," she says, her eyes wide as she takes my arm. "Powerful? I can't even get my children to go to bed on time. Now, writing a book about the Enneagram for a big publisher, that's really something!

"What I like," she says, "is being in the background—solving problems and giving others the credit."

"But you like to be noticed for that?" I ask.

She beams. "Would that be so horrible?"

About her success she says, "In high school I would never have been considered most likely to succeed. But I happened to be the girlfriend of the guy voted most likely to succeed."

Do you recognize Rhonda? Rhonda is a Two.

The Basic Premise

Twos are "people" people, and for them every business is a *people business*. Jim Autry, the former publishing executive, succinctly states the Two credo when he writes, "There is no business. There are only people." Mary Kay Ash, the cosmetics magnate and one of the most successful woman entrepreneurs ever, is a Two. "To me 'P & L' meant much more than profit and loss," she has written; "it meant people and love."[1]

Twos zero in on the emotional needs of individuals around them—their boss, colleagues, or customers—and then deftly, relentlessly, expertly respond to them. They are the extraordinarily prescient secretary or personal assistant and the empathic, nurturing, I-take-care-of-my-brood boss. Twos see themselves as—and often are—the power behind the throne.

As such, Twos have considerable power and influence. They can make their lack of formal authority seem fairly irrelevant. When I worked in a small government agency, the agency director's secretary, a Two, essentially ran the place. As the boss's gatekeeper—a standard Two position—she determined who got to see him and when, and what papers reached his desk. He was a Six who was grateful that she kept supplicants at bay. She knew his priorities; she expertly ministered to *his* bosses; and she took personal care of him: she was not offended to fetch his coffee and his lunch.

Twos can be true guardian angels of a project or an organization. They are responsible, engaged, and accountable. Genuinely empathetic, they build their lives around the people who matter to them. They sense when someone's feelings are hurt, and they know what to do to soothe them. They pick up on potential animosity between co-workers and make skillful efforts to bring them together.

For his part, the Two doesn't ask for much, directly. But there's a catch. Twos believe that by expertly meeting your needs, they should get theirs met, also expertly. Two runs a seductive bait-and-switch power game. "I am only here to help you get well," says the Two nurse, "and in order for me to do that, things must be done just my way." The Two takes control, but only for your benefit.

And what Twos want as their part of the bargain is for people they value (like you) to depend on and therefore appreciate them. Seductive, skilled at pulling those hidden strings, they are as adept at making others depend on them as Threes are at getting the job done. Gradually Twos become powerful and influential because important people rely on them.

They enjoy basking in this reflected glory, particularly in the appreciation they get for being the linchpin: central and essential. "Aren't I a damn fine therapist?" asks my friend Susan when she hears of the worldly successes of one of her clients.

Twos at their best offer heartfelt, customized service without strings; at their worst, they may implicate you in a tangle of unspoken obligations. Many Twos have elements of both types.

The Two's Favor Bank

Marley, a colleague when I worked for the government, is now a high official at the Department of Health and Human Services. A Two, she was described in the *Washington Post* as "running an exclusive favor bank." Nothing illegal here, just the gift of getting people to owe her a favor. For example, she specializes in finding the perfect person for federal jobs that need filling. Both employer and employee are delighted and feel indebted to her, not to each other.

But if a Two fails to receive what she feels is her due, she'll certainly get perturbed and may take imaginative revenge. Barry, a lawyer, said to my assistant, Samantha, "Geez, my secretary has scheduled me in back-to-back meetings today every hour without a break."

Samantha, a Two, recognized the problem without missing a beat. "Barry, did you forget Secretary's Day last week?"

"Yes, as a matter of fact I did," he said. "Why? They did something in the office, but I didn't know it was mandatory."

Barry, a Three, was oblivious to the connection between his oversight and his secretary's behavior.

Twos *need* to be appreciated; that's why they are so appreciating of others. The corporate magazine at Mary Kay Cosmetics is called *Applause*. "Everyone loves praise," says Mary Kay. "One of the most important steps I ever took was when I began imagining that every single person I ever met had a sign around his or her neck that read, 'Make Me Feel Important.' I respond to this sign immediately.

"If you give somebody a 40¢ item in a $1 box with $100 worth of recognition, that's a thousand times more effective than giving a $100 item in the same box with 40¢ worth of recognition." Her famous sales awards ceremonies—in which she rewards her top performers with diamond rings, mink coats, pink Cadillacs, and expensive vacations—"strive for elaborate staging and glamour worthy of a Cecil B. DeMille production."[2] At these award ceremonies, all the winners thank Mary Kay for making it possible, and rightly so.

Psychology

Unlike Ones and Eights, who were punished as children, Twos remember being encouraged and rewarded. These were children who focused on relationships; they were cherished as helpful, attentive, and caring. Twos learned early on that their path to success in the world was to be lit by the adoring smiles of the people around them. An attorney of my acquaintance who is a Two (specializing in adoptions) told me that when she was a young girl and her parents went to church, she would make all the beds in the house, just for the pleasure of seeing how delighted they were when they returned.

But the behind-the-scenes life of a Two in childhood was not so rosy. Twos often were responsible beyond their years for cooking and cleaning, for taking care of siblings and even their parents, who both dwarfed them and depended on them. Twos may have had plenty of time and attention from parents and important others, but at heart they believed they merited this attention for their expertly performed Two services, not for their true selves.

The result is that Twos—feeling that they are indispensable for their services but not really seen for themselves—feel inflated about their impact and deflated about their real self-worth. They are proud and humiliated at the same time.

Twos became Daddy's little girl and Mommy's little man; they were the teacher's pet, the star protégé, sometimes the brown nose. They became masterful at meeting the needs of authority figures in their life through flattery and service. In being needed they found their (false) identity. Rhonda, the university vice president, told me that when she was ten years old her best friend suggested they run off together. "Oh, I could never run away," she said. "I'm all my parents have. What would they do without me?"

As children, Twos believed that looking out for yourself, meeting your own needs, was selfish and shameful. As grownups, Twos continue to think of their own pesky needs as intrusive and of satisfying them directly and openly as selfish.

A Two may appear completely self-sufficient, the queen bee, either beneficent or imperious, without real needs of her own, and with a hoard of people who rely on her. Or she may seem a slavish devotee or acolyte to her boss or the master in her field and be ready to act on it. The Two is at her best when she is the conscious mistress of this tension: balancing individual self-worth with legitimate interdependence.

The Good News

Twos are enchanting genies. To those they have aligned with they seem to say, "Your wish is my command." Barbara Eden's genie in the television series *I Dream of Jeannie* was a classic Two. She was always frustrated by her master's desire to run his life without relying on her magic.

But many Twos are genies of a subtler sort. The Greeks believed that each entity has a guiding spirit—a "genius"—that inspires them. The high side of Twos is their uncanny ability to zero in on your unique "genius" *and then nurture it.* This can be very heartening, and you may not even know it's happening. You'll just be extremely pleased with yourself.

The best Twos ask, "How can I help you *as a person* do your job better?" Andy, a Two manager of a computer sales and service operation, noticed that one of his sales employees was lagging behind. He didn't reprimand him. He called him into his office for a long chat. He found out about the employee's experiences as a recent immigrant and the difficulties he was having adjusting to America. "I felt that if I got to know who he was, I could make it easier for him to succeed in his job. As soon as I got to the place where I knew and liked him, I knew it would be okay. He felt that I had my eye on him and was rooting for him. He turned things around very quickly." Twos manage people one at a time, responding to individual needs.

People Skills

Twos are expert at twisting your arm, but it may feel (at least at first) like a wonderful massage. "Carter loves that I can relate to the people on the board in a personal way," says Rhonda, the university vice president. "When he talks to people he has an agenda. Sometimes this means he's not paying attention to them personally. Once we were trying to get a wealthy donor to join our board of trustees. Carter told him at a meeting all the benefits of being on the board, talked about the university's financials, the facilities, and our needs for the future—and Carter simply didn't notice we were losing the guy. He actually started nodding off. Finally he got up to go and he said to Carter, 'Well, my wife makes all the important decisions.' I knew I had to do something fast. I looked up at him with my big eyes, gave him my warmest smile, put my arm through his, and said, 'If I were your wife, I'd tell you to do it!'

"He melted! And of course he did join the board. Later, Carter said, 'How do you get away with that palaver? I wish I could.'"

Enneagram Twos are the "universal solvent." They get along with a wide variety of people, accessing different personas for the different universes they operate in. Twos report that they are *sincere* in these different personas. So a Two may be seductive and subservient with a boss but a diva with her employees. For most Twos, both roles feel authentic and appropriate. (Contrast with Nines, also highly accommodating, who maintain the same persona and approach for both boss and employees and everyone else.)

Twos are the cheery specialists of small kindnesses at work, appreciating people exactly the way they long to be appreciated, remembering birthdays, weddings, and special needs. They write cards to commemorate births and promotions. They organize the office to collect for gifts and condolences. Twos are also quick to express gratitude—which is, of course, what they want from you!

Mary Kay still personally makes cookies for the saleswomen who are promoted from consultant to director. Says Mary Kay, "Some of the women even take a cookie home for a child or for a consultant in her unit—simply because 'it was made by Mary Kay.' So it's obvious my little personal touch matters to them."[3]

Rhonda has a candy bowl right on her desk, a model Two prop.

Customer Driven

Twos are customer driven, in contrast to Threes, who are market driven. Three says, "I'm in this business, let's go get customers!"—and then they can provide extraordinary customer service. Two says instead, "I'm serving these people, so I must be in this business!" McDonald's, a Three operation, wants to sell as many of the same hamburgers as possible. But Twos respond to individuals. "I can't just think in terms of tasks or routine," says Jack, who runs a family jewelry business. "I think in terms of people. I need to have a person in the picture. If it's *you* that wants something done, it doesn't matter what it is, I'm very glad to do it." The old Burger King jingle must have been written by a Two: "Have it your way at Burger King!"

"I get very happy when I see acknowledgment in people's faces," says Mimi, a Two who works for a big singles introduction service. "It means a lot to make other people happy and feel good. When I can't make people happy, I really do feel that I've failed."

Twos expect those below them to be as proudly customer driven as they are. "What I give my managers is their autonomy," says Kevin, a Two who is the manager of a department store. "Your department is your store. I expect only one thing in return: Don't let a problem with a customer land on my doorstep before I hear about it from you. By the time a customer comes to me, I want to be able to tell him that the problem has already been fixed. That's the standard of service around here."

The Ultimate Insiders

Although they may seem eager and sometimes naïve, Twos are the ultimate insiders. They know their organization as well as anybody because they know what the people are up to.

In the process of relating to everybody, Twos learn what's happening. Jackson, a Two bureaucrat, told me, "My boss says, 'I've never been around a man who talks to people as much as you do.'" But Twos can listen just as well, depending upon what is required to get people comfortable. "I consciously ask questions," said Marilou, a receptionist. "People like talking about themselves sooner or later." At SAS Scandinavian Airlines, the story was that whenever three employees would gather together, Jan Carlzon, the chief executive, would join them for a chat.

The Bad News

Twos are ambitious. At their worst, these seemingly sweet and supportive people can be ruthless powermongers and manipulators. Twos are not shy about intruding on people or messing in your business. Some Twos go so far as to be emotional vampires, so unctuous and subtle and expert that the victim may be sucked dry before he even realizes that the Two was thirsty. A stereotypical example is the Two mother who gives her son two ties for his birthday. When she next sees him he is wearing one. "What's the matter," she asks, "you didn't like the other one?"

Low-side Twos have *chutzpah,* a brazen sense of entitlement. Many years ago, a Two who was a direct competitor of mine asked with wide-eyed innocence if she could have my client list. "Competition will be good for everybody in the business!" she said with a straight face.

Twos can be ambitious groupies of the powerful. They can butter up whomever is in a position to advance their purposes, their career, their influence, their problematic independence. Unless you have what this Two wants, you may be ignored, used, or abused in the service of the Two's dedication to his leader. If you do have what he wants, he will sell his soul for a compliment or a stroke or what you have that he needs.

Power Through Helping

Twos, like Sevens, are self-inflating. Pride, often barely disguised, is their vice. "The worst part of working as a saleswoman," says Helen, a Two, "is that customers keep asking for me. It's embarrassing for me when the other sales people have nothing to do." Once I was working on a project team with a Two, and I, expecting very modest sympathy, complained about an obnoxious manager we had to deal with. "Oh, he never gives *me* any problem! I just know how to talk to him," she said, satisfied with herself.

Twos care greatly about what others think of them. They want to be seen as the best, most sensitive, most selfless givers, as independent and without needs (or, alternately, as dependent on your largesse, if that does the trick). Being seductive is an essential part of this image; they magnetize others by their charisma, their sweetness, their sexiness, or even their motherliness. Most seductive of all is their astonishing ability to offer up just what they know you need.

Being all things to all people (that is, all people who matter to them) can sometimes result in confusion for these emotional chameleons about who they really are. Since they insist that others support their idealized self-image as givers par excellence, they appear independent while they are really dependent on the opinions, judgments, whims, and especially the needs of others. By finding their identity in being needed by others, Twos sometimes avoid dealing with what they really need for themselves or what's best for their business.

I once consulted with a family manufacturing business in which Sandra, the owner and widow of the founder and a Two, wanted to retire and pass the business on to her three sons. But she couldn't seem to find a way out. One son was in charge of sales, another of the factory, and the third ran the office. When any of the sons had a problem in his sector he consulted with Mom, who, without consulting the others, made adjustments that affected them. When this aggravated the others, Sandra would make further adjustments with the best of intentions. Although Sandra professed a great desire to leave the business, she and her sons agreed that the business was too dependent on her personally. How would they manage without her? Whenever the sons would try to work things out directly with one another, Sandra couldn't help but intervene. "Why shouldn't I try to make things easier?" she asked. Eventually Sandra saw how she made herself indispensable by stirring things up; she kept control of the business under the guise of helping. Once she acknowledged the part of her that didn't want to leave, she was able to go.

Manipulative Flatterers: The Beam of Light

Even though Twos put the spotlight on others, they control the action considerably by deciding where the bright beam is directed. In a consultation I did for a firm of management consultants, I spent the day meeting the partners individually in the conference room. In charge of me and of the event was one of their secretaries, Julie, a Two. She set up the conference room with flowers, many choices of hot and cold drinks, cookies, candies, and fruit. Somehow she knew I was allergic to wheat. We had wheat-free muffins. She checked in with me periodically all day; each conversation with her seemed like a beam of light and love. ("I'm just wonderful," I thought.) I began to muse about putting her on my staff. Then, between sessions, she asked if she could speak with me. She wanted to know if I would consider hiring her. I said I absolutely would. I was completely enchanted.

In midafternoon her boss stopped in for a few minutes. While he was there Julie glanced at me. Her look was so different I was startled. It's not that she was unfriendly; I simply saw that the beam of light and love was now completely directed at him. There was nary a ray for me.

I related this story to Marlene, a Two retreat center director, who exclaimed, "Oh, yes! That's the whoosh effect. Whoosh, and it's gone! I pick whom I'll champion and when."

Like Sevens, their mental counterpart, Twos are generally available for a better offer. Twos often experience this sequential monogamy as a kind of constancy; others may see it as fickleness. Evita Perón, a Two, attached herself to successively more powerful patrons for rapid advancement until she became the "mother of the nation." Her dying wish was that after she passed on, the poor should write their requests to her.

Twos feel comfortable using flattery as a means to an end. Mary Kay says the key to keeping customers is to lavish "so much value, care and attention" on them that "they would feel *guilty* even thinking about doing business with somebody else" (my emphasis).[4]

I met a Two in a large industrial organization who was attached as a staff coordinator to two competing research and development teams. She had the charming but perverse habit of inventing compliments that each of the warring parties might have said about the other and repeating them to each group. Why should it matter that the original encouragement was "pretend"? Wasn't it good for the organization?

Working with a Two

Influencing a Two

In working with a Two, your most effective appeals are to your mutual relationship or your need for personal support. Note the truth of how much your fortunes are intertwined and how the success of your project depends on the Two and on her behind-the-scenes exercise of power.

In your discussions, emphasize the effects of your proposals on people, especially specific people who are important to the Two. (Compare with Nine, who would be less interested in the impact on individuals than on the group as a whole.)

Avoid logical arguments to persuade. Remember how Linda, the pharmacist, wore down her Two boss in the chapter about Ones? Don't harp, as she did, on fairness, ethics, or standard procedures; although she got her raise, she nearly ruptured their relationship. On the contrary, it's better to note in any given situation that the rules deserve bending because real people with real feelings are involved.

How a Two Makes Decisions

As we have seen, Twos are most likely to understand problems as people problems and to consider the impact of decisions on people. "I make decisions easiest when I focus on a particular person," says Cheryl, the owner of a chain of beauty shops. "How does my decision affect this person? Even a decision that's about me, I think of someone else in order to get it going."

Twos are the least likely on the Enneagram to chew things over. Like Sevens, their mental counterpart across the Enneagram, Twos shoot from the lip: big talkers, they listen to themselves as they are talking to hear what they have to say, and they rely on quick hunches and impressions rather than judicious reasoning or firm convictions.

Content takes a back seat to emotional connections. In situations in which mental rigor or substantive linear thinking is expected, Twos may seem lightweight. But in situations where accomplishment through people is central, Twos are the Enneagram's heavyweights.

The Two Leadership Style

The Two's magnetism and natural feel for how prestige works attracts important others to become part of a mutually beneficial network. Twos don't hesitate to entice powerful people to associate with their enterprise. Twos can be super-salespeople because they see clearly and can point out elegantly (or shamelessly, depending on the need) exactly what the targeted benefactor stands to gain from this association.

At their best, Twos are the "servant leader." This is a concept developed by Robert Greenleaf, a longtime manager at AT&T, who was inspired by Herman Hesse's *Journey to the East*. In Hesse's tale we see a band of men on a mythical journey. "The central figure of the story is Leo who accompanies the party as the *servant* who does menial chores, but who also sustains them with his spirit and song. He is a person of extraordinary presence. All goes well until Leo disappears. Then the group falls into disarray and the journey is abandoned. They cannot make it without the servant Leo. The narrator, one of the party, after some years of wandering finds Leo and is taken into the Order that had sponsored the journey. There he discovers that Leo, whom he had known first as *servant*, was in fact the titular head of the Order, its guiding spirit, a great and noble *leader*."[5]

Indeed, a humanistic management style now in vogue proposes inverting the pyramid of the organization chart. "The entire structure of organizations needs to change," says Norman, a Two hotel manager. "It needs to be turned upside down." He displays an organizational chart for his hotel with the employees who serve customers at the top and himself at the bottom, a clever place for a Two. This makes Norman far more indispensable than if he were at the top—like most CEOs—where he could be lopped off without the entire structure collapsing! "I let all associates know I work for them," he says. For the best Two leaders, management itself is a support function. "To be a lone chief atop a pyramid is abnormal and corrupting," writes Greenleaf. (An Eight would not find it so.)

Max De Pree, the former CEO of the furniture maker Herman Miller, says leadership is "a serious meddling in the lives of others."[6] Two managers are not shy about being actively interventionist. They send their employees to conferences and to training. They delight in offering personal counseling.

For Twos, the art of leadership is not following principles (as with One) or cutting to the bottom line (as with Three). Real success for them is measured by their effects on customers and employees. De Pree, right on point, says, "The signs of outstanding leadership appear primarily among the followers. Are the followers reaching their potential? Are they learning? Serving? . . . [because] reaching our potential is more important than reaching our goals."[7] (This philosophy would startle most Threes.)

Similarly, Greenleaf says of servant leadership, "The best test is: Do those served grow as persons; do they, while being served, become healthier, wiser, freer, more autonomous, more likely themselves to become servants?"[8] For a Two leader, people are the focus—not information, as with a Five, or strategic planning, as with a Seven. Twos empower, engage, or light a fire in others. "The new leader is a listener, communicator, and educator—an emotionally expressive and inspiring person who can create the right atmosphere rather than make all the decisions himself," says Jan Carlzon, describing his customer-driven approach at SAS Airlines. "These traits were once regarded as feminine [but] intuition and sensitivity to other people's situations are traits that are essential for any manager."[9]

Two leadership is ideally suited for the kind of situation where an employee is ready to go but is feeling a little hesitant. The Two can be the mother hen providing confidence, support, and encouragement for the chick to leave the nest, but expecting a full report and many thanks when he returns.

The Two Work Style

Twos are masters at "managing the boss." They naturally know how to make their organization or their boss look good if they want to, and the bosses fall in line as they imagine that the Two's ideas are their own.

Twos don't have to be encouraged to get with the program They are willing to work late and hard to get something done for a boss they support. They don't need the explicit instructions required by a Nine or the specific authority you might need to give to a Six. They know what needs to be done, and they simply do it.

But make no mistake. Even though Twos are masters of the behind-the-scenes, these emotional types are comfortable with real power—with being around it and with exercising it. They want to be among the actors in significant situations. They know precisely the payoff they are looking for and how to direct the credit to themselves when they need to, even in jobs that may not seem like power positions.

"I loved being a waitress," says Marilyn, who now runs a day care center. "If they had benefits and I thought my back could take it I'd still be doing it. When you wait tables you're in control. You can double your tip with a look. You don't have to say anything."

Working with people they get along with easily is a big plus for a Two. Zeke, who hires out as an office temp to support his budding acting career, puts it this way: "Who do I like to work with? It all comes down to whether I can get you to like me. I don't like working with people if they *insist* on being dissatisfied or don't understand give and take. People who don't know what they want are fine with me. My job is to find out what they want and provide it. When I do, then the rewards are really big. I love working with people who appreciate me and my contribution."

The Two Learning Style

Twos may be highly intelligent, but they are rarely bookish. While Fives may relish a day (or a year) alone with a good book or a good modem, Twos long for more face-to-face interaction with people. Twos do well in workshops, discussions, and other situations in which they can exchange stories, feelings, and experiences. They learn best when they have an opportunity to connect with others, show off their people skills and charm, and be admired for enhancing the learning experience for others.

The Two Organization: Legendary Customer Service

Two organizations are people oriented. Customer satisfaction—and often employee satisfaction—are cornerstones of a Two organization. At the best Two companies, human resources functions (like training, personnel, employee assistance programs, profit sharing, health insurance) take center stage. Technological innovation or tight cost controls, in comparison, might be neglected if they are not seen as having any effect on customer or employee satisfaction.

Nordstrom, the department store famous for extraordinary customer service, is a Two organization. Its entire rulebook fits on a card and reads: "Rule

#1: Use your good judgment in all situations. There will be no additional rules." Compare this to the Midwestern furniture manufacturer with a One culture that hands each new employee a 114-page rulebook.

Nordstrom avoided computerized inventory controls until very recently. James Nordstrom argued, "Computers will only tell you what you've sold, not what the customer is asking for that you don't have." So Nordstrom carries by far the largest inventories, with the widest range of styles and sizes per square foot, in the industry.

Herman Miller, the furniture maker, was a leader in developing support systems for workers with AIDS, and the company—a Two organization if there ever was one—gives much thought to innovative benefits like child care and flextime.

It must have been Two organizations that pioneered the current vogue of "convenience benefits" for employees. An industrial plant in North Carolina sends its own mechanics to employees' homes to fix home appliances. Baptist Hospital of Miami takes employees' clothes to the dry cleaners, has the cafeteria cook employees a made-to-order take-home dinner, and offers employees a full body massage on-site. Many employees appreciate convenience benefits like these, feeling they liberate their time and increase their flexibility. The catch is when companies add services in order to gain control over employees, who must then work harder and longer with less maneuverability. Such captive employees may be barely aware that they are held hostage. This is the Two pickle.

Some Two organizations focus their Two beam of light so much on their clients that they forget (in true Two fashion) their own employees' needs. I've consulted at a wonderful social services agency where employees spend their entire days hearing about other people's tragedies but rarely consider their own problems. These energetic workers come up with every possible solution or referral. When I was there last, a fellow came in who couldn't afford to buy a birthday present for his son. First they called all over the city to see if there was an agency who could help him, but to no avail. So the staff took up a collection. "Thank you! Thank you so much!" said the poor man, who knew what to say to Twos. But more often the benefits of helping are not so crystal clear, nor is the gratitude, and so the burnout rate remains high.

Getting the Best from a Two

Instead of putting others first, or appearing to, Twos evolve when they value their own feelings enough to act on them directly. This is the perspective of Two's High Performance Point Four. (Freed of the urge to manipulate, Two can really be there for others.) When Twos are stressed, they overdo their autonomy and run over others at Stress Point Eight.

Two's Ally Point is Three. Twos are energized by staying on task. When they are not distracted by trying to win others over they make a real difference in their world, which is their true goal. One is Two's Shadow Point. Twos avoid One's rigid rulemongering, but they are grounded when they stay connected to One's keen sense of principle. When Twos balance principle (One) with the requirements of task (Three), they put their own ego aside and access the humility, the virtue of Two.

Marlene's Story

Marlene, a Two, is the executive director of a country club and seminar center in Florida. She's famous for her trademark people skills, which keep the atmosphere friendly and personal. "When someone passes my open door and doesn't say hello, I wonder why," she says.

Leslie, an Eight, was on Marlene's board of directors. "Leslie was very politically active," relates Marlene. "She not only was important in state politics, but she was very influential on the board.

"Leslie convinced the board that she should have an office at the club to do some development work. She got the board to give her a $5,000-a-month honorarium to go with it. But all she did was work on a friend's political campaign. She was doing her own business on the phone all the time!"

Stress Point: Eight

Twos need to feel assured that they are affecting others and are in control of their environment. If they aren't allowed to help, if they don't get recognition for what they do, or, especially, if they are suppressed, bullied, or disempowered, pressure builds up. Twos feel explosive and move to Eight.

Two at Eight is frustrated. She feels herself to be the victim of others' bullheadedness, abuse, insensitivity, stupidity, and lack of empathy and appreciation. Very often this seems like pure injustice to a stressed Two. But Eight is also a focusing wake-up call for Two. There is no more indirection. There is no more "Ms. Nice Girl." Eight forces Two to expose her game as a power game. Orders must be issued to others directly, without a sugar coating or manipulation, to correct the injustice or power imbalance. When necessary, retribution and revenge are swift and sure.

"Leslie drove me crazy. She was running up huge phone bills and getting paid for it. I overheard her say on the phone that she has free run of the joint! I'm not sure which is worse: that she was doing it right in front of me [Twos hate to be humiliated], or that I couldn't make her stop [Twos hate to feel powerless]. I was incredibly angry," Marlene remembers. "I felt like physically throwing her out of the building. I would've gotten away with it, too." In stress, Eight forces Two to express control and dominion directly. "Then she would have learned her lesson," says Marlene.

High Performance Point: Four

At Four, Twos find their much sought after independence and individuality. They confidently rely on their own feelings and positions. Two learns to tolerate longing, that of others and their own, instead of managing quick emotional fixes. Frequently Two's move to Four is demonstrated by a change in professional direction in which Two surprisingly actualizes a long-repressed artistic, creative, or humanistic venture.

When Twos access Four, they look inward instead of out to others. They keep track of their feelings and needs, the opposite of usual. At Four, Twos develop deep convictions that are not dependent on the opinions of others and that won't be denied. This gives Twos a legitimate premise for being independent and for having things their way—indeed, for having a distinctively personal way. "As much as I enjoy serving the needs of the Board and our members," says Marlene, "when I'm at Four I realize I'm the creator of a fairly strong vision for this place."

At Four, Twos naturally find the answer to the basic Two dilemma: What do I want for me?

Wings

Shadow Point: One

One is Two's rejected shadow. Two says, "I am people-oriented and flexible, loving and warm, not rigid and strict, and especially not critical like a One." One is a stickler for the law: "The same rule for all." Equity—adjusting for the individual case—is the special dominion of Two.

"Ordinarily I don't like formalities," says Marlene. "I like to wave my magic wand."

Twos who run from their One shadow avoid restrictions, rules, and inhibitions. Such are for the hoi polloi. Because of who they know and how much they give, objective standards don't apply. "We need just the rules you and I make, or, better yet, let's have no rules at all, just our mutual concern and support." Impersonal rule-based criticism—or any criticism at all, for that matter—can be a real downer to an approval-seeking Two.

As with many Twos, Marlene's relationship with rules was to bend them. "Rules?" she retorts. "I don't make them, I don't like them, and when they exist I try not to follow them." Many Twos are sticklers for the rules as applicable to strangers or to those with whom they do not have a personal relationship, but when it comes to those they know and want to court, or to themselves, most Twos will bend the impersonal rules for the sake of enhancing their cachet in a personal relationship.

Here Marlene was stuck. Leslie was breaking the rules, demeaning Marlene's power and prestige rather than enhancing it.

The Two who does not embrace her One shadow sacrifices necessary critical communication of the rules for relationships at her peril. Twos in a good relationship with their internal One do not apply the rules too formally or bend the rules excessively to accommodate their favorites. The rules make sense as appropriate guidelines.

Ally Point: Three

Twos long to accomplish great things, but their style is to work through others. When Twos are drawn to Three, they no longer overaccommodate the feelings of others, to manipulate them to like the Two or do what the Two wants done. Two in Three concentrates directly on the task at hand, on competence, on doing the job efficiently and effectively. Two is transformed when he can say, "This is my work. These are my goals. Without fooling or seducing or manipulating others, how can I directly attain them?"

Marlene remembers, "When I started out I would invite my employees to go to jazz clubs with me. I didn't really want to socialize with them, but I felt the best way for us to get on a good footing at work was for them to like me outside of work. In the office, I tried to act like a pal and was always terribly indirect in setting work priorities or making other demands on them.

"I used to say sweetly to an employee, 'When will it be convenient for you to turn this report in?' Now I say, 'I need this by. . . .' What I have learned is the difference between being liked by my employees and simply working with them—which, by the way, turns out to be all I really wanted or needed."

Once she saw the problem with Leslie in this light, Marlene put aside her wounded pride and made a plan to leverage her Three wing. "What can I do about it? If I threw her out," she told me, "that would be a waste."

When Marlene confronted Leslie, this is what she said: "This political campaign you're working on is terrific for the center, Leslie. Why not see if you can use your influence to hold your fund-raising events at the center. We'll give you a discount rate. It will be a good way to bring in new people and drum up business for the center." Leslie jumped at the chance.

Twos at their best work powerfully and effectively through others to effect a unique, personal vision. "Once I could see that what she was doing could be helpful to the center, and to me for that matter, if I channeled it right, I realized I had my Two powers back," says Marlene. "Then I could genuinely be in service to the center, which is what I want."

Cardinal Rules
If You Work with a Two

- Be generous with your praise, approval, affection, and approbation. While Twos are wary of false and manipulative flattery, they crave *genuine* admiration for their people skills, their big hearts, and their bottomless appetite for service. Let them know when they've hit the mark. "Wow, it's just what I needed!" "Just the way I like it!" "Just as I'd hoped!"

   If you are the sort of person (perhaps a Five) who doesn't believe in praising people for just doing their job, you need to know that Twos' lifeblood is emotional applause; they get vindictive when their "due" is withheld. Take a Two for granted and you're a goner.
- Never embarrass a Two. Twos dread humiliation. At Mary Kay, "Criticism is always sandwiched between two thick, heavy layers of praise."
- Speak from your real needs without whining. Twos respond well to need. It perks them up. In some ways, they are likely to know how to meet these needs better than you do. Natural nurses, Twos are great at triage. When catastrophe strikes they know how to prioritize and stay calm.
- Be personal.. The best thing you can say to a Two is, "Gosh, I couldn't have done it without you." The worst thing you can say is, "Mother, please! I'd rather do it myself!"
- To try to bully or lead a Two by the nose is to court disaster. Twos are power mavens par excellence; they will take the appearance of bullying from their actual boss (whom they in fact control), but not from you.
- Don't try to meet their needs the way they meet yours. You'll never be able to keep up, and anyway it's usually discombobulating for a Two to receive. But do let them meet your needs, to the extent that it's comfortable for you. That's how Twos build relationships.
- Twos will be grateful to you for any deposits you can make in their "favor bank" or any way you can expand their sphere of influence.
- Don't expect a Two to give pithy answers to questions like "What do you need?" or "What can I do to get along with you?" Two will say, "I'm the person who meets needs! I do the getting along with!"

- Don't be dismayed when you see a Two (or a Seven, for that matter) socializing on the job. That's how they recharge their batteries and even how they get their work done. Twos know that connecting with people is an important part of their responsibilities.

If You Are a Two

- Turn your legendary Two compassion on yourself: What are your real needs? Who really matters? Take time to find your own feelings, true interests, positions, and desires. This may mean looking inside yourself and spending time alone (gasp!).
- Back off. Butt out. Sometimes people need to solve their own problems and have their own space. Note your codependent tendency to rescue and make other people's problems your own. This person may not need your rescuing. Don't overempathize. Be clear about where your responsibilities end.
- Everybody else is not a (defective) Two: they won't be able to anticipate your needs as well as you anticipate theirs. Asking for what you want may not be as humiliating as it seems.
- When you can stop working through others, you've solved the Two's central dilemma: independence versus dependence. The answer is interdependence: seeing your importance in context and being able to receive what you really need.
- Make sure the content side of your work is being addressed, not just the people issues. Twos tend to think their problems are people based; sometimes it's just that the work isn't getting done.
- Learn to accept praise without discounting it.
- Deal straight, without manipulating. You believe you deserve special deals to match your special relationships, but this just continues the Two game, which dictates that you have to beguile in order to get what you want.

1. James Autry, *Love and Profit: The Art of Caring Leadership* (New York: Avon Books, 1991), 45; Mary Kay Ash, *Mary Kay* (New York: Harper & Row, 1987), 26.
2. Mary Kay Ash, *Mary Kay*, 158.
3. Mary Kay Ash, *Mary Kay*, 169.
4. Mary Kay Ash, *Mary Kay, You Can Have It All* (Rocklin, CA: Prima Publishing, 1995), 4.
5. Larry Spears, "Servant Leadership and the Greenleaf Legacy," in *Reflections on Leadership*, ed. Larry C. Spears (New York: John Wiley & Sons, 1995), 7.
6. Max De Pree, *Leadership Jazz* (New York: Dell Publishing, 1992), 219.
7. De Pree, *Leadership Is an Art* (East Lansing: Michigan State Univ. Press, 1987).
8. Spears, "Servant Leadership," 13.
9. Jan Carlzon, *Moment of Truth* (New York: Harper & Row, 1987), 36.

THREE

The Producer

AKA	The Performer, the Motivator, the Manager, the Marketer, the Achiever
Worldview	The world is a contest that I can win if I work hard and appear successful.
High Side	Eager, responsible, goal-oriented achievers; persistent, organized, enthusiastic
Low Side	Workaholic, manipulative, soulless hustlers
Leadership Style	Task-oriented meritocracy: lead by high-profile, sometimes autocratic, example; cheerleaders for success
Credo	Just do it.
Appeal to	The bottom line, effectiveness, efficiency, image, winning, what the competition is up to, the Three's career path or self-interest
Don't Appeal to	Warm, fuzzy vibes; the need to pace or slow down
Talk/Communication Style	Pitches and propaganda, advertising for self and others
Makes You Feel	Inspired, capable of your best, part of the team; and—sometimes—a little behind, too cautious, a little slow moving and lazy
Appearance	Bright-eyed and bushy-tailed, or bedraggled from overwork, high-energy dress for success
Good Work Setting	Fast moving, deal making, entrepreneurial, image conscious, competitive, where results are quantifiable and hard work and success are rewarded
Difficult Work Setting	Low prestige, waiting for others to make decisions, lost in a crowd

Books	*The Effective Executive* by Peter Drucker *The Gamesman* by Michael Maccoby *What Makes Sammy Run?* by Budd Schulberg *Competitive Advantage* by Michael Porter *Dress for Success* by John Molloy

Sayings	"Ready! Fire! Aim!"
	"Be the best that you can be."
	"Life is short. Play hard."
	"Fake it until you make it."
	"Keep up, keep up."
	"Real successful people have to cut corners and manipulate. That's the way things get done."
	   —John De Lorean
	"If you don't come to work on Saturday, well just don't bother coming in on Monday."
	   —Attributed to Jeffrey Katzenberg when he was at Disney
	"I never got a [high school] degree, and I've only worked half days my entire career. I guess my advice to you is to do the same. Work half days every day. And it doesn't matter which half. The first twelve hours or the second twelve hours."
	   —Kemmons Wilson (founder of Holiday Inns)
	"Massive consistent action with pure persistence and a sense of flexibility in pursuing your goals will ultimately give you what you want."
	   —Anthony Robbins, motivational speaker and author
	"Winning isn't everything. It's the only thing."
	   —Vince Lombardi
	"Everyone lives by selling something."
	   —Robert Louis Stevenson

Of the Three Persuasion	Donald Trump, Murphy Brown, Ray Kroc (McDonald's), Bryant Gumbel, Anthony Robbins, Sharon Stone, Arnold Schwarzenegger, Jack Kemp, James Baker III, Jack Welch (General Electric), Wayne Huizenga (Blockbuster), Werner Erhard,

Michael Jordan, Tom Monaghan (Domino's),
McDonald's, Federal Express, Hong Kong, the U.S.A.

High Performance	6 Builders of work teams, organizations, and communities; loyal idealists; appropriately strategic and cautious
Stress	9 Overwhelmed, spacing out, vegging out, blown fuses
Ally	4 *Energized* by connecting with heart's desire, true calling
Shadow	2 *Grounded* by being in service, by sensitivity to others' feelings and plights
Virtue	Honesty
Vice	Hypocrisy

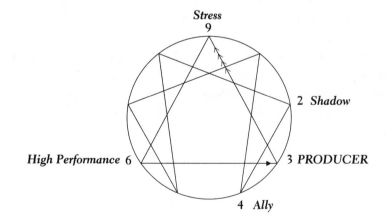

Getting to Know a Three
Kate's Story

Kate is director of marketing for one of the national cable networks in Los Angeles. Her bright, innocent, eager good looks make her seem honest and straightforward. A terrific deal maker, she acts as if she has an inexhaustible supply of energy.

When she arrives at her office, she picks up a stack of mail and memos from her secretary without actually stopping. She responds to her secretary's good morning with "I'll take the London calls first, then the New York calls, and the L.A. calls after that." Using a wireless headset so she can walk around with her hands free (and do something else while she's talking), Kate takes scores of phone calls a day, most of them from prospective advertisers on the channel, from cable operators who want to drop or add the network, and also from merchandisers who want to license the network's well-known logo or characters on network-owned shows for toys or clothing. Her secretary prioritizes the callers on a list that appears on a computer screen in Kate's office. Sometimes her secretary will flash a computer message to interrupt her with a more urgent call or note. To sit in her office and watch her make deals quickly on the phone is dizzying. Once she has confirmed a deal, her assistant, who may be listening on the phone, draws up a contract, which she sends on to the legal department.

When, after a corporate reshuffling, *Daily Variety* got Kate's new responsibilities (slightly) wrong, she went ballistic. She called up her company's PR chief and bit his head off for incompetence. "You don't understand," she said. "This is really critical. This is how everybody in the industry looks at me. They need to know who to have a meeting with, who to invite to an event. *Who I am is who I appear to be!*"

Within the cable industry she is much admired. A consummate juggler, she serves on several industry-wide committees and is very active in the Hollywood Council, a high-profile but exclusive political lobbying group, where she has many famous friends. As if that weren't enough, she volunteers for a group that serves hot home meals to people with AIDS and sits on the board of her son's private school.

She keeps a tight watch on the professional competition. Once she actually declined to fire a mediocre performer on the spot because she was afraid he would get a job right away with one of the competitors and reveal her network's strategy for a marketing campaign. She waited several months, until the campaign was launched, before she let him go.

As a youngster, Kate reports that she was "a great kid who got great grades.

At one time or another, I was the captain of every sports team I played on—basketball, soccer, and track." She was such a good baby-sitter that her friends stopped recommending her as a substitute for their regular clients. "The kids always wanted me back instead," she says. She worked her way through college by starting and running a housecleaning service; she wasn't too proud to work as a maid herself when she had to. At Harvard Business School she "felt kind of like a fraud. I just winged the financial stuff. But it was really worthwhile because I met some high-powered people who are some of my best friends—and contacts—today."

Says one of her employees, "I love working for her because she's so smart, energetic, and committed. There's no one who works harder or who's savvier about this market. She's also a great boss; she knows everybody's talents and weaknesses, and she helps us function as a team. She's like a coach who pulls in the right player at the right time, even though egos might get bruised. I always feel like she squeezes the best out of me. When she gets behind a project she makes it happen, and when she gets behind a person she makes him happen, too. She's great with recognition and awards."

Not every employee, though, is quite so enthusiastic. "Sometimes I feel like I'm an obstacle between her and the finish line. She just runs right over me. She's always in such a terrific hurry to get things done. If a situation is complex and deserves some serious reflection, it's almost impossible to get her to consider the pros and cons. I feel like I have to make an appointment just to say good morning. Plus, she's not exactly the kind of person you want to go to when your kids are sick and you're overwhelmed."

When Kate approached me to explore the Enneagram she said, "I want a step-by-step manager's guide for handling various problems. For example, what precisely do you say when some employee is sobbing in your office? I want to be considerate, but I have work to do."

Do you recognize Kate? Kate is a Three.

The Basic Premise

Threes shine in the workplace, their natural habitat. They want piles of *accomplishments*, and they want to be noticed for them. Ray Kroc, the Three who built McDonald's, called his autobiography *Grinding It Out*, which is the basic Three approach. But even though Threes are Type A workaholic grinds, they're *image conscious* as well, and they make a strong effort to appear to the world as charismatic winners.

"Just Do It," goads Nike, whose advertising targets Threes and Three wanna-bes. Threes have a bias for action. They are *pragmatists*. They know how things work and what it takes to make something happen. To a Three, life and work are about having goals, doing whatever you need to do (and being whoever you need to be) to attain them, while finessing obstacles that get in the way until, full speed ahead, you break the tape at the finish line.

For the Three, life and work are essentially *competitive* enterprises, and Threes are not squeamish about beating the competition. That's what the competition is for. "This [business] is rat eat rat, dog eat dog," said Ray Kroc. "You're talking about the American way of survival of the fittest." Jack Welch's famous insistence that General Electric's businesses be number one or number two in their market is pure Three. "If you don't have a competitive advantage, don't compete," he instructed.

America is the land of the Three. Self-starting, can-do Three skills are much admired; indeed, lots of folks pretend to be Threes, sometimes without knowing it, in a culture where our identity seems to hinge on our material achievement and success. The typically American theology of Norman Vincent Peale and Robert Schuller, both Threes, is not so much about a profound personal exploration as it is about being resilient, "believing in yourself," having goals, and acting on them. Peale's power of positive thinking, an applied optimism that may look similar to Seven, is in fact far more pragmatic and results oriented. Peale says, don't be "an obstacle man," a person who gets stuck in why things can't get done (that is, a Six). Get your act together and get on with it.

America's facility in marketing American culture all over the world is not surprising or accidental. Threes like to sell themselves and are validated when they do.

The Enneagram Three is the type famously described a generation ago by the psychiatrist Michael Maccoby as "The Gamesman":

> He is cooperative but competitive; detached and playful but compulsively driven to succeed; a team player but a would-be superstar; a team leader but often a rebel against bureaucratic hierarchy. *His main goal is to be known as a winner and his deepest fear is to be labeled a loser.*
>
> He is not compassionate but he is fair. He is open to new ideas, but he lacks convictions. . . . Life is meaningless outside the game. . . . But once the game is on . . . they come to life, think hard, and are cool. . . . While other[s] . . . find such high pressure competition enervating and counter-productive, for the gamesman it is the elixir of life [my emphasis].[1]

Threes like to be responsible for their own work, but they very much need a game with rules and a scoring mechanism so they can tell how they're doing. Threes always know what counts as winning, however it is defined: fame, promotions, influence, the key to the executive washroom, or an enviable reputation for knock-your-socks-off service, for slashing costs, for total quality management, or even for creating a progressive or humanistic work environment. Whatever the game is, Threes know how to play it.

Traditionally, though, the game is tallied with money as the marker: profits, salaries, benefits, equity, and capital. As oil magnate Nelson Bunker Hunt put it at a Congressional hearing, "Money is the way you keep score in life—I mean, in business." Sometimes Threes confuse work and life, and therein lies their struggle.

Image Conscious

Nothing succeeds like the appearance of success.
                    —*Christopher Lasch, social philosopher*

Threes are master *marketers* whose basic commodity is themselves. The ultimate conformists within their own community (whether it's Wall Street or Jump Street), they dress for success. This might mean Gucci and Armani in one world or Doc Martens and grunge in another. In any case, Threes have a nose for what it takes to get ahead. This allegory was told to me by a famous and successful Three entrepreneur, who keeps reprints of his company's *Forbes* magazine profile in his reception area, as an explanation of his business philosophy:

"You're flying over Stone Age people. You get into a parachute and jump out of the plane. As you float down, you see that they're carrying their fire in a satchel. You land. You approach them. You say, 'You people, you don't know a damn thing about fire!' You whip out your BIC lighter. You light it up. You know what's likely to happen? They'll eat you for breakfast!

"Now, same scenario: You jump out of the plane. You see they're carrying fire around in a satchel. You land and approach them. You say, 'You guys are great. I love how you live. Hey, you know what? I want to be just like you. I wonder if you would allow me to follow you around? I'll make myself useful.' The Stone Age people look at one another and say, 'What the hell. Follow us around if you want.'

"Now three or four months go by. You work hard to do whatever work needs doing. You make some contacts. Now you have the opportunity to go on a little hunting expedition with three or four of the real heavies of the tribe. When you're out there, you say, 'You know, I love how we live. We're at one with nature, we're at peace with ourselves. . . . By the way, where I come from, we do this fire thing a little differently. I don't know if it's any better, but I'd love to show it to you and get your opinion.' You whip out your BIC. You show them the fire. What's likely to happen? They're gonna make you the chief!"

So when Threes dress for success they are talking about far more than clothes. Threes dress their personas as well. They want people to know that they are doing a good job, that they are successful and hardworking. They appreciate public recognition. My client Marjorie has a mail order clothing business that she runs from a small town on the Oregon coast. Whenever she does something of note—winning a professional award, making an important presentation—she makes sure her industry's trade magazine gets the word. "It's all part of the game," she says.

"What do you like about your *self?*" you may ask a Three. He may well respond like Bert, a marketing vice president at a consumer products company, with a performance self-appraisal. "Every boss I've ever had has said that I get things done well and on time with a high level of detail. And everybody knows I'm decisive and a good closer.

"I'm always conscious of my standing in the company. It's very much of a 'What have you done lately?' scene," continues Bert. "I know that some people think I'm a 'kiss-ass,' but I prefer to think of it as '*proactive, preemptive schmoozing.*'" This interest in and talent for creating an impression on others makes Threes seductive and charismatic within the areas of their concern.

Threes can't help but divert energy into impressing others, often without consciously realizing it. When I asked a moderately successful mortgage banker why he spent so much time being active in professional societies and presentations instead of directly drumming up new clients, he said, "The business is all about creating the illusion of success." Threes are naturals at taking a meeting and leaving a good impression.

Psychology

Threes remember a childhood in which their parents valued achievement over everything else—certainly over feelings. Typically their parents gushed over their accomplishments but showed little interest in helping them over the emotional hurdles of childhood. "These excellent grades prove your value," says such a parent, sometimes in so many words. Like Twos, Threes came to believe that they had no intrinsic worth. "Your value is in your accomplishments, not in who you are or what you feel." Such a message is a profound blow to a child's self-esteem.

Threes decided to work harder and longer. These were the kids who had the newspaper routes and the baby-sitting jobs and who worked in the library after school. Likely as not, they also edited the school newspaper, headed up the honor society, presided over the student body, and otherwise proved they were worthy. Threes as children were overresponsible, hardworking adults well before their time.

Eventually Threes end up *selling* themselves instead of *being* themselves. Such nonstop marketing of self as a commodity—the essence of this type—is the really exhausting part of being a Three, more exhausting than the actual hard work they do. This is what Erich Fromm called "the marketing orientation" to life. According to Fromm, such a person "is not concerned with his life and happiness, but with becoming salable, like handbags on a counter." Naturally, Threes want to go for the highest price; no Three wants to be left in the sale bin.

The Good News

Threes focus on the task at hand. Especially committed and nimble within the realm of work, they do what it takes to get the job done without dragging along much extra baggage, unlike Ones, who push a rigid, perfectionist agenda, or Eights, who relish crushing the opposition, or Fours, whose creative work must be the most profound. Threes, simple, sleek, and direct, just want to win.

Pragmatic and Confident

Threes are the mavens of making things happen—of working where the rubber meets the road. Most Threes believe they can do anything they set their minds to. "If I don't like the way something is going," says Jan, who runs a professional association, "I just change it. When we had some board members who presented obstacles to my plans, I gracefully arranged for their departure." Threes are the quintessentially practical problem solvers.

Part of the reason Threes are able to do so much is that they don't worry about unseen problems (like a Six) or ruminate over countervailing considerations (like a Nine). They don't know that they can't do it or that it can't be done. "When we had to move our retail store," explained Jim, who owns a store that sells upscale garden equipment, books, and clothing, "we brought in a moving company. They said, 'We'll color-code you by department. It will take us ten days to move you.' I said, 'I don't have ten days.' We decided to move ourselves. We were operating at the old place on Friday and the new place on Monday, because we didn't know you couldn't do it over the weekend."

The ever-practical Three is looking for a new angle on a better mousetrap, not a radical paradigm shift. Sam Walton, the majordomo of Wal-Mart, bragged, "Most everything I've done, I've copied from somebody else."[2] Andrall Pearson, who has been a Harvard Business School professor and president of PepsiCo, said, "The majority of our strategic successes were ideas that we borrowed from the marketplace, usually from a small regional or local competitor." Such PepsiCo marketing coups as Doritos, Tostitos, and Sobritos, with combined sales of over a billion dollars, were originated by small West Coast competitors. "In each case what we did was spot a promising new idea, improve upon it, and then outexecute our competitor. To some I'm sure that sounds like copying the competition. To me it amounts to finding out what's already working in the marketplace and improving on it."[3] Pure Three. For a Three, imitation really is the sincerest form of flattery.

Built for Speed

Threes work quickly, leaving their co-workers in the dust. My friend Steve, a Three, is an international management consultant with a large firm. "We have a fancy voice mail system that lets me listen to all my voice mail on button 6, which speeds up playback," he says. "I'm sure everybody else listens to messages from me on button 4, which slows down playback."

"I write copy faster than any of my colleagues, partly because I type so damn fast," says David, a public relations copywriter. Says Lucy, who sells customized software to large companies, "I just find out what customers need and tell them we can do it. If they just want information, I give it to them and move on. I don't get bogged down." When it comes to making deals, Threes like to sign on the dotted line as quickly as possible.

In business, Threes are especially effective when such speed is important and it's okay to make mistakes, or where delaying is worse than the possibility of making a mistake. If they do make a mistake or offend, most Threes will be happy to make it up to you next time, on the next deal. Sometimes Threes think of themselves as perfectionists, but they are not absolutists, like Ones; for Threes, perfection is, in Bruno Bettelheim's phrase, "being good enough."

Market Aware

Like Gale Sayers, the former Chicago Bear, Threes are the swivel-hipped running backs of life who rely on their speed, agility, and commitment to go through an existing opening or around an obstacle. Contrast this with Eights, the power backs, who dynamite their own opening and plow straight through, like John Riggins, the former Washington Redskins workhorse. The elegant Michael Jordan, a Three, recalibrates his approach with Threelike grace while in midair, unlike the terrifying, dead-ahead power forward Charles Barkley, an Eight. In business, Threes' agility translates into the ability to turn on a dime. This means Threes easily drop or readjust extensive plans when the market or the customer changes.

"We beat the opposition not through superior analysis or better research or attention to detail, but by moving ahead lickety-split on the patently obvious," says Will, the Three marketing director of a Southern foodstuffs manufacturer. "Our talent is seeing what's right in front of our face and acting on it."

Threes always keep the market in mind, whether it's the retail customer, a vast audience targeted through advertising, or the boss down the hall. "Make no mistake, I am an expert in the areas we study," says Rebecca, a Three and one of the highest ranking women at the CIA. "But my main contribution is as a *packager.* I'm the one who has to sell the product to the customer—the policy makers. My analysts rely on me for that. I know what sells. I know how it should look. Sometimes the analysts don't like it when I cut up their product, but you can't be sentimental. I'm always thinking about whether the customers are buying what we are selling."

Failure Teaches Success

Threes focus on solutions, not problems. Because they are natural "try-it-outers," Threes understand that failure teaches success. This is, of course, a great spiritual truth. Thomas Edison said, "I've found a thousand ways not to build a lightbulb." For Threes, failure is a victory still under construction. When Tom Monaghan, the founder of Domino's Pizza, went bankrupt early in his career, he was more than 1.5 million dollars in debt. "I've become a reverse millionaire," he said. He went on, of course, to create a multimillion-dollar company based on speed, efficiency, and convenience.

Threes are profoundly inspirational because they are willing to take their shot: to show up in the arena, figure out what it takes to win, and then do it. Their high energy is infectious and motivates others. Threes are not so afraid of making mistakes or appearing foolish if they are likely to advance their game. An employee said of Sam Walton, "He is less afraid of being wrong than anyone I've ever known. And once he sees he's wrong, he just shakes it off and heads in another direction." Threes crave instant feedback. This is what the marketplace offers.

By acting, Threes inspire and enable the rest of us on the Enneagram to act. Likely to be the best role models at work, they know how to build a team and get it to function toward a goal. "I'm like Magic Johnson," said Denise, a Three project manager at an aerospace company. "When I'm in the game everyone on the team plays better. I know how to dish out the ball. Everyone gets their job done. And I make sure I'm enthusiastic about their contribution."

The Bad News

Competition brings out the best in products, but the worst in people.
                                                        —*David Sarnoff*

Like the bright and shiny Tin Man in *The Wizard of Oz*, who got too focused on his job chopping down a tree and rusted up in the rain, Threes get lost in their work. Also like the Tin Man, they need a heart.

Driven

Threes flee into productivity the way Sevens flee into good vibes or Fours into their feelings. They have the same answer to difficulties as the naïve but dedicated workhorse Boxer in Orwell's *Animal Farm:* "I will work harder." But as Boxer discovered, there's always more work. Like Boxer, Threes don't necessarily realize they're being manipulated by the system. For all their success, innocent go-go Threes can be oblivious to what's happening under the table. (It's no accident that their High Performance Point is Six, the expert on sub-rosa matters.)

For a Three, there's rarely time to breathe. "I never pause between tasks," says Dean, a project manager for an investment bank. "As soon as one is done, I'm already into the next. I don't even put away my materials from the first project. I just put them down and pick up the next set." Threes avoid getting bogged down because they keep moving—skimming the surface like an outrigger canoe—but there is not much time to reflect on the meaning of what they have done.

Threes tend toward the classic Type A behaviors: tense and tightly wound, they tap their fingers and toes while you try to talk in complete sentences, and they run full tilt until they keel over, like the old man on the tricycle on *Laugh-In.* "Then I start calling from my bed," says Jan, a management consultant. "The advantage of using the phone is no one knows I'm out of commission."

Brusque

Quintessentially practical, Threes put their distracting, untidy emotions on hold so they can get their work done. Human factors may get overlooked. "When I'm on the phone, I cut right to the chase," says Lucinda, a marketing director for a software firm. "Then I remember I haven't done the social niceties. So I reboot and ask about the person's family or whatever."

Often a Three's relationships suffer, both at work and at home. "I would say that when I'm in overdrive I win the battle and lose the war," says Jennifer, a disc jockey in Washington, D.C. "I'm so intense that I end up jeopardizing relationships with my boss and colleagues, and then I have to pay for it later.

"Once my husband (a Seven) and I were trying to plan a vacation. I checked with him, thought we had a deal, and then just made it happen. He was surprised. He didn't know I was going to buy tickets and make reservations. I was just trying to get it done, but he felt steamrolled. But we had our vacation."

The Inner Taskmaster

Threes have an Inner Taskmaster, much as Ones have an Inner Inquisitor. Virtually a Simon Legree on Benzedrine, the Inner Taskmaster says to the Three that her identity depends on continuing to produce. "Nobody loves me when I lose," said the struggling tennis prodigy Jennifer Capriati, a Three, pushed too far too soon.

Threes in thrall to the Inner Taskmaster act like and often believe that they have powers and abilities far beyond those of mortal humans. "In college, I was an intern for a city government agency in the District of Columbia," says Joyce, who now works as a corporate lawyer. "I enjoyed it, but I never quite fit, in terms of personality. When my term was up, the boss said to me, 'You know, you don't have to be Superwoman.' I remember thinking to myself, 'Shows what you know.'"

Although Threes talk an optimistic can-do game, a deep despair haunts these high-powered achievers. Without tangible proof of their achievements, they can't ignore the nagging suspicion that they're "nobody." They feel the weight of the world on their shoulders; if they don't work hard and act responsibly, they really don't have a right to be here. They are not worthy.

Hypocrisy

Threes think of themselves as principled, but because they are so focused on ends over means, their guiding principle tends to be pragmatism and their ethics are situational. Elizabeth, who worked in the development office at a university, got her dream job as the director of development for a large medical center only because many people went out on a limb for her, as she was somewhat less experienced than the other candidates. Three months later— when a U.S. Senate candidate asked her to be his finance chair—she was gone. "How could I not take this opportunity?" she asked. And who could blame her? But her friends and advocates at the hospital were left holding the bag. These dilemmas are not unfamiliar to Threes. Naturally able to make quick comparisons and act on them, Threes are unsentimental about cutting their losses or jettisoning commitments or people who are tangential to their goals.

In their eagerness to shine, Threes sometimes take credit for other people's work. "I was at a meeting, talking to the chairperson of our national board," Liz, a Three lobbyist recalled. "She was under the misconception that I had snared an important high-profile speaker for the upcoming convention. I let her compliment me profusely. Beth, who happened to overhear, said, 'But, Liz, I arranged for that speaker!' I had to admit she was right. I wasn't trying to lie. I was trying to impress the chair. It happened so fast, I didn't even know I was doing it."

Threes have been known to adopt a pose or summon up feelings to make the most of a situation, often without realizing it. Larry, a Three trial lawyer, says, "There are times, talking to a jury, or in a tough negotiation, when sincerity is the best policy. And frankly, I do sincerity really well."

Because the Three places full attention on the end—the sale, the finished project—the means may seem manipulative. "I know the word *manipulative* gets a bad press, but my job is to manipulate these twenty-six salesmen to knock themselves out for us and to feel good about it," says Fred, a sales manager. "It only makes sense to find out what motivates each of them—cajoling, threatening, begging, painting a pretty picture or a scary one—and remind them of it. What could be wrong with that if it helps them in their work, which is what they want anyway?"

Working with a Three

Influencing a Three

The secret of influencing a Three is to demonstrate your commitment to the task at hand. Says Hiram, the owner of an insurance brokerage, "I hate people who blow smoke. The way to influence me is to do the job."

To influence a Three, let her know what the *results* will be. In addition, it doesn't hurt to show how what *you* want will further *her* ambitions. Compare with Six, who wants you to expose your ambitions so they know what you are up to. Nines will need to ruminate with you awhile to feel comfortable. Not Threes. Threes want the goods, the faster the better. One time I made a proposal to teach the Enneagram to the employees of an airline. In a meeting with the human resources director, a Three, I had barely opened my mouth to explain the Enneagram when he interrupted, "Let's cut to the bottom line.

How is the Enneagram going to help my airline?" When I told him it would help his employees make more effective choices more quickly, he signed on.

Threes respond best to a bottom line–oriented, cost-benefit approach. Keep it simple: offer clear comparisons that show how going down one of two alternate routes is obviously better. Be realistic: if a Three thinks what you're pitching is pie in the sky, she'll lose all interest—but you may attract a Seven. Threes, unlike Sevens, are more interested in the possibilities that may actually happen.

You can learn much about how to influence a Three from Threes themselves. Take my agent, Mary. A classic Three, she's not particularly interested in plumbing the depths of people's motives (she leaves that to me), but she's always aware of what other people *want*. One time, she devised an imaginative way of allocating earnings in a contract she was negotiating for me. When the other party dug in his heels, Mary generated a spreadsheet that convinced the other party that escalating my down-the-line percentage was just fine. She pointed right to the bottom line, the most potent place for a Three. This kind of win-win approach can be persuasive for all types in business but is most especially the way the best Threes treat others and like to be treated.

Unlike Twos, Threes don't necessarily want to be your special friend. They want you to respect them for their competence and skill. At the same time, they're looking to see if you can be respected for *your* competence and skill. Referring to your feelings or making personal appeals doesn't usually cut the mustard with them.

How a Three Makes Decisions

Threes are confident, linear, here-to-there thinkers; they make a beeline for their goals. They don't need the perfect solution (like a One). They don't need all the data (like a Five). They don't necessarily need to know the downside (like a Six). They just need to get going. And when they do, Threes lack the nostalgia of the biblical character Lot's wife: they don't look back.

You won't need to pry a decision out of a Three so long as it is part of her work, her projects, her achievement focus. (A Three's spouse, however, may have to wait for a decision about where to go on holiday, or whether there will even be a holiday, because of the pressures of work.) A deadline helps a Three. (Nines, on the other hand, seem deadline resistant.) "Decisions come easily for me. I'm happy to make them. But I'm very busy and it's up to you to make sure that I'm looking at the right stuff and have whatever information I need," said Elyce, a new manager at a clothing manufacturer, to her employees at a staff meeting.

Threes have little patience for people who are not ready. "I hate wafflers," says Elyce, "and more than that, backtrackers, people who change their minds." To Threes, speed is of the essence. (Remember Monty Hall's frustration if contestants agonized too long over which door to choose? What is there to think about? Let's Make a Deal!) Says Ken Melrose, a Three who heads Toro, the lawnmower manufacturer, "I want to cut through preliminaries and go to the core of an issue. I don't have patience for extraneous material and analysis. I tend to tune out, having little time for all that detail. I believe most hour-long meetings can be synthesized down to twenty minutes."[4]

Threes, of all the types on the Enneagram, rush to closure. Jack, a Three management consultant, says, "The advantage of being a Three and also the problem, I guess, is that I can see where things should go. I want everyone to get there as quickly as I can, without getting distracted by other options. I don't trust anyone's judgment more than my own."

The Three Leadership Style

Much of modern management theory is about trying to teach people to be Threes. The current vogue of "just-in-time management," which squeezes out savings by delivering components and materials precisely when they are needed instead of warehousing them, puts a high premium on Three-ish planning and teamwork. In addition, Threes naturally manage by objectives, in Peter Drucker's formulation: designating and contracting for the desired goals and carefully checking achievements against them. By building in plentiful and measurable feedback, a Three manager constantly readjusts along the way with the goal always in mind. Threes are the best on the Enneagram at setting clear targets, assigning responsibilities, and holding people to them. "I don't like to read between the lines, and I don't like my people to read between the lines," says Patrick, the head of food services at a Big Three auto maker.

Threes are social Darwinists who believe in the survival of the hardworking, the committed, and the successful, and their preferred leadership system is a meritocracy. But originality is not their strong suit; for all their aura of leadership, they buy whole hog into their group's or organization's standards and practices, mastering these so thoroughly that Threes stand out by fitting in.

Not all Enneagram types embrace the organization's objectives as easily as a Three. Contrarian Sixes may struggle with whether the boss can be trusted; Fours may have contempt for economies of scale or for conquering the marketplace. Not surprisingly, management by objectives never caught on in France, a Four country accustomed to honoring unique, even eccentric leaders — people who in America gain respect as entrepreneurs or inventors or artistes, but who are less often found in companies as line managers.

If you find your Three boss's cheery "get with the program" enthusiasm *de trop,* chances are you can still coexist. Threes are adaptable utilitarians who will work with you even if they don't like you so long as you can get the job done (and don't mess with the team). I once had a client, the Three manager of a large computer and electronics store, who could not countenance the way a Five repair technician dressed and groomed himself. "Is he any good?" he asked the service manager. "He's the best," was the reply. "Well, then, I'll have to live with it," said the store manager. (Contrast this with One bosses, who at their worst obliterate employees who commit "sins" of personal behavior.)

But any sign that you don't take work seriously is likely to bring your Three boss down on your head. "It bothers me when people come to a meeting late," says Patrick, the food services chief. "I'm human, I understand about traffic, but I like people to make an effort. I have a healthy respect for work, and I expect others to have the same."

The Three Work Style

The Three work style centers on competence and effectiveness. Threes like to show that they know what they are doing (a good thing to remember if you supervise a Three). In general they set challenging but doable goals and take moderate but not excessive risks. They prefer frequent, concrete feedback on how they are progressing toward their goals. Prominent and structured appraisal, feedback, and reward systems are like manna from heaven for a Three.

Because Threes always have a game plan and like to charge ahead, they're not wild about meetings where consensus must be reached in order to proceed or where one department reports in detail to another before action can be taken. For this reason, they tend to do best in fast-moving environments where the relevant players are up to speed and the Three is not bogged down by decision-making laggards.

In certain environments, such as high-pressured sales and marketing, where individual results are displayed on a wall chart for all to see, non-Threes may feel oppressed by the constant pressure to perform, but Three employees rise to the occasion. I never cease to be amazed by my Three students who work as real estate agents. They thrive on the daily pressure of producing sales under threat of being fired. Indeed, they think it's justified. Awards like "top producer," "employee of the month," and "million dollar club" were made for Threes. "You know what I like about this line of work?" says Kevin. "You're great or you're gone!"

Caught in a self-made race that goes to the swift, and where appearances are reality, Threes naturally take shortcuts, as long as they won't show or the

Three won't be penalized for taking them. Threes know what's being graded and what's not and also where to put the chewing gum and the baling wire to fix things so that nobody will notice. If you're uncomfortable with your Three employee's quick fix, all you have to do is change the rules: "Some things haven't counted directly in your performance appraisals because they haven't been quantifiable, but they're so important to our organization that from now on we're going to take them into account. We're going to develop a scheme to see that your strategic planning efforts are evaluated and rewarded. We want to make sure that you take the time to bring your newer employees along, so we're going to have everybody schedule time for that, and then we'll get feedback from all concerned about how it's going." Most Threes easily will adjust to these shiny new priorities when you state them so clearly.

Your Three employee will be delighted if she can share her career goals with you and if you will help her align her job with those goals. Average Threes aren't great with people—they tend to see them as fungible—so it may come as a surprise for a Three that her boss is a resource, not an obstacle to be finessed.

Threes are often credited with inspiring teams to great feats, but on the low side, since they work harder and come in earlier and stay later than their team members, they can also have a destabilizing and demoralizing effect. (Threes always compete to be the team's Three.) "I'm the mechanical rabbit," said Tom, a manager of real estate salespeople and a Three. "They all try to catch me even though they never will."

The Three Learning Style

Threes learn through trial and error. Theory doesn't speak to them much, except perhaps as a rule of thumb; on-the-job training and practical experience are far more important. They like war stories, the case method, and working in teams with other smart, committed people where they can show their stuff.

And they're *fast*. Before you finish teaching it, the Three will be doing it. "I can watch the boss do a presentation and then get up and do it myself even better," says Peggy, a corporate trainer. But sometimes they learn too fast. A very well known and successful Three gives workshops on business ethics. He boils down complicated philosophical problems into quick fixes for the workplace. Something is gained in encouraging people to think about ethics, but much is lost in rushing over the intricacy of the problem to a facile solution.

Still, to teach a Three, you'll want to keep the lesson moving. Also keep it on practical applications. Unless you stress the lesson's relevance to real-world competence, the Three's attention will wander. Threes learn just as well by seeing how things *don't* work. They are as far as they can be on the Enneagram from the paralysis of analysis that afflicts the mental triad of Five, Six, and Seven.

Threes are quick studies, often with a wide range of abilities, but they are most motivated by the desire to excel at work. Helping them improve their people skills can be an uphill battle if you try to sell it on its own merits, so couch any such training in terms of its relevance to work. A World Bank economist who is a Three asked me at a training session, "Why should I study the Enneagram when I am already successful?" I told him, "You haven't explored the meaning of your success, so you can't build on it. And you resist being sensitive to others' realities, which would make you more effective. What do you think it takes to be a real leader of the development community?" Threes need the bottom line. He got it right away.

The Three Organization

In the Three organization, goals are specified precisely, as are measures of success. Efficiency and consistency are key values. At a cable television company in Southern California, management sets clear and precise performance goals for telephone customer service reps: how long each call should be, how many calls they should take in an hour, how many transfers and referrals they should make. Giant white boards in every office give instant, comparative feedback on such items as sales, account fulfillment, and complaint response.

Three companies are the prototype of whatever business they're in. When it comes to fast food, for example, nobody can do it like McDonald's can. Each McDonald's is something of a manufactory. Operating controls are exacting. Manuals and standard operating procedures offer precise job descriptions and specialized procedures for the grill person, the shake person, the fry person, the bun person. Grill people, for example, are instructed to position hamburgers from left to right (regardless of whether they are right-handed) in order to create six queues of six burgers and to turn the center rows more quickly because that's where the heat is. French fries are to be held for no longer than seven minutes under the heat lamp; after that, they're discarded. For each franchise, each day of the year has assigned to it a special chore: cleaning the bun machine, painting the parking lot, and so on.

The best Three companies are expert at responding to the market. "We have a public image of being slick, professional, and knowledgeable marketers who also happen to be plastic and shallow," according to James Kuhn, a former McDonald's vice president. "In fact, we are a bunch of motivated people who shoot off a lot of cannons, and they don't all land on target. We've made a lot of mistakes, but it is the mistakes that make our success, because we learned from them. We are impulsive, we try to move faster than we can, but we are also masters of cleaning up our own messes."[5]

Three organizations are most effective

- with a limited and focused product line
- when tasks are well defined and straightforward
- when rewards, status, and opportunities for advancement are clear
- when the market or customer is unfragmented and steady
- when the goal is efficient production and marketing of a uniform product or service
- when personalized product is unimportant to the customer
- when deadlines are clear and success is quantifiable.

At their worst, Three companies may succeed in the marketplace but run into trouble with their people, who are treated as mere cogs. "Keep up! Keep up!" is the battle cry, as employees compete with each other. There is high turnover and high dropout rate as the nonstop, no-holds-barred rat race takes its toll.

Getting the Best from a Three

Threes have put their feelings on hold—and such related benefits as meaningful relationships, a sense of joy, and a sense of calling—for the sake of the applause that comes from working hard. When they consciously balance their wings they become affected by the feelings of others (at Shadow Two) and their own feelings (at Ally Four). Then Threes can be honest with self and others, the virtue of Three. This frees up Threes to become committed, interdependent team members (at High Performance Six), instead of just being on the make for themselves. When overcharged Threes blow a fuse, they go to Stress Point Nine for an enforced rest, reconnection, and reevaluation.

Stress Point: Nine

When Threes overdose on work or lose their focus on task completion, they space out to Nine. These intently focused folks lose concentration, get lost in the minor details of a presentation, and become paralyzed by trying to include the views of all who are affected by a decision.

For Threes, not being able to get the work out and dealing with people who move too slowly are like being imprisoned in a tar pit. "Dealing with the bureaucracy around here, the slow pace of decisions, the number of people who nominally have input is very stressful to me," says Teri, a Three manager in the federal government. In such circumstances, instead of their usual sense of competence and control, Threes feel the victim of events.

Warren Bennis, a leading theorist of leadership, writes from the perspective of an overwhelmed Three about his experience as president of the

University of Cincinnati: "I had become the victim of a vast, amorphous, unwitting, unconscious conspiracy to prevent me from doing anything whatever to change the university's status quo." This is the invasion of Nineness. "Routine work drives out nonroutine work," Bennis continues, "and smothers to death all creative planning, all fundamental change in the university—or any institution."[6] From a distance Nine may look like an island of respite for the overworked Three, but it is more like the Loch Ness monster—slow moving, powerful, mostly below the surface, with a hellish undertow.

Of course, Nine can be very functional for a Three under stress. It is a circuit breaker. "When I have an overwhelming list of things to do, sometimes the only viable option seems to be to take a nap," says Patrick. "When I'm overdone, my computer just sucks me in," says Mickey, a Three writer. "I surf the Internet for hours." Three at Nine has had enough.

High Performance Point: Six

Six gives Three the ability to reflect on what he is doing. Six may feel uncomfortably tentative and calculating to a normally superconfident Three who leaps before he looks. The Six theme is about pulling back, figuring things out, and taking appropriate cautions. Six is the keel on the Three outrigger canoe. It provides stability below the surface.

Six is the place on the Enneagram where bluffs are called and hidden truths are exposed. At their best, Sixes are brutally honest—quite a different approach from Three's tendency to create the best possible spin.

Sixes create affinity groups that coalesce in support of an idea or cause; for them, Three-ish competition takes a backseat to the team. With real leadership, writes Warren Bennis, "People are part of a community. Where there is leadership, there is a team, a family, a unity. Even people who do not especially like each other feel a sense of community."[7] This is the perspective of Three at Six.

The higher side of Six is trust and faith. While Threes may seem confident, even to themselves, their frenetic activity is a sure sign of lack of trust in others and in themselves. When Threes go to Six, they learn to trust that forces, people, and systems outside their control can come through. They become *appropriately* responsible.

Wings

Torn as children between the aspirations that others had for them (at Two) and the pull of their own heart's desire (at Four), Threes experienced their feeling functions as immobilized. Their jerry-rigged solution was to flee into productivity and avoid the feelings and needs of others as well as their own. They are *grounded* by being sensitive to and serving others (at Shadow Two); they are *energized* by claiming their true calling (at Ally Four.) By balancing the wings, Threes go from human doing to human being.

Shadow Point: Two

Afraid of selling themselves out to others again, as they did in their youth, and losing their illusory independence, Threes repress their Two shadow: the pull of the feelings of other people. They don't want to get distracted from their work.

But owning their Two wing—being in service—grounds the work of Three in relation to others.

Threes assimilate the perspective of Two when they remember to ask, "What are people's feelings here? What can I do to recognize and assist them?" When Threes own their repressed Two, which wants to be in service to other people's aspirations, they move from meaningless, dreary workaholism to becoming the best who lead from the heart.

Ally Point: Four

Four is Three's ally, the precise tonic for the Three ego. So many Threes, well along in their successful careers, look at their lives and ask, "Is this all there is?" Four gives *meaning* to what the Three is *doing*, so that a Three influenced by her Four wing has a real sense of her unique calling. (All Threes pretend to have a calling—their work—but when they are allied with Four it is the real thing.)

Tom Chappell, a former insurance salesman who founded Tom's of Maine, manufacturers of organic toothpastes, deodorants, and related items, described the movement from Three to Four neatly in his book, *The Soul of a Business*. At the height of his company's success, Chappell enrolled at Harvard Divinity School. "What more could I do in life, except make more money?" he asked himself. As part of a search for values and meaning for himself and his company, he insisted that his senior executives study Martin Buber to develop a conscious relationship with customers (to treat the customers not as statistics, but as "Thous"), and to make the company a more intentional community. He boldly brought in the theologian Richard Niebuhr to explore the deeper meaning of their enterprise. He and his employees reported they found a more personal connection to their work and the company.

Cardinal Rules

If You Work with a Three

- Get on their list. You won't be able to get their attention unless you make an appointment to see them. Don't expect to drop into their office and schmooze.
- Be prepared and well organized so that you can get right to the point. Don't waste a Three's time. Spit it out. Give an executive summary. You can attach the supporting data, but don't make it required reading. Emphasize results and action points.
- Don't interrupt a Three in gear. "Don't break my concentration," says Three. "It makes me crazy." Instead, get with the program. Stand on the running board. Don't be a drag.
- Do what you say you are going to do. Threes are committed, and you should be, too. *Doing* is the area where Threes are most comfortable; if you are cavalier in the area of their greatest concern, you will suffer the consequences. Carry things through.
- Set clear parameters for success. Threes like to know the game is fair. Don't change the rules in midgame without explanation.
- Threes want to know that their efforts are noticed and rewarded. They like clear feedback; that's what they're working for. They especially like to hear that they're doing well.
- Threes like short-range plans and deadlines or at least reasonable stopping points for feedback. They hate unclear expectations or responsibilities that drag on without discernible boundaries.
- If your relationship with a Three is troubled, show her why a smoother working relationship will help her reach her goals. She's much less likely to be responsive to urgings to be more sensitive or less driven. "You know, I think there are some misunderstandings that may be getting in the way of work. Can we take ten minutes to check them out and maybe make some agreements about how to interact in the future?"
- Don't compete with Threes, collaborate. (Unless you are their competitor, in which case be sure to develop a distinct competitive advantage.)
- Don't depend on emotional strokes from a Three for a job well done. A job well done is what they expect.

If You Are a Three

- Learn that there is a difference between who you are and what you do, and learn how to tell what it is.

- *Don't just do something, stand there.* Note your automatic tendency to take over, whether or not it's a good idea. Stand back and let others take the lead once in a while.
- Make it part of your job to anticipate people's objections and concerns. You want to plow ahead with your eyes on the prize, but others see pitfalls and have reservations. How can you meet their needs for stability, security, and satisfaction?
- Make time for people in your schedule. Employees who are not Threes may not know they have to *ask* to be scheduled. Educate them. Instead of just saying, "I'm too busy. Go away," say, "I'm busy, but I have some time at four tomorrow."
- Develop a relationship with time and the forces of nature. Learn about the rhythm of ebb and flow instead of always charging full steam ahead. Don't bite off more than you can chew and then insist on chewing it.
- Note your tendency to close too quickly, to commit now and fix problems later. You'll do a better job in the long run if you invoke Six and ask, "Are we going too fast? Are we considering all the options?" Before you barrel ahead with an assignment, make sure you understand the implications. Do you need to be cautious?
- Practice honesty. The truth will set you free. Note your tendency to *embellish*, particularly around how you appear to others. Even if you win the rat race, you're still a rat.
- Don't feel so bad about wanting to work so much. Threes can work hard and long if the choice is conscious and not compulsive. You can give a lot through doing.
- Remember that "How are you?" can be a genuine inquiry, not just a conversational nicety.

1. Michael Maccoby, *The Gamesman* (New York: Simon & Schuster, 1976).
2. Sam Walton and John Huey, *Sam Walton: Made in America* (New York: Bantam Books, 1993), 47.
3. Quoted by Robert H. Waterman, Jr., *The Renewal Factor* (New York: Bantam Books, 1987), 169.
4. Ken Melrose, *Making the Grass Greener on Your Side* (San Francisco: Berrett-Koehler, 1995), 151.
5. John F. Love, *McDonald's Behind the Arches* (New York: Bantam, 1986), 7.
6. Warren Bennis, *Leadership by Warren Bennis* (Cincinnati: Univ. of Cincinnati Press, 1972), 26.
7. Bennis, *Leadership by Warren Bennis*, 28.

FOUR

The Connoisseur

AKA	The Romantic, the Artist, the Auteur, the Individualist, the Tastemaker, the Creator
Worldview	My work is affecting and authentic, with depth, grace, insight, and style, yet something is missing. If only things were different. . . .
High Side	Sensitive, aesthetic, refined, intrepid, audacious, get to the heart of the matter
Low Side	Depressive, disdainful, self-involved, hateful, envious, spiteful, arrogant, hard to please
Leadership Style	Intuitive, bold auteurs; uncompromising divas
Credo	"Beauty is truth, truth beauty, That is all you know on earth, and all you need to know." —Keats
Appeal to	Their creativity and self-expression, their elite standards and unique contribution, their emotional skill, depth, and power
Don't Appeal to	Convention, a fast buck, emotional or artistic compromise, "Everybody else is doing it."
Talk/Communication Style	Soulful; dramatic; lamentations; meaningful silences; strong, feeling-toned words: picture painters
Makes You Feel	Deep and special; and—sometimes—trivial, superficial, dowdy, and beneath contempt
Appearance	Stunning, lush, of a piece, rich, considered, artistic, often elegant and classy, sometimes shocking and outrageous
Good Work Setting	Opportunity to express self; an uncommon environment that's full of heart

Difficult Work Setting	Bureaucracies, assembly lines, routine work
Books	*The Heart Aroused: Poetry and the Preservation of the Soul in Corporate America* by David Whyte *Why Me? Why This? Why Now?* by Robin Norwood *Quest for the Best* by Stanley Marcus
Sayings	"I could've been a contender." —*On the Waterfront* "It's not enough that we should succeed, but our enemies must also fail." —La Rochefoucauld
Of the Four Persuasion	Stanley Marcus, Diana Vreeland, Marlon Brando, Patsy Cline, Francis Ford Coppola, James Dean, Elizabeth Taylor, Martha Graham, Janis Joplin, Anaïs Nin, Edith Piaf, Anne Rice, Percy Bysshe Shelley, John Keats, Vincent van Gogh, Gore Vidal, Sylvia Plath, Oscar Wilde, Tennessee Williams, the artist formerly known as Prince, Simone Weil, France
High Performance	1 Steady, principled action
Stress	2 Excessive helping; compulsive intrusion; hysterical and desperate
Ally	5 *Energized* by an objective vantage point
Shadow	3 *Grounded* by doing the ordinary stuff of business, including merchandising and marketing and financials (ordinarily rejects the crass commercial bottom line)
Virtue	Equanimity
Vice	Envy

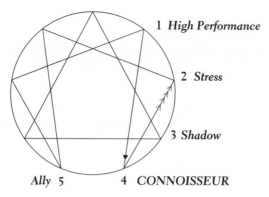

1 *High Performance*

2 *Stress*

3 *Shadow*

Ally 5   4 CONNOISSEUR

Getting to Know a Four

Peter's Story

Peter, an attorney with an M.B.A., is a partner with a securities firm in New York. A financier, most elegantly attired, he has served on the boards of several performing arts companies. He's had some public successes putting together debt instruments for local governments in crises; he was credited with skill-fully responding to the potentially explosive concerns of various political and community interests.

Peter describes his current project as "complex and confidential. It's the most compelling work I have ever done. I had occasion to tour one of the city's hospitals for a bond issue we were putting together, and I was very per-sonally affected. It was like being in a third world country. So I put together this project. It has the potential of reinventing a portion of the health care de-livery system so that it will respond to individuals. If I can get the right people involved—and I already have the mayor interested—quite a bit of human mis-ery that we accept as normal and necessary can be avoided." For Peter, "fi-nancing is about people, about responding to aspirations and longing, or why would it matter?"

"Peter has a reputation for quality," says one of his partners, "which brings in the best people and brings out the best in people. They want to work with him because he makes every project passionately one of a kind. He makes a deal meeting into a theatrical event, which he orchestrates with precise prepa-ration. These can be volatile or tricky situations, and Peter just handles the flow of the deal—especially people's feelings, but even the paperwork—like an impresario."

Not everyone supports him. Says Peter, "Some of my partners think this medical project far too complex and costly for the firm, with very little direct benefit. They're concerned I won't be holding up my end. But this work is far more worthy than anything we've done.

"But my partners," Peter smiles thinly, "really don't understand me. I've always been something of an outcast here. I was the first person that the original four partners hired, right out of business school. So I've always been one down, not quite an original founder. And that is not fixable."

"His work sets the standard," says another. "My only problem with Peter is that he is a little preoccupied with his own internal emotional complexity."

Do you recognize Peter? Peter is a Four.

The Basic Premise

If Twos are outward-looking "people people," Fours are their mirror image: introspective, *passionate romantics* whose domain is the psyche. Deep feelings, creativity, and self-expression are the coin of Four's realm.

This naturally places Fours in artistic endeavors of all kinds. They are producers, curators, designers, actors, artists, and writers *and* their agents, advisers, and critics. But they can also be lawyers, bureaucrats, and management consultants who have a special flair, whose passionate, sensitive, poetic style distinguishes them.

Like Fives, Fours are self-starters who follow their own interests and vision. But Fives are minimalists, who can survive quite well on a little input. Fours, on the other hand, like to tap their own considerable wellspring of feelings, which is the key to their gifts.

Authenticity is the touchstone of this style. It is Fours' urgent insistence on the *deepest feelings* and the *highest standards* that distinguishes them. Fours flee from superficial conversation, from cheap imitations, from kitsch. I enjoy going to Wal-Mart when I'm on the road, but I can't get my Four colleague to come with me.

Most Fours possess a breathtaking capacity for aesthetic presentation that can leave the rest of us feeling clunky and inelegant. A character in Nicole Hollander's comic strip, *Sylvia*, "The Woman Who Does Everything More Beautifully Than You," is a Four, as was Oscar Wilde, who said, "I have the simplest of tastes; I'm easily satisfied with the best." Not surprisingly, Fours are the most distinctively attired of any Enneagram type. While Twos dress sweetly or seductively and aim to please and Threes dress for success, Fours are usually trendsetters within their set.

Fours are the least willing of any Enneagram type to accept that they might *be* a type. (Curses on those who would reduce you to an Enneagram type.) But Fours are so protective of their uniqueness that this tends to typify them. Their longing to be special can mean that an ordinary workaday job is pretty tough for a Four. "I can do nine-to-five drudgery and routine," says Joy, a Four who is an aspiring actress but who works as an administrative assistant, "as long as I remember that I'm playing a character." Such a sense of role playing is quintessentially Four-ish. (Threes role-play as well, but they are playing themselves.)

Unlike Nines, who are sometimes content to be a cog in a machine, Fours want their work to be personally meaningful. They like to feel their impact. Rudi owns a highly regarded art publishing company in New York City's Soho district that prints limited-edition graphics, each signed and numbered by the artist. Few of his prints are distributed through conventional sales channels; most of Rudi's business comes through a network of personal relationships he maintains with people throughout the world. "I'm not interested in building a distribution network," Rudi states flatly. "I'm interested in building relationships with sophisticated clients, one at a time."

In the workplace, Fours gravitate to where commerce and deep feelings meet. "It may sound overblown, but I think of my work as not only creative but also spiritual," says Margery, the editorial director of a publishing company in New York. "To develop writers who have something to say and to find their special audience is a worthwhile venture, even today."

Fours thrive on drama. You'll often find them on the scene when people are fired, when partnerships or family businesses are starting up or are on the rocks, or when takeovers and turf battles get overheated. That's when Four's special talents for navigating human crises and extremes of feeling come in handy.

Ben, for example, declined to work in his family's business, a chain of shoe stores, until it became clear that the business was in trouble. Then his interest and energy perked up. Ben got his relatives to elect him chairman of the board, and, with expert advice, he guided the company through and out of chapter eleven. He held a fragile coalition of creditors, shareholders, and interested others together through the force of his own personality. Then he hired key people capable of putting the company back on an even keel.

Whatever their considerable talents and skills, Fours are most at home within their own rich, often turbulent, emotional life. They're distinguished by their deep, dark, introspective feelings and moods. Indeed, to the people they work with, the powerful feelings of Fours can sometimes seem outsized, overwhelming, and counterproductive. In fact, once Ben put his key people in place, they forced him out because they considered him too emotional and erratic.

Central among the Four's feelings is *melancholy*. Fours experience a characteristic sadness about life, a wistfulness, a sense that things are not what they could be. Something is missing or has been lost: a person, a reciprocal relation-ship, the opportunity to be recognized. In the workplace, Four's attention goes to the parts of the presentation that are not quite right, the colleague who is not there who needs to be, the colleague who is there but should not be, the flaw or the emotional strain in the group. "Nothing is ever perfect in the advertising business," says Jerry, an account executive and a Four. "So you try to put your heart on the page, knowing you'll never get it quite right. And then you go on."

The Four's melancholy in the right circumstances can be a source of cre-ativity and depth. When the troubled poet Rainer Maria Rilke was offered the opportunity to be psychoanalyzed by Freud, he declined; he feared losing ac-cess to his creative demons. But many Fours have experienced a more serious crisis of feeling as well: an immobilizing depression—not a creative place at all, but a hopeless one.

In the workplace, while Threes identify with their idealized self-image of accomplishment and Twos ferret out *your* idealized self-image, Fours identify with a tragic self-image in which their blessings are curses and their curses are blessings. They are blessed with sensitivity and emotional insight that is painful, but in the right circumstances their pain can be the source of great creativity and emotional authenticity.

Psychology

Many Fours remember a time in their childhoods when all was right with the world; then, often suddenly, the whole experience of living changed with a devastating dispossession. For many, it was the loss of a parent's love through divorce or death. For others, it was a shocking change in the family's circum-stances. Whatever did or did not happen, Four's experience is of paradise lost and innocence ended, and, as such, it is particular to Fours. All Fours carry such a powerfully felt memory of loss and separation, and this sense of es-trangement is why they experience life as so poignant.

Tamara, a psychotherapist, lived like a princess in the Panama Canal Zone—her father was a civil engineer—until she was eleven and her family re-turned stateside. They no longer had servants or a huge house; their life was now ordinary instead of grand. Helen Anne, principal of an exclusive private el-ementary school, reports that her family lost all its money when her father's brokerage went bust in a scandal. Joe, a career counselor, was blissfully happy growing up on a farm in Oregon, where, although he was only twelve at the time, a young girlfriend became what he now remembers as the love of his life. Then Joe's family moved to Los Angeles, where he was mugged several times.

"What happened?" asks the Four. "Where did it all go? What did I do wrong?" A longing to be made whole again captures the Four's heart and becomes the Four's central driving force. As loss inevitably recurs in their lives, they ask, "Why me? Why this? Why now?" (as in the title of Robin Norwood's book).

Fours spend a lot of time trying to find the *reasons* for the loss. They take the loss personally, blaming some fateful flaw in themselves. They feel cursed and condemned to exile. They fear they are somehow not enough: not grand enough, not fascinating enough, not attractive enough, not profound enough. Or they feel that they are too much: too deep, too authentic, too emotionally open, vulnerable, and intense. Their dignity wounded, they become *overly* dignified, overly elegant, and overly profound, sometimes even snooty.

This most special wound keeps Four unique, if only in the depth of her tragedy, and not quite knowable to the rest of us. When Four holds her alienation and melancholy gracefully, as the most evolved Fours do, she can be genuinely elegant and soulful.

As adults, Fours, like Sixes, live in a world of negative expectations. Both worry when things are going well. But where Sixes are afraid something or someone is going to get them, Fours are afraid they will be ignored, abandoned, or humiliated. But as with the Six, it is the expectation, not the reality, that is murderously controlling. Fours have the habit of rejecting first, before they can be abandoned. They do this by being elitists or by feeling hopeless. "You'll never quite make it to my standards," projects the Four boss. "I'll never be understood by the team," thinks the Four employee; "they're too superficial, too insensitive, too focused on winning."

At the core of the Four's emotional response is a catch-22: a Four desires what she lacks; if she gets it, it's no longer desirable. A Jules Feiffer cartoon shows his famous modern dancer all in black—a Four, of course. "I want it! I want it!" she cries out for several panels. A sugar daddy puts presents and stacks of money at her feet. "Here it is," he says. She considers the pile. "I don't like it!" she says. Inevitably, Fours are dissatisfied. They are addicted to the feeling of longing and aren't always comforted by the actuality of having. This can make them great martyrs, as they privately, sadly compromise in order to go on.

The Good News

For all the turmoil that characterizes their personal lives, Fours' powerful passions make them bold executives (and employees) with a strong hand. Like Eights, they know what they want and they insist upon going for it. They are not shy about expressing and standing by their inner voice. Elizabeth, a director of human resources at a manufacturer, will stop a meeting of top management in its tracks by saying, "We are avoiding some unconscious feelings here, and I believe I know what they are." Everyone listens.

Fours are masters at navigating and describing the inner landscape. The efforts currently being made to "bring soul to business" are led by Fours or Four wanna-bes. Just as for a One, nothing for a Four is casual. ("Life is earnest," my Four mother used to say.) Natural symbologists attuned to the unconscious and to myth and metaphor, they search beneath the surface for deeper meanings. Rae, vice president of a nondescript firm that delivers packages in New York City, puts it neatly: "You wouldn't think the workaday world would be an ideal fit for me," she confides, "except that business is the true myth of our times." Like Rumpelstiltskin, Fours at their best spin the straw of ordinary life into gold.

Life for a Four is not a rational process, and neither is business. Life is about discovering what you are; business is the same. "We are very, very good at that, at the process of figuring out who we are," says John, who heads a public relations firm that caters to the record industry. "Trying to fit ourselves into somebody's image of who we should be is ridiculous. It doesn't work that way in this business."

With many Fours, it is not their job but their artistic avocation that is the centerpiece of their lives. Henry manages a warehouse in St. Louis because it gives him time for what is most important to him: creating holograms. The job also appeals to Henry's artistic temperament: he *enjoys* a poignant Four-ish disaffection working as "just" a warehouseman, the way Orwell worked as a clerk and Gauguin in a *bureau de change*.

At their best, Fours are stirred by a sense of purpose. They align with causes, volunteer for social movements, and empathize with those who, like the Four, suffer most: the poor, abused, neglected, or misunderstood.

Unique

Fours like to be special by knowing and feeling more deeply than others do. This skill often serves them well in their work. In a CIA office where other women dressed in drab business suits, Juliette, an intelligence analyst, stood out with her elegant dresses and flawless makeup. She read extensively in the literature and culture of the small country she was studying, which was fairly unusual among political analysts. Using the Four's antenna for drama, she sensed that the nature of a domestic dispute the leader of the country was having with his wife had implications for the way he ran his cabinet. She wrote a brilliant internal paper making several bold predictions about government policy and decision making. She was right, and when her predictions became true she received an award, an accelerated promotion, and a reassignment to a large country team, which allowed her to work with several of the foremost experts in her field.

Interestingly enough, this turn of events proved to be problematic for Juliette. Once she began working with other experts, she no longer felt special; her interest flagged and her career began to wilt. She became depressed. So she left the analytic team and went abroad for a year to study an exotic language and culture, one that promised the special knowledge and experiences that would keep her uncommon upon her return.

Fours at their best know *exactly* how to put their Fourness to best use. Give them a context in which they can flower, and they don't merely decorate the organization, they touch its soul.

Connoisseurs

Fours are connoisseurs who appreciate the best. They discriminate, not like the rest of us, between good and bad, but between the fine and the finest. Indeed, the finest is none too good for Fours. They want to be known as the elite quality producer, provider, or purveyor. When all of the champagne houses in France were being bought by conglomerates, Taittinger's, perhaps the most pursued, chose a different route. Said Claude Taittinger, the president, "We decided to remain 'artistes' and produce a limited quantity of the very best champagne." This is the Four approach.

Fours are great appreciators of beauty and great proselytizers on behalf of it. Unlike Fives, who would be cautious about intruding on their customers, Fours take on "the Four's burden": the task of educating and refining the tastes of their customers and colleagues. Here is Stanley Marcus, former chairman of Neiman-Marcus, in his Four memoir *par excellence, Quest for the Best*:

> We were rigorous in maintaining our standards of taste, be it in merchandise, advertising, or other activities in which the store was a participant. This required a certain presumptuousness on my part in setting standards with which some of my associates disagreed at times. I recall an incident in which I criticized our candy buyer for having too large a proportion of her stock in milk chocolate, rather than in the dark bittersweet. Her merchandise manager came to her defense arguing, "This is what the public wants. What right do we have to tell them to eat dark chocolate?" I replied, "Milk chocolate is a yokel taste. Chocolate-educated customers will be turned off by seeing so much milk chocolate and we will lose their trade. I'd rather satisfy them than the yokels, if it comes to choosing up sides, but I think we can please both by simply reversing the percentages between the two kinds of chocolate. *It's our job to educate the customers as well as to sell to them.*" My directive was followed and eventually our customers switched to the dark chocolate. [My emphasis.][1]

Fours' connoisseurship, even more important, extends to people. Like Twos, they have the talent to catalyze your specialness. While Twos encourage your external talent, Fours nourish your private depth by insisting on their own. As Martin Buber reminded us all, "It is the duty of every person . . . to know and consider that he is unique in the world." Fours, passionate seekers after their own inner nature, like to remind you of yours.

A Sense of Drama

Because of their early experience of dispossession, Fours make a special effort to set down roots (underground growth is Four's specialty). They want special places to express their uncommon passions, and they often create extraordinary environments that make strong personal statements. Classic Four businesses such as Victoria's Secret and Bloomingdale's were originally successful (before they were taken over by large Three conglomerates) at least in part because they created lush, romantic environments that could transport their customers to another realm.

"This setting evokes feelings. It is nonordinary reality," says my friend Rob, the head of a management consulting firm with stunning offices filled with sculpture and tapestry. "You can't help but feel we're doing something special."

You'll often know when you're in a Four's environment because you'll experience what I call the "gasp factor." My old classmate Phil is a lawyer with a large firm in a tall, boring office building in Chicago. While his colleagues inhabit cookie-cutter offices with standard-issue furnishings, Phil has outfitted his office with a pair of Turkoman rugs, a polished granite desktop, and an original Mark Rothko, along with a few personal photographs from his travels through central Asia. Says Phil, "I'm certainly not trying to impress people. Anyone can throw money at a decorator. But an environment that represents your true self brings out the best in other people." (Other Fours, in other environments, may emphasize stark, Zenlike simplicity, but the basic principle remains the same. Some Fours will not tag their specialness to their environment at all.)

The Bad News

The Need to Be Special

A colleague of mine, a Four, wishes to write a book about the Enneagram, but only about Fours. "Really, that's the only number where my heart is," she says. Spoken like a true Four.

In a business setting, the Four's desire to be special can sometimes be expensive. Alfredo, a leather goods executive, wasn't content to show products in the best display cases available. He filled the company's New York showroom with expensive furniture and covered its walls with fine art. When his boss in Europe found out, he sent it all back. Alfredo was furious and, unrepentant, exclaimed, "They made it look like a warehouse!"

Unlike Ones, who feel entitled to rewards based on what's right and fair, lowside Fours feel entitled to recognition based on their specialness. But don't expect them to ask directly (for fear of being humiliated). "Putting your hand out is degrading," says Paul, a hospital department manager. "If my contribution is not obvious, then I'm not in the right business."

Drama Kings and Queens

At their worst, Fours are drama queens and kings who *feel*—truly, madly, deeply. From within their passion, there is only one best way—theirs (which makes them the emotional version of Ones).

Yet despite their tempestuous emotional lives, Fours aren't always skillful with emotions. Fours have the capacity to plumb the depths of their own psyches, yet they're so self-absorbed that they often fail to empathize with others or understand how they and their emotions fit into a larger context. Capacity is not the same thing as mastery.

Fours' problem isn't that they put their faith in their feelings but that feelings are the *only* place they put their faith. Fours have swallowed whole the notion that "you are your feelings." They don't see that (their) feelings are only part of the picture. "If you start making adjustments for the sake of the marketplace, then you aren't being true to your art, which can be something ugly," says Rudi. "When I was starting out, I was highly suspicious of the business order. I realized I had to develop my own style, and that became my goal: *to succeed with style, my style.*" This approach becomes dangerous for Fours when insistence on style takes precedence over the realities of the marketplace.

At their worst, Four bosses or employees live life at emotional extremes and with little fondness for those who don't. And because much of working life is ordinary or even boring, though legitimate and essential, Fours may rebel against standard procedures by cutting corners, by claiming privilege, or by creating a roller-coaster of emotion—all in the name of adhering to their grand vision.

Fours invariably complain that their sensitivity, creativity, depth, and avant-garde approach make it hard for them to deal with the commonplace and trivial. "I never schmooze. It's hard for me to relate superficially to people, to make small talk, to butter them up," says Andrea, who runs a very successful service that advises high school students applying to college. "I insist on going very deep, very quickly. I understand that some people will fall by the wayside. What people want or expect is one thing. But what I sell is my business."

Like Ones, who are committed to their version of what is right, Fours can be brutal in pursuit of their vision of truth or beauty. They are sometimes willing to destroy others in a vain effort to remake them, annihilating co-workers when there is no need for complete devastation. "If I saw that someone was just going through the motions, if it was *ordinary*," said Marianne, the editor of a magazine, "that was contemptible. They deserved what they got. I hate when people don't seize the opportunity to make something special. When they do, the effort always shows, even if they missed the mark."

Melancholic

Nothing is harder to bear than a series of good years.

—*Goethe*

Fours need the blues to set their compass by. At work they may keep themselves unhappy by playing the victim, by pushing success away, or by not appreciating what they have. At an extraordinarily well attended fund-raising dinner for the foundation she runs, Ellen could still say, "People don't appreciate the impact we make."

Indeed, Fours, who naturally make invidious comparisons anyway, take competitive pride in their negativity. "You think *that's* bad?" a Four may respond (sometimes silently) to your troubles. "If only you knew what *I'm* going through!" They are negatively inflated, much as Twos and Sevens are positively inflated.

Most Fours have suffered from depressive periods, which can be long and debilitating. One Four I know, a director of organization development, sometimes lies on the couch in his darkened office and stares at the ceiling for hours. The members of his staff pass the word to warn each other. "He's doing ceiling therapy," they say. Clinical depression is beyond the scope of this discussion, but it is important to know that a Four in a bad patch is likely to feel not merely sad but also hopeless. And when Four feels hopeless, it's not a good idea to say, "Cheer up! Everything will be all right. I'm sure we'll get the Diefenbaker account!" You will seem like a Pollyanna on mood elevators. Instead, honor his frame of mind, make him comfortable, and take care of business. You can acknowledge his melancholic feeling without feeling melancholic yourself. "Let me know if you want me to check on anything or if you need to talk. Meanwhile, I'll be meeting with Mr. Diefenbaker this afternoon," you might say.

Working with a Four

Influencing a Four

Although their volubility and taste for drama makes them seem outgoing, Fours are actually introverts, in the strict definition of the word. That is, they look to their internal experience to assess reality, gauge where they are, and renew themselves. Fours center themselves on their own creative and emotional nature. Try to pressure a Four to change his views on a matter of taste or style, and you'll get amazement or contempt. You won't be able to challenge a Four's criteria directly with a logical argument. A better bet is to concede the aesthetics but broaden the focus. "Look, you're right about the aesthetic deficiencies of that brochure. But how creative can we be given the time and budgetary constraints that we have and given our somewhat conventional target audience? Let's try to make as much as we can of this difficult situation." Creativity in difficult straits is Four's *specialité de maison*.

Sophisticated Fours know they sometimes go overboard when they're expressing feelings or defending their position. These Fours know they occasionally need someone to save them from themselves. "What do you mean, my speech was too emotional and too long?" Harriet, a marketing manager, said to her trusty Six assistant. "That's why you were there—to give me the high sign. Why didn't you?"

Like Eights, Fours want you to match their strength with your own. When an Eight or a Four encounters another who is willing to stand toe-to-toe (with Fours it's emotional rather than physical, like Eight), then they can feel their full power. Don't try to "handle" them. "It drives me crazy when people aren't up front with me," says Alana, a Four television producer. "If you try to 'handle' me, you'll miss me for sure. Meet me with your real self." Authenticity goes a long way with a Four.

How a Four Makes Decisions

Fours operate on feeling-based intuition. "I don't have these long-term plans," explained Calvin Klein. "I just operate instinctively."[2] They don't care for market research, which, after all, reflects plebeian tastes. Fours will instead rely upon their own talents to tell them "what's missing" and "what's right" and "what's real" and "what's best." Morrie is a wholesale jeweler. "I don't know anyone's judgment I trust more than my own. Listening to customers is a sure way to screw up your merchandise," he says.

As members of the feeling triad, along with Twos and Threes, Fours make many decisions by comparison. Ask a Four, "Which is the higher quality? Which is the bona fide? Which do you like better?" and you'll get a quick answer. They don't necessarily care for a more objective approach, especially on issues they feel strongly about. Fours experience decision making as a peeling of their personal onion: they are consciously looking for the truth at the center.

The Four Leadership Style

A Four leader is typically a romantic, passionate, impulsive star who holds to a strong personal vision and leads with the force of her personality. Unlike a Seven, who inspires people to new *heights*, the Four leader inspires others to new *depths*—of feeling and authenticity. A Four's authority, like that of a Five, comes from what she knows. And, like Five, Four's chief strength and greatest weakness as a leader come from the same place: her unwillingness to compromise her vision.

"Where is the passion?" asks the Four boss. "What is the deep, authentic truth here?" Four is always trying to develop a relationship with the heart of the matter. Once he sees it, he must achieve it, and he won't let anything or anyone stand in the way. This can make Four leaders heroic cultural revolutionaries who put radical and forward ideas into action or neurotic prima donnas who stand in the way of progress and common sense, depending on your point of view. Their demand that their passions be plumbed to the depths of authenticity can push some employees to do their best but can frustrate others whose contributions burn up in the Four's super-hot kiln.

The Four boss may be widely admired and influential, but he can also be imperious and unapproachable. Moods are *critical*. When Brian, a Four movie executive, enters his office in the morning, he either says a warm good morning to his secretary or he barely nods. His secretary then reports on the boss's mood to all concerned. Brian himself related this drama to me; he encourages the arrangement. "It gives people a good idea of whether they should make their pitches or hold them for another day, depending on *their* mood," he says.

Sharing creative leadership for a Four can be difficult. I was once paired with Sandy, a Four, to create a multimedia project based on the Enneagram. She announced the fundamental Four requirement straight away: "Of course, I couldn't be edited," she said. "I need complete artistic control."

Because Fours strive so hard for an impeccable vision, sometimes a minor detail, like making a profit, can fall by the wayside. Diana Vreeland, the famous editor of *Vogue*, promoted a world of high-gloss plastic outré fashion that could exist only in her fantasies. Models in unwearable clothes were shot at great expense in exotic locales, all of which she insisted was vital to the project. She ignored the budget and eventually got herself fired. They gave her job to the Four-ish Three Grace Mirabella, who emphasized comfortable classic clothes that women could wear to work. Passionate Four leaders do well, on occasion, to remember their followers. (See Shadow Point Three.)

The Four Work Style

Fours are full members of the competitively prideful triad that includes Twos and Threes. Twos take pride in how helpful they are. Threes take pride in how accomplished and efficient they are. Fours are especially proud of their aesthetic sensibility, their deep emotional insights, and their struggles to remain true to their vision, which they want you to notice and appreciate. Being forced to hide their light under a bushel is painful for a Four.

Because Fours don't want to see their efforts as ordinary, they often refuse to see that aspects of their work might, in fact, *be* ordinary. When they confront a workaday problem, they may look high and low for a complicated answer while completely overlooking a mundane solution readily at hand. When Judith, a personnel manager, was developing a referral system for people with emotional problems, she hired some of the nation's most prominent psychologists and authors to help her think about it. The group had fascinating discussions, but Judith probably could have found an adequate set of procedures in existing texts.

Frequently in emotional flux, Fours can be inconsistent because they are mood driven and react personally to others rather than applying objective standards like Ones (see High Performance). Fours relate best with co-workers when boundaries are clear, management is consistent, and evaluation is based on objective criteria rather than the boss's idiosyncrasies. You can help Fours in your employ be creative without being volatile and temperamental if you make sure they feel valued and give them outlets for their creativity. Then they don't have to insist on their specialness by other means.

Although Fours like to feel they have a place at work, they struggle as team members. Seeking consensus as a group member is anathema to a Four; their personal vision is too compelling. They much prefer to reach a general understanding at the "heart level" or "soul level" or, alternatively, to do all the work themselves. They are much better as special consultants or facilitators to the team or as coaches who remind the team how meaningful and powerful the work they are doing really is.

The Four Learning Style

Fours want to be "in a personal relationship" with any material they set out to learn. Many Fours say a version of what Robin, a marketing manager, said about the best training programs: "The subject reveals itself not when you assault it head-on but when you allow it to reveal itself to you, and you to it." Four teachers and trainers know to leave space for the *mystery*.

Fours don't like being one of many, so group learning doesn't always work for them. Fours prefer a personal relationship with the teacher and, when possible, private instruction or initiation where they can demonstrate their special facility and verve; they like to learn in the back room from a genuine mentor who conveys special wisdom about taste, quality, and emotional or spiritual reality.

To get a Four on your side, make it clear why you're teaching the information, what the essence is, and why it's valuable. Fours also respond well to tasteful, quality handouts, graphics, or videos. (Many other types won't even notice, but Fours always comment on them.) Let Fours do something creative with the material—perhaps designing or writing—to make it their own.

When you are working with a Four, it is helpful to seek permission. Fours understand courtliness. Ask respectfully, "May I guide you further?"

The Four Organization

Give the customer what Tiffany likes, because what it likes, the public ought to like.
                              —Walter Hoving, former chairman, Tiffany and Co.

By nature, Fours are less interested in volume sales than in filling a special niche, often at the top of the market, often defining the quality standard in the market. Fours create the genuine article: Mont Blanc pens, Godiva chocolates, Rolex watches. They are masters of elegant presentation, such as Bergdorf Goodman or Tiffany or Henri Bendel (where exclusivity is the byword).

Although customers of Four companies will be impressed, such companies are not primarily service oriented, as are Two companies. Compare earnest, eager, helpful Two enterprises such as Nordstrom with glitzy Four enterprises such as Barney's or Neiman-Marcus or Claridge's Hotel in London. An eager, smiling Nordstrom clerk who can't help you find what you need may well recommend a competitor. That's not likely to happen at Barney's, where their prime concern is to provide you with the rich experience of themselves—the commercial version of what I earlier called the gasp factor. At the Oriental Hotel in Bangkok, a Two organization, staff is everywhere, on your heels and at your side; service is *the* central salient feature; the decor is neither lavish nor impressive. At a Ritz-Carlton, while service is a byword (and the motto is "Ladies and gentlemen serving ladies and gentlemen"), their aim is to create a "memorable experience" (their words, their experience), of which exemplary customer service is only a part.

The leaders of Four organizations are crusaders for quality, and employees who try to make decisions based on the usual profit calculations may be relegated to second-class citizenship. In the long-ago early days of Hewlett-Packard (it was a different world then), cofounder David Packard caught this spirit when he chided his executives about a product that turned out to be a clunker. "Somewhere, we got the idea that market share was an objective," he said. "I hope that is straightened out. Anyone can build market share; if you set your price low enough you can have the whole damn market. But I'll tell you it won't get you anywhere around here."[3] Packard counted on the quality of his products to shine through in the marketplace so that consumers would disregard their cost. Indeed, the company's cachet was only enhanced by the gibe that *HP* stood for "High Prices." (If you're selling special goods to a unique population, high prices are part of the bargain.)

Another version of the Four organization is among nonprofits. Emotional idealists, they take up a cause, like World Vision or People for the Ethical Treatment of Animals. Four organizations are the best containers for profound emotionality, for tragedy, and for communicating the same for a heartfelt response.

Getting the Best from a Four

Instead of being swept away by their feelings of distinction or despair, Fours evolve when they act dependably, faithfully, and ethically, the perspective of Four's High Performance Point One. When Fours are stressed, they feverishly intrude on others at Stress Point Two. Balancing material achievement (Shadow Point Three) with objective detachment (Ally Point Five) gives Four a sense of equanimity.

Helen Anne's Story

Helen Anne is the principal of Burnham School, an exclusive private elementary school north of Los Angeles. The school is homey and colorful, with students' artwork displayed around beautifully landscaped grounds; it is attended by scions of the rich and famous, especially from the worlds of film, theater, and the arts. Helen Anne works hard to develop a superior curriculum, with especially enriching programs in the arts and sciences.

At an institution like Burnham, evaluating a potential student's parents is nearly as important as evaluating the student. Parents are expected to support the school by serving on committees and by making financial contributions, and Helen Anne takes what she admits is a "devilish pleasure" in conducting the long and sometimes grueling interviews with parents of prospective students. Celebrities fail to impress her. "Oh, they applied to get into Burnham," she will say of a family with a household name, "but we had to reject them."

When Helen Anne called me in to consult, she was feeling overwhelmed and discouraged and was actually thinking about resigning. A board member who was an accountant and management consultant, Bill, a Three, was fighting several of her projects, including a small planetarium Helen Anne envisioned and new instruments for the orchestra. He was also putting pressure on her to formalize the school's admissions and personnel policies, telling her that she operated too much according to her own whims.

Bill's reaction was confrontational and direct. "We can't afford the planetarium," he told her bluntly. "You seem to have no sense that we're a business. I think you're actually hostile to the idea that we have to make a profit. You have to watch the bottom line."

Helen Anne replied, "No, *you* have to watch the bottom line. I'm here to nurture the minds, imaginations, and souls of the children. Find the funds," she said. "I won't compromise on quality."

But the standoff couldn't last long, as Helen Anne knew. Bill had too many friends on the school's board of directors, Helen Anne had a long history of insisting on her way, and if push came to shove, she'd lose. When I met her, she felt forced to yield to Bill's demands and was bitter about it. Feeling brutalized and abandoned, she had lost her enthusiasm for her work.

Stress Point: Two

Under stress, Helen Anne had moved to Enneagram point Two. At Stress Point Two, Fours lose their center, focusing on others and feeling like they've sold themselves out (the worst thing possible for an individualistic Four who identifies with her own vision). They fear that they have lost their due. "I gave my whole life to this school. I sacrificed my own needs over and over again to keep this school in business, and now they tell me I am not respecting the bottom line," she lamented, feeling herself the victim of others who did not see her true gifts.

But Two also helps Four get through stress. Two is a wake-up call, which shakes the Four out of *self*-involvement. Attending to the intentions of others focuses the will. Helen Anne was stressed by the conflicting interests—she didn't like compromising on educational matters—but, annoyed as she was, she was enlightened by them as well.

High Performance Point: One

Fours need what Aristotle called *ethos*, or ethical character. One offers a principle-centered realm in which right and wrong are clear. At High Performance Point One, Fours move from a chaotic world centered around mood and feeling to a moral universe that makes sense. At One, Fours, who try to avoid the rules of the game by being the exception, find that sometimes the rules *are* the game.

Fours find power by distinguishing between feelings, the province of Four, and values, the province of One. For Helen Anne, her feelings *were* her values, and she refused to compromise them. When Fours can gain access to their High Performance Point One, they understand with great clarity that their ethos—their character—can't be compromised.

Moving toward One helped Helen Anne see the usefulness of formalizing the school's admissions policy instead of relying on impressions and whims. The new rules left plenty of room for her to exercise judgment. Although everyone felt that Helen should retain significant decision-making power in admissions, all were happier having the criteria codified and made available to parents and others. She next tackled codifying and revising personnel policies, since she previously had made individual deals with the faculty and staff, which led to jealousies and resentments. "Rewriting the policies was the right thing to do," said Helen Anne. "That isn't to say I enjoyed doing it. But I can see the benefits."

Wings
Shadow Point: Three

Fours run from their shadow Three, the part of themselves they want to deny. Threes are conventional, practical, and ambitious, charismatic experts at the mundane. They are oriented to the marketplace, to sales, to winning. Fours suppress the idea that they might be any of these.

That's why Helen Anne had such trouble with the school's financial director, Bill, who represented precisely these rejected themes. Once she acknowledged the part of herself that was competitive and aspiring, she found it much easier to collaborate with him. Of course, Helen Anne wanted the school to have a sound financial foundation—that in fact none of her visions could come true without it.

Ally Point: Five

Fours believe they intensely experience *life*. Actually, what they intensely experience is *their feelings*. Awash in a sea of feelings, Helen Anne needed to find dry land. Five offers an objective place to stand, that quiet place within, where a Four can see clearly without drama or embellishment. As she moved from focusing on herself to focusing on the facts of the situation, Helen Anne was able to harness the power of a detached observer. Bill became less the boor and more the person who was raising interesting facts and issues. She found she could work with him. Together they created a fund-raiser for the planetarium.

Cardinal Rules

If You Work with a Four

- Fours like process, not rigid goals. Say "paint me a picture" or "tell me the story," not "just the facts ma'am," to allow the Four to communicate important impressionistic material.
- Be careful when you offer a carrot. Don't offer money or perks and think it will persuade a Four to abandon her vision. You won't get anywhere if you say, "Do it my way, quick and dirty, and you'll get a big bonus."
- Honor the Four's unique depth and insight. (Fours usually don't need your help to feel special, but they like being recognized.) If you want him to work hard and well, show how a project needs his personal touch. So much depends on Four's enthusiasm for the project. If you make it personal, the Four will make it successful.
- Don't minimize a Four's feelings. Never ask, "How can you feel that way?" Never tell a Four to "lighten up" or "look on the bright side" or suggest that something's "no big deal." It only makes Fours wrap themselves more tightly in their feelings.
- Don't presume that you know what will satisfy a Four; you're probably wrong. Fours must find their own way. And remember that their brand of satisfaction may be unrecognizable to you. Accept the mystery of their feelings.
- Be empathic with a Four rather than helpful. The Two cheerleading style is a stressor to Fours. Instead of giving Fours the answer, give them the opportunity to express themselves.
- Telling a Four to lower her intensity will seem like you are asking her to be dishonest. Much better to ask Four to widen her focus to include additional factors and information.
- The creative idea is everything. Fours want to feel that their creative ideas have been received, understood, and appreciated.
- Be a good "container" for the Four. Be strong, stable, and steady. Speak the truth without an emotional charge.

- Make clear your commitment to a project. Being critical will seem like the Four's old abandonments.
- Let the Four make things beautiful.

If You Are a Four

- Your feelings need not determine everything you do. Learn to *name* them rather than *be* them, to convey them rather than act them out. "Look, I need to make some points that I have very strong feelings about." You may even choose to keep some feelings to yourself.
- In a sense Fours, who so treasure their sensitivity, are the emotional versions of Eight. They need emotions big and boffo in order to make sure they matter. The next time you're about to succumb to a tidal wave of feeling, ask yourself why. Is it out of habit? What are you avoiding? Ordinariness? Mundane responsibilities? Getting your work done? What are you choosing to miss?
- Never give up. Despair shadows the Four. "Many times I've noticed that I've given up in situations where had I persevered the outcome would have been different," said Gareth, a Four publishing executive. Fight to see how all is *not* lost.
- Don't stew if you can help it. Move your body instead. This is good advice for all; Eastern medicine and Western bioenergetics alike teach that depression is a depression of energy flow, to which movement is an appropriate response.
- Are you using your judgments of a colleague's lack of depth as a way of dismissing his genuine contribution?
- What hard facts about the working processes of your business do you leave to others? Mastering such pragmatic information can be a springboard for intuition and artistry in business.
- Don't confuse compromise with appropriate give-and-take. The ability to collaborate and to factor in practical considerations can make your projects stronger.
- Don't take everything so personally. Period.

1. Stanley Marcus, *Quest for the Best* (New York: Viking Press, 1979), 148.
2. From an interview in *Advertising Age* (May 18, 1992).
3. Tom Peters and Robert Waterman, *In Search of Excellence* (New York: Harper & Row, 1982), 184.

FIVE

⬠ # The Sage

AKA	The Thinker, the Guru, the Wise Man/Wise Woman, the Idea Smith, the Observer, the Philosopher
Worldview	I am the master of my private world, built by superior commitment to special knowledge.
High Side	Wise, perceptive, analytic, respectful, thoughtful, sensitive, kind; masters of information; self-starters; objective, privately passionate about ideas, concepts
Low Side	Cold fish; arrogant, pointy-headed intellectuals; stingy, unreachable loners; patronizing and pedantic
Leadership Style	The Philosopher King/Queen; leadership by remote control
Credo	*Cogito ergo sum* (I think, therefore I am).
Appeal to	Intelligence, scientific method, theories, mental models, intellectual competition
Don't Appeal to	Spontaneous impulses, emotional longings, societal expectations, conventional wisdom
Talk/Communication Style	E-mail, theses, treatises, and lengthy briefs
Makes You Feel	Dazzled by their intellectual tour-de-force, awed by their cool objectivity; and—sometimes—a little less bright than you thought you were
Appearance	Cool and pale; bloodless; sometimes nerdy, sometimes patrician
Good Work Setting	Ivory towers; behind closed doors; anyplace where there are few interpersonal demands, rules, or limits

Difficult Work Setting	Aggressive, fast-paced, highly interpersonal, demonstrative environments where expression of strong emotions is required and there's no time to think
Books	*A Christmas Carol* by Charles Dickens *Gates* by Stephen Manes and Paul Andrews *The Dilbert Principle* by Scott Adams *Crisis in Candyland* by Jan Pottker (on M&M/Mars)
Sayings	"I want to be left alone." —Greta Garbo "The only isolation I have known in my lifetime I felt in the presence of others." —Jean Harris "Knowledge is power." —Francis Bacon "Seek simplicity, then distrust it." —A. N. Whitehead
Of the Five Persuasion	Jerry Brown, David Souter, Greta Garbo, Ebeneezer Scrooge, Thomas Edison, Bill Gates, Warren Buffet, Garrison Keillor, Siddhartha, Neil Young, Neil Armstrong, A. C. Neilson Co., Bobby Fischer, Brian Lamb, Howard Hughes, Hugh Hefner, Bob Dylan, J. D. Salinger, Yoda of *Star Wars*, comic-strip character Dilbert, C-SPAN, Albania, imperial China
High Performance	8 In the arena, engaged, taking bold risks, making the vision real; willing to fight/confront to get it done; fully embodied and open-hearted
Stress	7 Impractical, indulgent castles in the sky; mental hysteria; intellectual diarrhea, nonstop talking
Ally	6 *Energized* by being part of the company, in solidarity with teammates; willing to take public positions and act on them
Shadow	4 *Grounded* by claiming rejected emotionality, sensitivity, and passion
Virtue	Detachment
Vice	Avarice

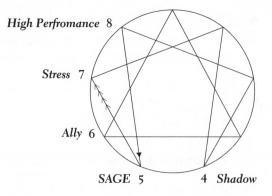

Getting to Know a Five

Roger's Story

Roger, a pale, lanky film director with thick Coke-bottle glasses, is well known in Hollywood but not particularly known well among the people he works with. When he makes a movie, he plans every shot in advance; most are wrapped in one or two takes. He seldom talks with his actors, usually relaying what few directions he has through the first assistant director and then watching the results on a video monitor.

"Roger is one of the finest directors I've ever worked with," one of his stars, an Academy Award–winning actor, told me. "Someday I hope to meet him."

Roger's production company keeps its offices at a large Hollywood studio. The studio has distribution rights for his films, but they have almost no contact with Roger. Roger intentionally keeps his budgets low and always comes in well under budget so that no one will bother him.

Roger's approach to recreation isn't much different from his approach to business. Behind the walls of his deserted-looking compound in the mountains north of Los Angeles hides a magnificent, regulation-sized basketball court. During the fall, famous actors and influential executives fill the court and the bleachers. Invitations to play in Roger's private league are much sought after and hard to come by. No one really knows what the prerequisites are—except Roger.

When Roger isn't playing, he sits on the sidelines and watches the games on several video monitors. He also supervises a full video crew—three cameras and a technical director staffing a switcher console—that videotapes every game. Each Monday morning Roger faxes to all the players the results of the weekend's game, including every possible individual and team statistic. The arcana of the league fascinate him, and he spends a great deal of time tracking them: he keeps the league standings, schedules the games, and even arranges for player moves and trades.

At work or at play, Roger seeks to be master of the game. Little happens in his private universe without his knowledge or approval.

Do you recognize Roger? Roger is a Five.

The Basic Premise

Fives are profoundly *private* and *sensitive* people. Imaginative, audacious, and nimble within the world of their mind, they hold an intimidating, sometimes awe-inspiring command of their subject, project, or company. This *intellectual mastery* can make them charismatic gurus who are a gold mine of relevant ideas and information or inaccessible recluses who hide behind and hoard their precious data.

Save or spend, information is the coin of the Five realm. Fives are the *illuminati* of the Enneagram—secret initiates who treasure their secrets, whether they be academic facts, technical procedures, departmental policy, skeletons in the company closet, or the competition's weak spots. Famous for their collections, they may accumulate large libraries, shelves full of stamps or coins, classic cars, display cases of toy soldiers arrayed in famous battles, or other unusual memorabilia. Fives work extraordinarily hard to acquire complete sets: all the volumes, all the versions, all the pieces, all the knowledge. A good number of Fives have told me that when they discovered the school library as a kid, they made a plan to read every book in it. And then they did, from A to Z.

Fives strive to stay in tight control of their world, but it is a remote control—at a distance, and without risk or engagement. They avoid life's entanglements—obligations and needs, volatile feelings and enthusiasms—which might make them vulnerable or beholden to others. Operating frequently in the background, austere Fives steadfastly guard against outside demands on their precious space, time, energy, resources, or money. They do so by thinking ahead and working out formulas, frameworks, and theoretical constructs that will enable them to survive, and even prosper and create, from well within the strong boundaries that mark their private world.

Fives are *observers* of life, which tends to remove them from it. Strangers in a strange land, they study or figure out how to act, which may lead to a kind of "as if" behavior, a kind of interpersonal awkwardness, so that they may seem to know the words but not the music. We've all seen this character in books and movies—people from outer space, brilliant but struggling with the nature of earthling feelings, charming in their impeccable but naïve observations, as in the Martian in Robert Heinlein's book *Stranger in a Strange Land* or Jeff Bridges's film character *Starman*. Their innocence is often profound but insofar as they seek to observe and understand from a vantage point on the outside, Fives are neither spontaneous nor engaged.

In a *60 Minutes* segment about Finland, Morley Safer reported of that remote, isolated country that "the national mission seems to be to not be noticed." The Finns, he continued, are "the shiest people on earth . . . so intensely private that to be noticed is an embarrassment, to take notice an affront." This is the Five approach. The Finns have the highest per capita use of the Internet of any country in the world by far. Communication by computer is the Five ideal.

Fives' gift to the Enneagram is the degree to which they honor the pristine faculties of mind. As the story goes, the philosopher Bertrand Russell, a Five, was once asked, "Lord Russell, you have so much intelligence, would you trade an ounce of intelligence for an ounce of love?" "Oh, no," Russell replied. "I *like* intelligence."

Lord Russell was being a bit provocative, perhaps, but the way to a Five's heart is definitely through her head. They are the Enneagram's natural philosophers (a word that comes from the Greek and means "lovers of knowledge").

But like Yoda, mentor of Jedi Masters in the movie *Star Wars*, *all* Fives conceal their magic behind an artfully fabricated facade. Their disguise may be that of a nerd (especially for Fives in science or technology), an eccentric but brilliant executive, or a drab bureaucrat. Fives sometimes hide behind outgoing (but well-rehearsed) charismatic facades as well—they can be the powerhouse entrepreneur or hail-fellow-well-met—as long as that guise serves a protective function.

They appear surprisingly often as the heads of corporations, having risen through the ranks on their expertise as scientists or specialists who are also strategists. Camouflaging their reticent, vulnerable Five selves behind an ingenious range of characters can be a Five specialty; actors Greta Garbo, Robert De Niro, and William Hurt come to mind.

No matter what role they play, their tactics in the workplace will be Five tactics: they will win through superior preparation and intellectual firepower; by carefully controlling the environment and the players; by paying astonishing attention to observing events and detail; and, as we shall see, because they have the best analytical "software" on the Enneagram. Fives are willing to be very aggressive, as long as they have time to think and prepare.

Foresight and Hindsight

Fives *crave predictability.* They get it by previewing: by vacuuming up raw data and working things through in advance. Husbands and wives of Fives

often report that on the way to a social event their spouse wants to know everyone who might be there and may even rehearse conversations based on who's
expected.

Ron, a Five attorney with a large law firm, says, "I like to know what will
happen at a meeting—the agenda, of course, but also who's going to be there,
what kind of demands they are going to make, and how to deal with them.
Then I map out the whole meeting in my head." Ellen, the president of a
small liberal arts college, always held small, informal meetings with members
of her board of directors and senior staff in the days before scheduled board
meetings. She wanted to know what everyone thought in advance. (A Three
would be hard pressed to allot time for such extensive preparation. That's
what the meeting is for.)

Says Louisa, a manager of systems analysts, "When I've got a stack of telephone calls I have to return, I make notes and script out what I'm going to say."
Rick, another Five manager, reports, "Although performance evaluation sessions are an important part of my job as a supervisor, I detest them. Usually I'm
so busy trying to figure out how to cope with the employee's reaction—let alone
my own—that I'm barely there. Later on I can look back and think, 'That went
great' or 'That went badly.'" Fives wear poker faces, not only because they value
their secrets, but also because they're not always reacting in the present.

After the meeting or event is over, Fives look back over the details. Hind-
sight is where the Five is usually most at home with himself, mentally reviewing and perhaps reengineering what happened. Fives can reconstruct
conversations and remember minute details. They are, once again, in control
of feelings, self, and domain.

For Fives, preparing for and reviewing everyday experience is a profoundly
respectful undertaking. While the rest of us may plunge into an event and
then move on to the next without taking a breath, evolved Fives anticipate
and then savor experience, sipping it slowly like an excellent tea. "Afterward,"
says Louisa, the manager of systems analysts, "I relax. I think: 'Okay, that was
interesting or pleasurable or hard.' That's when I have my feelings about it. I
do a lot of pondering after the fact."

Psychology

Fives are thin skinned. As a result, they spend a significant amount of time on
boundary maintenance, building a strong, sometimes impenetrable psychological fence, and then living well within it.

As children, Fives developed intellectual mastery as a defense against intrusive others. They built a wall against a tide of parental demands or in response

to a lack of support. "My mother was extremely anxious," says Marc, a Five. "When I was growing up, she worried about me constantly, always fussing over me. I took refuge in my room, where I taught myself to build radios. Eventually I got a ham license. I still spend a couple of hours in my ham shack every day."

"We lived on a farm and I was my mother's main social contact. I was responsible for listening to her long chattering in order to entertain her," another Five, now a psychotherapist, told me. A Five who feels neglected may erect the same kind of wall. "I remember the moment when I was ten years old," a social scientist who consults to the largest corporations confessed. "I looked at my parents and it hit me: they didn't know how to help me get on in the world. If I depended on them, I just wasn't going to make it. I'd have to do it all by myself. And I have."

The young Five feels forsaken because her need for space or attention is ignored, a feeling of anguish and loss similar to a Four's. Fours chose to experience their longing, pain, and desires in the world in a frustrating effort to be made whole. Fives instead chose to withdraw from these feelings. They decided on a minimalist approach: to get along on very little, not to rely on people, and not to want much. Fives are the classic *counterdependents*. There is always a part of Five that doubts that real interdependence—an "I and Thou" relationship is what theologian Martin Buber called it—is possible.

For Fives, withholding feelings—even from themselves, maybe especially from themselves—carries a certain satisfaction. Each of the types enjoys exercising a particular muscle. Twos like difficult emotional cases because they can give their Two powers a good workout. Eights seem to seek out the unjust, arrogant, and pretentious so that they can deton-Eight them. Fives take deep pleasure in minimizing their emotions and their enthusiasms, and more pleasure yet in their ability to do so. They don't mind if someone (perhaps a Two) tries to draw them out; they enjoy flexing their Five muscles in an emotional tug-of-war, sticking their heads out a bit, perhaps as a tease, and then pulling back into their private sanctuary.

The Good News

It is their very distance from emotional excess and group pressures that lets Fives see so clearly and dispassionately and often so imaginatively. Free from distraction and demands, Fives are exquisitely brilliant, pristine conceptual thinkers. They are *idea smiths* (as opposed to Sixes, who are ideologues). Fives develop, analyze, and test ideas. And more than that, they are *idealists*, who believe in the power of ideas.

Yet the Fives have little compulsion to affect or change others, as Sixes and Ones have. Fives seek to notice and understand, like a psychoanalyst. They have too much respect for personal boundaries (their own and others) to impose their will on their colleagues, lest someone try to do the same to them. The Five prime directive is to observe life without interfering in it. (Of course, within their boundaries they retain tight control of their world.)

Fives at their best are the most *generous* of the Enneagram types. They don't give themselves away, like Nines, or give themselves with strings attached, like Twos. Fives are restrained and thoughtful, and their gifts—because they don't give them indiscriminately—have real value. One of their greatest gifts to others is the gift of space: as far as the Five is concerned, he's on his own and you are, too. For this reason highside Fives can make excellent bosses, especially for self-starters or independent thinkers.

Despite what might appear to outsiders as a certain ascetic minimalism, Fives have capacious inner lives and are strongly affected by others. Although they may seem unfeeling on the outside, they are in their way as sensitive as Fours within. A hello from a casual acquaintance can mean a lot to a Five. Because they scrutinize each bit of information, a little input goes a long way.

Intellectual Firepower

Fives have the best mental concentration on the Enneagram. They are terrifically imaginative, often unconventional thinkers who are naturally able to solve complex problems. At their best they can be *splendid analysts, fact-sifters, and pundits.* Fives stand outside the crowd, which gives them a unique vantage point for commentary. They are scrupulous about the facts. Their sober perceptions are unbiased in a way that each of the other eight types are not (although their distaste for the flow of feeling can lead to other distortions). It's very rare for a Five to go off half-cocked. In an emotionally overheated environment, Fives can be prudent and reliable and will courageously stand by their independent perceptions.

Fives excel at planning and have a certain gift of foresight—the ability to imagine the future—partly because they don't like to be surprised. Sevens also like to plan, but they think globally, whereas Fives like to extrapolate from their specialty or their narrow experience to larger systems. "I don't see my job as running this place per se," says Dave, a Five who is director of an HMO. "My job is to deal with the fact that we're being bombarded with new information daily. What's happening in the health care industry? What are our competitors doing? Are we keeping up? What I bring to the table is the ability to assess facts and piece them together into theories and strategies."

Fives love to search for that special piece of information that offers leverage, defends against trespass, or bolsters their security. It might be an angle on the market, a stray bit of technology, or a passing facial reaction of the person they are with. Whatever it is, you can be sure that once she finds it, the Five in your employ will file it as part of a larger framework or build an entire hypothesis of her own around it.

As a corollary, Fives are wondrous observers of detail. Once during an Enneagram workshop I mentioned that I couldn't find my glasses. Jake, a studio executive, was in the audience. He said, "They're on the floor behind the passenger seat of your car." He happened to glance in my car as he was coming in. This same ability allowed Jake to determine at a glance when the products his studio licenses have not been manufactured according to the strict terms of the licensing agreement.

Restrained

The best Fives—so sensitive to boundaries—are modest and respectful of others. Like Ones, they can be deferential and polite, even courtly. Ones follow etiquette because it is the right thing to do, Fives because it is a set of understandings that helps prevent people from intruding on one another. For Fives it is central to respect sensitivities and boundaries—their own and those of others—so they are cautious in interpersonal relations. Sometimes their caution is misinterpreted as coolness or rejection, but many Fives are open to close alliances and even intimacy as long as their boundary processes are respected.

Fives' quiet and reserved demeanor often belies an aggressive business spirit. Just because Fives are quiet doesn't mean they lack ambition. The key to Fives is not so much their asceticism or isolation as their single-minded commitment to intellectual passions. Investor Warren Buffet became the richest man in the United States (until he was supplanted by Bill Gates) by finding cheap stocks and then by being excruciatingly restrained about when to invest. Buffet says that if you do very careful homework, you need only make a few investments in a lifetime. Threes can be more easily suckered because they so want to be in the race that they will take any horse. Fives can just walk away.

The Bad News

Their single-minded dedication can make Fives strict taskmasters. Their tendency to avoid "human issues" may make them seem ruthless and cold. When a Five bank executive called his tellers "human ATMs," he couldn't understand the ruckus he caused. "After twenty minutes, my computer is warmer than he is," said the employee of a Five bureaucrat.

Withdrawn

Even though Fives may unwittingly stand out as original or eccentric, their wish is often to hide, to quietly make their real self invisible. When Supreme Court Justice David Souter was attorney general of New Hampshire, he gave up the grand, ornate attorney general's office to an assistant and kept his own office in a small room across the hall. It's been said of Souter that his black robes have added color to his wardrobe.

Because Fives relish solitude, they're experts at discovering clever ways to hide. Jake, the Five who noticed my glasses in the back of my car, is the head of merchandising and licensing for a major Hollywood studio. His office is bursting with products from various manufacturers who have bought a studio license for a movie character or logo: giant stuffed animals, games, inflatable toys, jackets, hats, T-shirts, and posters. His desk is behind the door, camouflaged by the stuff, and impossible to see when his door is open. Only a Five could hide behind an open door. When you walk into his office you may not see him—you have to call out and wait for a response. I have found him several times working on the floor behind his desk.

Fives often make themselves invisible by closing their doors. Fives are famous for not answering knocks, messages, or notes. Some may avoid their office altogether and work in a special place like a conference room, the library, or at home. Others just flee, as did a client, a multinational computer company executive who became caught in the middle of an explosive conflict between his two deputies about who had authority over what. He suddenly felt he was needed on several other continents, and he traveled constantly until an outside consultant could resolve the matter. And still other Fives never go anywhere. A best-selling writer on pop psychology who lives in Manhattan says, "I make a point of not leaving my ZIP code." He spends most of his days watching television talk shows, which is the major source of material for his books. He observes human life from a safe distance, remote control in hand.

Stingy

Fives are, as one Five chief financial officer put it, the "cheap operating officers" of the Enneagram. They like to acquire and hoard. There are many stories of fabulously wealthy Fives like Bill Gates, Berkshire-Hathaway's Warren Buffett, or the Mars brothers (M&M/Mars) traveling coach and staying in very inexpensive hotels. The famous Five miser and billionaire J. Paul Getty had a pay phone installed for his oil executives who visited his estate. "When you get some fellow talking for ten or fifteen minutes," Getty explained, "well, it all adds up."

As executives, Fives tend to impose strict financial discipline and tight cost controls. They are unsentimental about letting go of people or businesses. But sometimes Five stinginess can result in management that is penny wise and pound foolish. Microsoft didn't acquire appropriate computers to run their own business until well past their need, according to Bill Gates's biographers.[1]

Fives see the safest path in holding close what they have. In his book *Man for Himself*, Erich Fromm described what he called a "hoarding" orientation. These people

> have little faith in anything new that they may get from the outside world; their security is based upon hoarding and saving, while spending is felt to be a threat. They have surrounded themselves with a protective wall, and their main aim is to bring as much as possible into this fortified position and to let as little as possible out of it. Their miserliness refers to money and material things as well as to feelings and thoughts. . . . These people tend to feel that they possess only a fixed quality of strength, energy, or mental capacity and that this stock is diminished or exhausted by use and can never be replenished.[2]

Fives are stingy most of all with themselves. "If you want to talk, call up a talk show," said a likely Five, hidden behind a newspaper, to his wife in a *New Yorker* cartoon.

A Five herself may not see her behavior as stingy. Says Louisa, the manager of systems analysts, "I have no intention of denying people. I don't think, 'I'll hurt them by withholding myself.' It's more like, 'What can I do? I only have a limited amount of time and energy. I have to be protective of it.'"

Tunnel Vision

Fives tend to be overly clear, overly focused overanalyzers, with an unbending adherence to what they consider "hard facts." Calvin Coolidge was traveling on a train (so the story goes), when a companion looked out the window, saw a flock of sheep, and remarked, "Seems they've been newly shorn." Coolidge looked and replied, "On this side."

Fives objectify what they analyze, whether people, systems, or groups. Their technique is to overilluminate a subject with an intense beam of laser-like attention; while their observations are usually accurate, they sometimes lack context, which can skew their interpretation.

A presentation to a Five boss can be something like a dissertation defense. Harold Geneen of ITT was famous for his vast command of budget line items, which he dissected along with presenting executives. "The numbers will set you free," said Geneen, who imprisoned himself and others with them. Geneen was known as an information hound and a proponent of "professional management," but he went from one of ITT's collection of companies to the next, cutting costs. So focused was he on the numbers that he never developed his managers. So focused was he on each compartmentalized unit that he rarely let true synergies develop among companies.

Even well-meaning Fives may give information but not direction. Bob, the director of information systems at a hospital, took a terrific amount of criticism when the hospital went on-line with a new computer system and software. Bob had spent an enormous amount of time picking just the right hardware and software. But he completely forgot to arrange for training on the system. He thought everyone would pick it up as he did, by reading the manual and poking around. Like Fours, Fives may emphasize their work product and forget about the consumer.

Intellectually Arrogant

At their best, Fives are humble because they know how little they know. That seems to have something to do with real wisdom. But many Fives were intellectually pampered "whiz kids" who grow up to be "wise guys" with contempt for people who can't keep up with them. "I hate dumb," says an otherwise congenial Pentagon analyst who specializes in military hardware. "That's the dumbest thing I've ever heard. How can you be so stupid?" is the well-worn phrase often flung by a famous Silicon Valley executive. Complains Tom, a Three who works for a Five boss, "No matter how on top of the material you are, he has an unerring instinct for asking the single question for which you are unprepared and then gloating about it."

Working with a Five

Influencing a Five

Because Fives seem emotionally withdrawn, many people try to get through to them by coming on strong, loud, and emotionally big. "This has got to be done! Right now! Are you on board? Hello in there!" you might bellow to get a Five's attention. This has about the same effect as yelling English loudly at someone who doesn't speak the language. It's a big mistake.

Fives are actually extremely sensitive and attentive to what other people want. But they are also afraid of being talked into something they don't want to do. Your enthusiasm for an idea may actually push a Five to reject it. "When someone tries to bully me, I get flushed," says Martha, a manager of research chemists. "I feel myself turn bright red—and the answer will be no. I hate when people try to push me. I'm especially suspicious when they make their case in terms of feeling or desire. Where's the analysis? Where are the numbers?"

To persuade a Five, make your pitch judiciously. When appropriate, emphasize an excellent deal on the numbers alone. Show how your desired outcome is the logical choice with supporting facts; don't push. "You don't have to say yes right now. Think about it." A first refusal isn't necessarily the end of the game. Fives need time to get used to what seem like demands, and time to explore their own feelings. Go away and give them time. Martha comments: "After they've left, I relax a little bit. I start replaying it and thinking it through. I see how, in fact, we can do it, or at least a part of it. I usually come around, but by degrees."

How a Five Makes Decisions

Fives are in the analytic triad (Five, Six, and Seven), so they want to know what makes things tick. They look for natural laws, formulas, and theories. Because Fives are cool and detached, complex or emotionally charged decisions (especially someone else's) generally don't rattle them. Able to focus dispassionately, they want their decisions to be logical, unfettered, and elegant.

Decision trees, which are a clever Five invention, are a good example of the Five's formulaic approach. These analytical tools, which can teach others to think like a Five, break complicated decisions down into several choice points. At each choice point—each fork of the tree—a value is assigned to designate its desirability or likelihood, depending on the process. Following different decision paths yields different numerical outcomes. Using a decision tree quantifies decisions in a logical way and lets you preview all possible scenarios and outcomes—just the sort of thing that Fives enjoy doing naturally.

All this takes time and requires *thoughtfulness*. To feel secure in their decisions, Fives need freedom from the pressure of people, events, or schedules. To help a Five decide, give him information, evidence, facts, and logic. And then give him time and space to use his famous Five powers of concentration.

Fives don't simply *make* decisions; often they declare them, once they emerge from their inner sanctum. Their decisions may seem like edicts—*faits accompli*—to subordinates, because Fives rarely share their personal process.

As a result, Fives can seem as intimidating as Eights. I once consulted with Gene, the vice president of research at a large multinational firm, and his work team. Already familiar with the Enneagram, the manager of human resources warned me that Gene was gruff and brutal, a sure Eight. Gene sat stone-faced through a day and a half of instruction about the Enneagram at an off-site retreat. Then he announced to all, "I am a Five." Jaws dropped all around the table. "But you just announce what you want and expect us to do it," said someone; "surely that's Eight." "I take your reports," said Gene, "and I go off by myself and think about them. You and your work are extremely important to me. I take my time to decide what to do, and then I come in and tell you." We spent a good amount of time discussing this surprising behind-the-scenes look at Gene, whom they always considered bossy but who thought of himself as contemplative.

The Five Leadership Style

While Eights are organizers and stabilizers of turbulent *physical* environments like big oil (Mobil), Fives are masters of untamed, unpredictable *intellectual* environments like cutting-edge computer technology (Silicon Graphics or DEC). The notion of Fives as mere nerds wedded to their microprocessors is misleading. Fives like to be in charge and can be ambitious and even relentless in pursuit of control and booty. Think Bill Gates as well as the absent-minded professor.

The best Five leaders make you feel part of a group of special initiates with access to special knowledge that is your responsibility to shepherd and refine. The Five leader's gift is to hold to the project *concept* but to be super-flexible about how to get there, as new technical and market information develops in the course of a project. (Ones, in contrast, are rigid about their processes but sometimes forget the goal. Fives strive for insight, but One says, "I'd rather be right than prescient.") The best Five leaders are able to juggle lots of new and complex information. Nimble in the realm of ideas and research, Fives can be highly responsive to technical and customer feedback.

However, in their focus on the job at hand, they sometimes lose track of the human game. Howard Hughes and Hugh Hefner, significantly different personalities but both master-of-my-universe Fives, managed their empires by remote control. Rarely talking even to their top executives, they communicated through copious memos, exerting strong control over minute details. They worked in isolation, often in the middle of the night—Hughes in a guarded hotel suite with shielded windows, and Hefner locked in his apartment at the Playboy Mansion. They both left strict instructions not to be disturbed for any reason for weeks at a time. In his heyday, Hefner (one of the great observers of the age) took no phone calls that were not in response to his own. Hughes took no phone calls at all. Hughes's wife, Jean Peters, had to communicate with him through an operations center.

Five leaders exert strong control over information. Their authority comes from their expertise, knowledge, or skill, coupled with their unemotional, owl's-nest point of view. (Owls have intense focus and silent, unerring flight.) People want to follow Five leaders because Fives know stuff worth knowing—either the most sophisticated, the most profound, or most at the cutting edge—and they have the integrity to stand by it.

Some Five leaders use information to manipulate. They parcel out data only if they're convinced you must have it—and maybe not even then. As an accountant said of his boss, "Fred dispenses information on a need-to-know basis. If you need to know, he won't tell you." For all their concern with details, both Hughes and Hefner left their subordinates feeling they didn't have enough guidance on important matters, let alone the authority to proceed on them.

If your boss is a Five, you'll probably experience her as an interpersonally hands-off, disengaged manager—unless you are the holder of some information she wants, or are in the path of some control she needs. Lowside Five bosses won't mollycoddle your feelings and are not likely to spend time or money on extensive training or, at their worst, even simple instruction.

Human relations can be problematic. "Dan is a terrible manager," said his colleague Julie. "He tells employees to learn their job or leave it. He doesn't share his vision of how he wants things to come out. One time I said to him, 'Dan, maybe you need to sit down and have a conversation with this guy instead of just busting his butt.' He said, 'But Jenny, I wouldn't be busting his butt if we were singing the same song.' I said, 'Dan, you need to share the lyrics with him.'"

In general, Five managers don't like to ride herd over the people they manage. Suzanne, a prep school finance manager, says, "I like the people who work for me to be independent. I encourage them to make their own decisions, just like I do." Employees who need a great deal of emotional hand-holding are torture for Fives, who pride themselves on their self-sufficiency. "I've always done everything myself," says the Five manager. "Why can't you?"

Some Five managers may check out when a situation requires intense personal involvement. Many Fives understand their workers' psyches but feel uneasy with the warm give-and-take that builds relationships. "I try to be nice," says the manager of customer accounts at an East Coast wholesaler, "but I'm really not interested in small talk or when people bring their emotional problems to work. I honestly don't know how they expect me to respond." The best Fives, though, can be quite warm, intimate, and loyal once they know that you respect their boundaries.

The Five Work Style

Fives need privacy, time, and space; they like to work independently with plenty of secluded time to think. All Fives are naturally monastic with a hermit side even if they lead an active secular life. Look down the rows of cubicles at an aerospace company, where engineers contemplate their narrow, technical specialties alone, day after day, and you'll see a Five culture not much different from that of a secluded abbey.

Fives are self-starters—for the pursuits that interest them. "Unlike some people, I'm self-motivated," says an aerospace engineer. "If I get interested in a topic I'll comb the Internet; I'll read a lot of books on it. Of course, I don't really care whether my boss thinks it's relevant or not."

In the workplace, Fives are wary of the demands of their co-workers, their staff, their boss, even of the job itself. They like to work independently in an environment that doesn't make demands on them with silly reporting rules or excessive meetings that take them away from their work. (Compare with Nines and Sevens, who are happy to meet all day long.) They don't like to be closely supervised. "I like to do things alone, particularly when I am in hot pursuit of some obscure information that no one knows much about and I do," a marketing researcher for one of the automobile manufacturers told me. "I've always had positions where I'm fairly high up in the organization," says Suzanne, the prep school finance manager, "but nobody really knows what I do. My goal is to make sure the right paperwork makes its way out of this office, because that allows me the freedom to work behind closed doors."

Fives hate having to grease the wheels of business with chitchat. They see social exchange as draining. "I resent having to be nice to get things done," says Betty, who runs a research team at a government agency in Washington. "I despise having to socialize with people at work I don't necessarily like in order to make sure they provide minimal service of my accounts when I need it. My work speaks for itself. I shouldn't have to kiss ass."

This aversion to socializing can surprise a Five when a business event turns personal, as Margaret, who coordinates international manufacturing, discovered when she hosted a reception for a colleague from India. "When the guest of honor arrived, I was all aflutter," Margaret recalled. "She was very outgoing, a big person who was right in my face saying how happy she was to meet me and how she hoped I would come to India because the India operation could really use my expertise. She had her hand on my shoulder, and she was really in my face. I had nothing at all to say to her. *She was taking up all the space!* For the whole event I found myself retreating from her, a woman whom I had spent a couple of years hoping to meet."

E-mail is like manna from heaven for most Fives because it directly and dramatically transcends their major reservation about interpersonal contact: its oppressive demand on space and time. With e-mail, senders and receivers can be anywhere, and you needn't converse in real time. You needn't spend much time schmoozing on e-mail, either ("How's the wife?") like you must in face-to-face meetings. The most important benefit of e-mail is that it greatly accelerates the flow of ideas, just what Fives like.

With the help of e-mail, Fives are expert at putting together "virtual teams"—like-minded people whom they can consult any time of day or night. Flesh-and-blood real-time teams are more problematic for most Fives to deal with.

Fives are motivated workers with unique talents, but they can have trouble fitting into a business world that demands cooperation with people of lesser ability. "My idea of fun is to work with really gifted, responsible people on an interesting topic," Betty told me. "Getting to think hard and well about interesting topics that allow for meaningful, structured, limited social contact is pure magic. Finding such a situation is not easy."

Of all possible interactions, an *unexpected* confrontation is the worst for Fives, *particularly when it's heated or personal in nature*. They either withdraw into their shells or become snapping turtles, defending their privacy by blasting the intruder with a barrage of high-powered ideas. When appropriate, the best way to bring a problem to a Five's attention is to make an appointment to do so. Tell him what you will want to talk about in advance.

The Five Learning Style

Fives learn best in situations where roles and expectations are clear and where they themselves are not personally exposed or obligated. They are imaginative, conceptual folk who appreciate orderly, organized, well-conceived lessons.

Fives also like to work things out for themselves, by themselves. Often highly visual people, they learn easily from books and other written sources of information. But while Fives can digest *factual* information at warp speed, they are likely to flee if the situation requires them to share their own passions and sensitivities. Impressionistic, improvisational teaching that is intellectually sloppy makes them uncomfortable.

"I always learn things better and believe them more when I read about them," Louisa comments. "Conferences and workshops usually make me feel claustrophobic. My real learning happens after the event when I reread my notes."

The best of each type watch themselves soften over time. Recently I gave a seminar at a university, and a famous Five member of the faculty in his seventies came in and sat in the front row. He kibitzed with me all day long. Finally I got the nerve to point out that this was very unusual for a Five. He said, "Oh, twenty years ago I would have sat by the door and taken extensive notes or listened to a tape. Live and learn."

The Five Organization

The Five organization is an information meritocracy. In a healthy Five organization, "who knows what" matters more than titles, and respect for data is more important than standard operating procedures (which are central for One).

The best Five organizations treasure their information. They consider themselves fiduciaries for the data, facts, news, and knowledge that have been entrusted to them. C-SPAN, the Cable Satellite Public Affairs Network, which covers congressional proceedings along with a sometimes mind-numbing, sometimes intoxicating run of public policy conferences and call-in programs, is the quintessence of Five enterprises. C-SPAN covers events without editing and without comment. They observe intently but are not part of events. C-SPAN has that spare and honorable humility that is one of the best qualities of Five. (Ones like C-SPAN, too: "C-SPAN lets you do the judging.")

Brian Lamb, the founder of C-SPAN, is a Five. On his program, *Booknotes*, where he interviews authors of books of current affairs and history, he asks questions that authors are rarely asked and are often startled by, such as, "What do you write with?" or "What is your writing schedule?" Lamb takes passages from a book and will ask an author what he means by them; there is no question that he has meticulously read the book. Compare with CNN's Larry King, a Seven who makes a practice of *never* reading the books of the authors he interviews.

At their worst, Five organizations *hoard* information and other resources. M&M/Mars, the candy and pet food manufacturer (its brands include Snickers and Kal-Kan) is a famously penny-pinching and paranoid Five organization. According to *Crisis in Candyland* by Jan Pottker, the two reclusive Mars brothers who run the company are billionaires, but they travel coach, use discount tickets for hotels, and rent subcompact cars. Mars is described as a "corporate hermit" whose "penchant for privacy makes Howard Hughes look like a socialite."[3] Executives give no interviews and permit no photographs. The Mars brothers don't have private offices; they have desks in a big room (without partitions) so that they can keep up on what everyone else is doing.

Poor communication is common in flawed Five organizations. Casual meetings are out of the question because they're seen as a drain on time and resources rather than as the social glue holding a system together. Memos and e-mail become the order of the day. At the engineering division of a huge aerospace and company, AVO—"Avoid Verbal Orders"—is a division byword. All management directives are put in writing or on e-mail. Face-to-face contact is avoided.

Getting the Best from a Five

Instead of hiding behind their role as observers, Fives evolve when they become willing to wield power in the world to do good. This is the perspective of Five's High Performance Point Eight. When Fives are stressed, they gush with ideas (which can look like a kind of mental hysteria) at Stress Point Seven. But Seven is also a wake-up call for Five to stop holding himself and his ideas back.

Five's Ally Point is Six, the willingness to become engaged enough to take sides. Fives are energized by joining their team or community. Four is Five's Shadow. Fives avoid Four's intense emotionality but are grounded when they stay connected to their genuine passion. When Fives balance their feelings (at Four) with their sense of intellectual engagement (at Five), they can choose to observe with true detachment, the virtue of Five.

Paulette's Story

Paulette, head of the human resources department at a Midwest insurance company, has the cool, patrician demeanor characteristic of many Fives. She had been a company librarian but took some company training courses and rose into management when her department was reorganized.

Paulette was candid about preferring to do her own work alone, which was juggling statistics. "What I hate is marketing this department: getting people in the organization to know that we exist and what we can do for them, and then getting them to sign on. When I'm doing that I'm out of my comfort zone. I'd rather be at the computer."

Other managers within the company fostered a collegial atmosphere by collaborating and consulting with their people as they did their work. Not Paulette. Paulette preferred that her employees drop a report in her in box. She would edit or even rewrite the whole thing and present it as a *fait accompli*. Her writing was often brilliant, but employees were left feeling ineffectual. Paulette lost five of her ten employees to other departments within the company in the space of six months. The turnover had become obvious to those above her, and she realized she could ignore it no longer.

Paulette's employees reported that although she had a reputation as a knowledgeable and imaginative problem solver, she was sometimes seen as weak, indecisive, and withdrawn. "People don't think she'll fight for them in the company or help develop careers," one employee told me. Her Eight boss told me, "She just doesn't want to take her lumps. I give her plenty of opportunities to lead meetings or speak up at meetings, but she shrinks from that." Paulette responds, "He never gives me any advance notice. He just bellows out, 'Hey, Paulette, you wanna be up here?' I don't do well in those situations."

Her secretary, Jennifer, a Two, said. "She just comes in and closes her door and starts work," she said. "People here think she's an ice goddess."

Stress Point: Seven

Fives have extremely ordered minds wherein each idea is given thoughtful consideration. When they are under stress the rapid, disorderly flow of ideas and input is disorienting. When Paulette was under stress her head would spin with dizzying ideas, much like a Seven. Paulette was one of several persons competing for a significant promotion. She was terrified to be visible, take a stand, and fight. When interviewed she talked nonstop about all the ideas and possibilities she saw for the new position. She barely took a breath. The hiring committee was put off by her ungrounded enthusiasm.

When we talked later, she said, "It's not totally a bad thing. At least I put my hat in the ring, instead of retreating like I usually do."

High Performance Point: Eight

Fives are afraid of being overwhelmed or intimidated. Eights overwhelm and intimidate. What a coincidence! Five and Eight, flip sides of the same coin, are both centrally concerned with power and control over the environment. To keep control, Fives implode and Eights explode—the extremes of this power continuum, the Five-Eight line. To avoid alienating her staff even further, and for the sake of herself and her career, Paulette needed to balance withdrawal with an Eight's active engagement. While Fives defend against contact, Eights propel themselves into it. Fives perform in a flow state when they effortlessly, fearlessly engage with people, when they are willing to be visible—"to take their lumps"—and to embody their ideas, insights, and positions. At Eight, Five learns that understanding without action is only life's consolation prize.

Part of Paulette's job, like that of any manager, was to help nurture the careers of her people. Paulette thought she was doing just that by rewriting their reports, but she came to see that she was abdicating her responsibility for mentoring her staff by simply redoing their work. At Eight, she learned how to nurture and protect her brood. She was willing to mix it up with them, offering strong opinions and advice. She learned to stand up for their work (and for her own) within the company.

Wings

Shadow Point: Four

Sensitive Fives have their finger in the Four dike, fighting against being overwhelmed by a torrent of feelings. Although Fives define themselves as people who are not swept away by feelings and who may indeed seem aloof and cool, the shadowy secret of Five is that they are extremely sentimental and filled with longing. Fives are grounded by owning and acknowledging their shadow's profound emotionality.

Paulette's employees would have been shocked to learn how much she knew and cared about them. She was reluctant to let them know it for fear of getting "too involved" or being too exposed or dependent. She decided to deal with "the human factors," as she put it, by having a short heart-to-heart with everyone every morning. It worked like a charm. "I spend about thirty minutes now just saying good morning to people!" she told me, rolling her eyes. "Then I get back to my office, close the door, and reintegrate."

Ally Point: Six

Five's Ally Point is Six, where she isn't afraid of taking sides. Fives, whose habit is cool neutral objectivity, are energized and engaged by Six's characteristic creation of enemies and collaborators. Sixes are anything but neutral. They take positions and argue them. Participation can be intoxicating for a Five who has been merely a voyeur. When Fives move toward Six, their Ally Point, they learn to value and act on loyalty and commitment to people or ideas larger than themselves.

Six and Four (fear and longing) are as "hot" as Five is "cool." Balancing access to the wings gives Five the chance for real Eight power. When Paulette began to let her views and positions be known and made it clear that she would fight for them and for her people, she gained a visibility and a credibility that she did not have before. In a sense, she hadn't allowed people to be loyal to her before because she wasn't a strong enough presence. No longer hidden from view or ignored, she found her department coalesced around her newly expressed positions; sometimes people disagreed, but everybody was in the game. The newly visible Paulette was seen as more committed to her own job and more of a leader and an influential force in the organization.

Cardinal Rules

If You Work with a Five

- Meetings can be hard for Fives. Give them as much information before the meeting as you can: what will be discussed, who will be there, and what must be decided. If possible, Fives like to make decisions after the meeting.
- Fives love inside information. They want that special piece of knowledge that will give them the edge or provide a relevant insight. It's the mental equivalent to Three's "competitive advantage." Include as much supporting data as you can. Fives delight in the details. What may be too trivial for you may be the central fact for a Five.
- If you stray too far from the agreed-upon or acceptable area of inquiry, Fives may experience even normal questioning as cross-examination. Be direct, precise, and concise. Don't pry.
- Don't fill every space in the conversation. One Five whose silence was interrupted barked, "I'm thinking. Don't you ever think?"
- Fives need their privacy. At one company I worked with, a Five who was assigned a cubicle took her important phone calls under her desk.
- Shut the door and hold the calls when you're meeting with a Five, especially if you're talking about something sensitive. Create a safe, bounded physical and emotional space, a cocoon for the two of you.
- Sevens, Fours, and others: Don't expect emotional fireworks in response to your great ideas (to say the least). And don't become even more enthusiastic to try to get a reaction. You'll only get more diffidence, more holding on, or worse.
- Fives like to feel prepared, so give them plenty of advance warning. A managing partner of a consulting firm announced that I would be giving a seminar in a month. "But," said a Five, "this is the first I've heard of it!" "Well," said the manager, "this is the first I'm telling you of it." To the Five, that didn't matter. Remember the old Army guidelines for speech-making: "Tell 'em what you're going to tell 'em. Tell 'em. Then tell 'em what you told 'em."

If You Are a Five

- The world of work is collaborative. Align with production-oriented people so that your can bring your ideas to life. (You only need one such person.)
- Check the effect your communication has on others. To you it may seem like you are offering helpful if obscure ideas or facts, but to others it may seem like you are a condescending and arrogant know-it-all.
- Risk expressing your position first. Let other people align around you.
- Risk expressing your position at all. Other people are not mind readers— or at least not as much as you are.
- Don't always play it safe and hide. Consider whether the braver choice— making your real feelings and opinions known—might not be the better one.
- Listen up. Try to get out of the habit of thinking what you're going to say while the other person is talking.
- Check to see if you have some contempt for the human factors in plans. It's an attitude that tends to be counterproductive when you make plans that involve humans.
- Learn the difference between secrecy and privacy. It's appropriate to keep much about you private, but you don't need to keep everything secret.
- Make agreements with your boss and co-workers that describe your boundaries, what you need, and what your plans are, even if they are in flux. Strain to let people know, when appropriate. Don't just disappear with no explanation.
- Let your colleagues know that you're on the team, that you support its goals, and that you want to be helpful. Let them know when and how you're willing to be available. Give it up. Ask, "Is there anything else you need to know?"
- Moderation in all things, especially moderation.

1. Stephen Manes and Paul Andrews, *Gates* (New York: Simon & Schuster, 1993).
2. Erich Fromm, *Man for Himself* (New York: Henry Holt, 1947), 65.
3. *Fortune*, November 27, 1995.

SIX

The Troubleshooter

AKA	The Faithful Skeptic, the Devil's Advocate, the True Believer
Worldview	The world is dangerous; the truth is hidden; appearances are suspect; I need trustworthy allies.
High Side	Dragon Slayers and Knights Templar: loyal, truthful, warm, dutiful, imaginative, funny, clever, committed, discreet, pragmatic, self-sacrificing, builder of coalitions, supportive team player, fighting the good fight
Low Side	The persecuted persecutor; paranoid, suspicious, blaming, attacking, cowardly bullies
Leadership Style	The Reluctant Authority (who can be warm or fretful or contentious or highly authoritarian, but *always thinking*); takes *protective action* against the enemy: the competition, the boss, the employees, the government; reacts to real and imagined provocation; solidifies the side; protective of inner circle or employees
Credo	Be prepared.
Appeal to	Preparing for battle or survival, to the noble cause; to rational analysis, to taking calculated risks, to "what's really happening under the surface"
Don't Appeal to	"Because I say so." "There's no reason to worry. Things will take care of themselves."
Talk/Communication Style	Caveats, complaints, constraints, concerns
Makes You Feel	Distrusted, cross-examined; awkward, like the enemy; *or* trusted and warm, part of the team

Appearance	Worried, tentative, aggressively defensive *or* funny and ironical, warm and reassuring (either way, organized around fear); or heroic
Good Work Setting	Clear roles, responsibilities, and authority; cards on the table; where preparation, caution, and constant questioning are valued; where the good guys and bad guys are clear; sometimes dangerous adventure
Difficult Work Setting	Like Huxley's *Brave New World:* uncertain, changing environment where the basic premises, theories, or alliances alter without notice or explanation; working under a volatile, judgmental, impenetrable, all-seeing authority
Books	*Trust* by Jack Gibb *Managing* by Andrew Grove *Will* by Gordon Liddy
Sayings	"It's not what you say that counts, it's what you don't say." "Readiness is all." — Hamlet "It wouldn't be prudent." — George Bush "Let's be careful out there." 　— Sgt. Esterhaus, *Hill Street Blues* "Question authority." — Abbie Hoffman "There are moments when everything goes well; don't be frightened, they won't last." — Jules Renard "Only the paranoid survive." 　— Andrew Grove, CEO, Intel "The British are coming! The British are coming!" 　— Paul Revere
Of the Six Persuasion	Woody Allen, Sigmund Freud, Crusader Rabbit, Gordon Liddy, Bob Dole, Andrew Grove, Abbie Hoffman, George Bush, Jay Leno, Steven Seagal, Spike Lee, Lt. Columbo, Richard M. Nixon, Hamlet, Jane Fonda, Ted Turner, Fran Leibowitz, Mary Matalin, Camille Paglia, J. Edgar Hoover
High Performance	9 Trusting the natural flow of events and people to do their job; faith in the team

Stress	3 Manic doing; overdrive; overresponsible; imprudent rushing ahead
Ally	7 *Energized* by positive potential, exciting possibilities, fun, positive conspiracies
Shadow	5 *Grounded* by being a cool, detached observer instead of a partisan or a target. Grounded by getting all the information or data or facts
Virtue	Courage
Vice	Fear

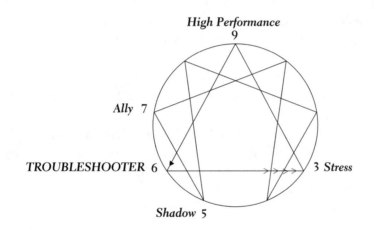

Getting to Know a Six

Sarah's Story

Sarah is the managing editor of a well-known weekly trade magazine in New York. To outsiders she seems warm and ingratiating, with a self-deprecating Woody Allen–style wit. But to those who work with her she is indecisive and cautious. "It's not that Sarah doesn't trust herself," said one of her employees, "but that she trusts other people less."

She can be secretive, dispensing information cautiously. "I wasn't told half the things I needed to do my job, because she was so tight-lipped, even with me," said a former senior manager who reported to Sarah. "But her deputy and her treasurer—the inner circle—seemed to meet constantly. We used to wonder what the three of them talked about all day long."

"It's not that I'm paranoid," Sarah says in her own defense. "But you have to expect the worst in this business. People do make mistakes. People tell you things that aren't true. People break their promises. And there are a slew of people who would like to see us fail. Stuff happens. I'm just realistic, not paranoid."

She loves keeping her hand on the pulse of what's new in the trade and keeping closer watch than anyone knows on the competition, but her reaction to anything new at the magazine is typically cautious. "Let's not be haphazard," she likes to say. "Let's think things through." Her tendency to procrastinate is well known, and people are often stacked up outside her office waiting their turn to ask her questions or get her approval. Sometimes she takes months to return e-mail messages.

When people do fail her, her fury is filled with blame; others' mistakes seem intentional. What went wrong is someone's fault—probably the fault of people who are out to get her. She spends a good deal of time speculating by whom and for what reason she is being undermined, whether in-house or by the competition.

Yet, as much as she rides her own people, she never lets outsiders criticize them directly. Once, when one of the most influential members of her board of directors called a reporter to complain about a cover story, she told the director, "Who's side are you on? You can't make secret end runs around the chain of command. If you have any problems with the magazine, you go through me," she said. "I hate when people force me to be the big authority," she told me later. "But I'll do it if I absolutely have to."

A substantial number of her employees are completely devoted to her. "It may take a while to get on her good side, but once you're in, you're in," says one staffer.

When the magazine is on deadline, she is magnificent. No longer hesitant, she has a sure hand and a clear vision of what she wants, and she says so. "I'm in this business because I love deadlines," she says, half joking. "Otherwise, I'd never get anything done."

Her favorite magazine features are about little guys challenging the industry bigwigs. This sometimes leads to out-and-out arguments with the publisher, who wants the magazine to be less political and more attractive to advertisers. She usually wins these arguments. A committed fighter for her convictions, she's not afraid to put her job on the line. For this many admire her, but some think her arrogant, brittle, and unable to compromise.

Do you recognize Sarah? Sarah is a Six.

The Basic Premise

Sixes are the *worrywarts* of the Enneagram. Of all the types, Fours and Sixes anguish the most. Fours anguish emotionally; Sixes are caught on a mental treadmill. They question their own abilities. They fret about what others are up to. They worry that they are going to be screwed—by their bosses or their employees or the competition.

Sixes are the goalies of the Enneagram, hyperalert defensive specialists who are as afraid of being scored on by their own team as by the opposition. They keep their guard up against real or imagined threats. They look behind appearances for what's really up. Precisely opposite to Threes, who believe that what you see is what you get, Sixes know that hidden motives and unspoken agendas drive what people say and do. Even without necessarily knowing what they are defending against, they take every precaution. It can't hurt.

For Sixes, worrying is more than a safety net; it is a familiar touchstone, a homing device. Indeed, for the Six the absence of worry is disconcerting. Many years ago, my partner Joan began to teach a relaxation technique at a retreat we were leading for the senior managers of a consumer products company. She mentioned that they could use the technique before important presentations. The CEO said, "I don't think this relaxation stuff is all good. Sometimes before an important meeting, I feel at ease. I know I'm ready. I know I know my stuff. That's when I worry most. When I don't worry, I worry."

But like noble knights on a crusade, Sixes fight the good fight. Sixes are *loyal* to their friends and *dutiful* about their responsibilities. They are especially concerned about their leader: is he abusive, unfair, self-interested, or incompetent? Will he take care of us? Sixes either completely trust that he will or are tormented with fear that they will be done in.

Sixes may not seem worried on the surface or even feel anxious to themselves. Such Sixes are easygoing and warmly placating in an effort to reassure and *disarm* the people they think may be dangerous (the authorities, the customers, the employees, the competition). Other Sixes are tightly wound; they overprepare for disaster or remote contingencies like a tough-minded survivalist. But, however they appear, all Sixes are *anxious*; whatever their temperament, the nature of Six is to imagine the worst.

In fact, fear or doubt or worry is the preoccupation of the Six's life, and Sixes tend to deal with it in one of two ways: flight or fight. *Phobic* Sixes flee possible dangers. They keep a low profile by seeming meek, apologetic, guarded, conciliatory, nonpartisan, nonthreatening, or ingratiatingly funny. Frequently the humor is self-deprecating (disarming), but it can be mordant or mean. Sixes make jokes because they are afraid.

Fighting Sixes, by contrast, don't wait for the unknown dangers. Chin thrust up and out (hit me if you dare!), daredevil Sixes seek out their fears in order to confront them directly. The ranks of gangsters, police officers, the military, the militias, and bungie jumpers are heavily populated with these counterphobic Sixes. Like Mary Matalin, a counterphobe Republican who married James Carville, a prominent Democratic campaign tactician, counterphobic Sixes boldly sleep with the enemy. Many Sixes have elements of both types.

Sixes have a sense that life is hard, that they have to struggle for what they get; they feel like they are graduates of the school of hard knocks. There is frequently a charge with those for whom things seemed to come much easier, the way that Richard Nixon, a Six, admired, envied, and resented Jack Kennedy, a Seven.

Six's compelling, hard-won, signature virtue is *courage*. With potential conspirators and land mines everywhere, Sixes have to be courageous just to get through the day. Unlike low-side Eights, who are often just mindless bullies, Sixes *do* feel afraid.

Yet even though Sixes know they are in jeopardy, they go on anyway. They develop a tenacity and fortitude that is courageous and life affirming. The capacity of even a deeply distressed Six like Richard Nixon, who was roundly vilified in several political incarnations, to repeatedly come back for more against all odds is startling. As Woody Allen put it, "Ninety percent of success is just showing up." And the inclination to keep showing up is pure Six resiliency. Sixes are *survivors*.

Psychology

Invariably, Sixes experienced a crisis of faith in authority when they were young. Sometimes authority was overbearing; sometimes it was lacking. The young Six may have idolized an important authority and was then betrayed. Perhaps an incompetent or unreliable parent did not keep important promises. Not uncommonly, Sixes had an alcoholic parent; the young Six couldn't count on that parent from one day to the next. Nixon's close associate Bryce Harlow said that "as a young person [Nixon] was hurt deeply by somebody he trusted. . . . He never got over it and he never trusted anybody again."[1]

Sometimes, for political or social or other reasons, the family needed to keep a low profile for fear of being ostracized. Sometimes there was a *big secret* that the child needed to keep but wasn't sure she could. One Six remembered that her father went bankrupt, and when her family moved to another town, she was instructed to say that he had sold his business for a profit. Not letting the secret out was always on her mind. Another Six, whose father worked for the CIA, said that his father would suddenly be gone for long periods of time without explanation and that he knew not to ask for one.

These violations of trust, family secrets, intrigue, and collusions were emotionally dizzying. The ball seemed hidden. The Six became frightened. The Six realized he had to depend on himself, but in the presence of such strong emotions and preoccupations, the young Six couldn't think clearly. The result is an adult life focused around an effort to be superhumanly clearheaded—to pay intense attention—coupled with both tremendous doubt about his own perceptions (which as a child didn't pan out) and immense suspicion about others, especially authorities.

As an adult, a Six worries about the people with whom he has to deal and rely upon. Will he be betrayed again? Can he trust the boss? Can he trust his colleagues? Can he trust you? How will he know?

Some Sixes resolve (or avoid) the "who can I trust?" question by choosing certitude, by acting faithful and devoted to a person, a group, or a set of principles; this is what some cult members do or some police officers or some psychoanalysts. These are the people philosopher and longshoreman Eric Hoffer called "True Believers" in the boss, the work team, the company, the product. Other Sixes bypass the same questioning by doubting everyone so as not to be taken in. These are the "Devil's Advocates," suspicious and antagonistic. "Don't trust anyone over thirty," said Abbie Hoffman. Either stance gives the Six a sense of respite from persistent questioning and worry.

Sixes *want* to believe—in themselves, in others, in what they see. Their problem is they are constantly looking for proof that it's safe to do so. But until Sixes find a reliable authority—that would be themselves—they must be wary and not trust anybody, and certainly not you.

The Good News

Sixes have the considerable advantages of the power of negative thinking. Looking for what can go wrong and who can do it to them keeps them alert and present.

Debra is a Six real estate developer and commercial landlady. "Naturally, I am concerned about all the things that can go wrong," she says. "So my deal memos are very extensive, covering every premise that I can. Invariably people say to me, as a national tenant did today, 'We've never had quite this extensive a deal memo before.' My lawyer tries to rein me in. He says, 'You just *can't* pre-pare for every possible contingency.' But I do great deals *because* I worry. When a situation actually comes up, I know exactly how it's going to be dealt with."

Sixes take events seriously; they are concerned about properly understand-ing what's really happening and letting their colleagues know. "I feel I've done my best at a board meeting," says Ryan, a Six who is the executive director of a foundation, "when I clearly communicate my views about the problems we face in a rational, calm way, and I can bring people around to my way of thinking."

Concerned with details and particulars, the best Sixes are focused, reli-able, and responsible. Their tendency to think everything through can keep Sixes clearheaded and logical. Thoughtfulness is just the ticket for complex decisions that require lots of information, opinions, and input. As natural skeptics, insightful Sixes can offer wonderfully constructive assessments and imaginative perspectives.

The best Sixes have faith in their own experience and powers. The low side of Six is mere faithfulness—mindlessly following a leader or mindlessly opposing one.

Problem Solvers

For most Sixes, vigilance, procrastination, and compulsive worrying have proved more than functional. To see these traits as defects or personality disor-ders is to miss the point.

Sixes want to deal with the problems. Harvey Mackay, author of *How to Swim with the Sharks Without Being Eaten Alive* (the ultimate Six title), ad-vises, "You'll always get the good news; it's how quickly you get the bad news that counts. . . . A capable manager gets the good news before anyone else. An outstanding manager gets the bad news first." Says Andrew Grove, CEO of Intel, "It's very important to protect the conveyors of bad news."

Sixes have the best DEW (distant early warning) systems on the Ennea-gram. Ask what they think the potential problems will be, and they will be quick to tell you. When a prominent religious and political leader began a European tour, the organizers asked a British public relations executive, a Six, to help plan the trip. He ultimately declined, saying too much could go wrong. But he rattled off nearly thirty items that would need to be attended to. The organizers, recognizing the gift that had just been handed to them, used his catalogue of potential disasters as a checklist to plan everything.

When Sixes focus on the problems, they want to know that you are equally alert and concerned. Sixes don't necessarily panic when they hear bad news; indeed, it usually focuses them. Dave, the regional manager of a chain of retail outlets, remembered a regional manager he reported to when he was a store manager. Generally the store managers liked to emphasize their successes and minimize their difficulties, but Dave was different. "I knew the regional manager already knew pretty well what was working. He was most interested in the difficulties we were having," Dave recalled. "Most people were intimidated by his snooping around and his interrogations, but I was very forthcoming with our problems. We went back and forth with them. That was his way of teaching me the business.

"Once, I made a purchase that was far too optimistic. Of course, I reported the problem and we discussed what had happened. Normally I'd be penalized for that, but he just distributed the excess to some of the other stores without a hassle. Some of the other managers were surprised; he usually gave them a much harder time.

"Looking back," said Dave, "I think the regional manager wanted to feel confident that we were willing to name the problems and deal with them. I think he realized he could trust me to be on the team. When he retired he made sure that the powers that be knew I could do his job the way he did—he was incredibly loyal that way—and I was promoted over several others." Dave's regional manager, of course, was a Six.

Loyal Team Players

Persuaded that the world is us-against-them, Sixes really value loyalty and teamwork. A Six boss wants to know which of her employees is on her team and whom she can rely on. "I expect everything but loyalty," said Brenda, an advertising executive. "I demand loyalty."

Throwing in your lot with a Six customer can help clinch the deal. "When I was interviewing investment houses to handle our portfolio," the city manager of a midsized Southern city, a Six, told my Enneagram workshop, "I asked what would happen to their electronic records if there was a civil catastrophe. They thought I was kidding. I wasn't. I expected a detailed plan. But what convinced me to put our money with the New York brokerage we finally chose was that they required their professional staff to keep all their personal investments with their firm. At least we're all in the same boat. I like that."

If you prove you are trustworthy over time, brick by brick, steadfast Sixes will go the distance with you on projects and hang tough against naysayers and outsiders. This is your central job if your boss or someone on your work team is a Six, and it is no mean task.

Good Detectives

Since they are so interested in what's happening below the surface, Sixes are gifted people watchers and natural psychologists always on the lookout for revealing behavior. Frequently their colleagues do not know this; Sixes collect considerable data on co-workers completely on the sly.

In order to be inconspicuous, a Six's inquiries are indirect, like those of a detective on a case. He watches for clues; hesitations in speech and failures to meet small commitments are very meaningful to him.

My friend Thomas, a popular regular on my Six panels, is a martial arts instructor. In class he wears sixty pounds of body armor and teaches people to attack him—a good Six job. "I watch people's body cues very, very carefully," says Thomas. "I watch their facial gestures, I watch their hands. If they have them behind their backs, I notice whether or not their hands are relaxed. I look at their feet to see if they lean forward or backward. I'm looking for *information leaks.* The words may say one thing, but I watch to see whether the body agrees with what the words say." *All Sixes are checking for congruence between what is said and what is meant.*

Harvey Mackay feels that his success is based on gathering intelligence on customers. "At Mackay Envelope Corporation, you wouldn't believe how much we know about our customers. The IRS wouldn't believe how much we know about our customers. All our salespeople fill out a sixty-six-question profile of each one of their customers. We're not talking about the customer's taste in envelopes, either. We want to know, based on observation and routine conversation, what our customer is like as a human being—what he feels strongly about, what he's most proud of having achieved, and what the status symbols are in his office."

Unflappable in a Crisis

While they are always fearful of what might happen, Sixes actually feel relieved and confident when events justify their worry.

Larry, a Six, is a buyer for a large carpet store and warehouse one block from the Mississippi River in Davenport, Iowa. With the farm economy in the doldrums, the business was in trouble, and Larry stewed nonstop about losing his job. But after freak summer floods devastated the store and ruined much of the inventory, Larry was a different person. Cool and collected, even upbeat, he calmly helped the owner set up shop as best he could, advertised a flood sale across four states, and helped the store's neighbors with a grace that amazed everyone. He seemed to make an enjoyable experience of the crisis. "Well," he said at the time, "what else is there for me to do?"

Sixes are in heaven when the worst is out in the open and there are no hidden perils to worry about (until they figure out what to worry about next).

The Bad News

Sixes can be as inflexible as righteous, moralistic Ones, but unlike Ones, who are more than happy to tell you what's wrong with you, Sixes have a bunker mentality. They feel safer harboring a secret judgment or a grudge. (They may think you are doing the same thing.) For Sixes, as with Fives, secret knowledge is power; they're much more comfortable when you don't know what they're thinking.

Pessimistic

Don't bring me anything but trouble. Good news weakens me.
—Charles Kettering

Sixes catastrophize. "I have learned that my initial reaction to most problems that are brought to me is to make them worse than they are," said Tom, an automobile executive. "Now I try to reserve even my private judgment until I get all the facts."

Even written contracts are chancy. What's a Six to do?

A client of mine, a Midwest manufacturer, told me that he urged his risk manager to find a way to "double insure" some potential factory exposures to liability. "I seriously want two insurance policies," he said. "I don't want to collect a double recovery. I know that's illegal. I just want to make damn sure that our insurance company fulfills its obligations." This Six wanted insurance for his insurance.

Sixes are people who wear both a belt and suspenders. They know that every silver lining has a cloud. I showed my father, a Six, my new computer with all its bells and whistles, its extraordinary graphics. We surfed the Internet, his first time. We downloaded some articles. We left e-mail for a friend of his. I could tell he was impressed. I asked, "What do you think, Pop?" After a minute he asked, "Who do you call when this thing breaks down?"

For Sixes, their compulsion to anticipate the worst often blocks spontaneity and creativity, dampening initiatives to innovate, commit resources, or take risks. An electronic publisher, a Three, reported on a former partner, a Six: "Joe and I were putting together a computer database for the trade. He talked to a jillion industry experts. He became aware of a jillian pitfalls. They said it was superfluous; they were innundated with material already. Joe got cold feet and begged off. I trusted my instincts and went ahead. The database caught on immediately. I realized that my Six partner was trying to figure out, not why people would buy the database, but why they wouldn't!"

Preoccupied with Authority

Authority looms large, sometimes too large, for Sixes. They feel preoccupied by any authority others may have over them; suspicious of it, they tend to magnify it and responding with defiance or submission or ingratiation.

Unsure what authority they *really* have themselves, and unwilling to exercise it for fear of being a target, they tend to minimize their own power. (Compare with Eights, who inflate their own power and invalidate that of others.)

Their difficulties with authority make Sixes exquisitely sensitive to the power structure in which they operate, to the jockeying for position, and to the ways the company may be unfair or arbitrary. When the director of a Los Angeles city agency asked Judy, a new Six manager, to let him know when she went out to lunch so that he could make sure someone covered her phones, she refused, indignantly confiding to me that his request was a poorly concealed invasion of her autonomy and authority, a power play. She soon began to persuade the staff, complacent until then, that the director was violating regulations by having people work overtime and keeping lunch hours too short. Three months later—to the director's great relief—she quit in a huff.

Finger Pointers

Sixes and Ones are the biggest finger pointers on the Enneagram. But unlike Ones, who are critical of others but really blame themselves, Sixes ascribe their own feelings and failings to you. "You seem to have something on your mind. What aren't you saying? What are you hiding?" projects the Six. The more worried they feel within, the more they search for the source without, casting blame and accusations on others.

This projection process is actually an odd way of staying connected, a mental version of "reverse empathy." By placing thoughts and intentions in other people's heads, the Six can understand—or imagine she understands—their experience.

Working with a Six

Influencing a Six

Without question, the best way to get a Six to see things your way is to lay out clearly and systematically the existing and potential problems and dangers in your proposal and how you mean to respond to them. This gives a Six the sense that you have your priorities straight: that you are concerned, as much as he, that everyone may end up in the tank.

To a Six, not presenting the negatives makes you look as if you haven't done your homework. "There is an invidious trend among my managers to gloss over the performance appraisals of their staff," says Fred, a senior U.S. government manager, a Six. "This cover-up is going to stop. If the performance appraisal doesn't include a balanced report, emphasizing where the difficulties are—and I mean something legitimate, not that they 'work too hard'—I'll send it back."

Be prepared to expose your own self-interest. Sixes don't find selflessness completely credible (which can make life difficult for people-pleasing Twos). Says Doug, an executive recruiter and a Six, "I absolutely will not recommend people for a position who cannot tell me what's in it for them. This nonsense that 'Oh, I want to be here because I'm good with people' won't cut it. I like 'This work pushes my skills to the limit,' or better yet, 'Bossing people around agrees with me.' But 'people who are good with people' make me leery."

How a Six Makes Decisions

Unlike for Nines, for most Sixes decision making is not a problem. They have facile minds and make decisions quickly. The problem is that having made a decision, they immediately question it and then begin to stew.

To Sixes, such herky-jerky vacillating seems like the only prudent way to decide anything. But if you don't share their inner sense of uncertainty (you won't unless you're a Six), the care they take in checking and rechecking is bound to seem excessive.

Sixes are most at home in their heads, as we have seen. They decide by *analysis*. In contrast, sure-footed Threes instantly decide by *comparison:* "Of the alternatives we have, which is better?" Unhurried Nines decide by *historical analogy*. They ruminate through past events, customs, and traditions, looking for a match to the current situation. Sixes like to deconstruct a problem into its component parts and sort things out logically. While nobody knows the component parts better, Sixes very typically overfocus on apparently portentious details and trivia, neglecting the forest for the trees.

Don't be in a hurry if you need a decision out of a Six. Instead, encourage her to "think about it." Sixes love to do that! And, besides, they'll do it anyway. Six's natural tendency is to say no to a new idea. Don't force it. As people with authority issues, they resist pressure. (This is good advice for dealing with Six's paranoid triad mates, Five and Seven, too.) Share your reasoning, facts, and arguments with your Six colleague. Then give her the space to think about it on her own.

Since Sixes assume that people's intentions are obscured (as Sixes have obscured their own), whatever is said or done at a meeting is understood at some level as tactical jockeying. The ball is hidden. The Six, on the alert to begin with, is hypervigilant now that he is obliged to keep a close watch on a roomful of people. Six wants to know everyone else's position before taking a position himself, which of course makes spontaneous, on-the-spot decision making very difficult.

The Six Leadership Style

Uneasy lies the head that wears a crown.

—*Shakespeare*, Henry IV

Sixes are masters at getting all the wagons in a circle to defend against a common enemy. In a such a situation they can be real leaders. George Bush, a Six, was careful to line up broad-based domestic and international support before beginning military operations against Iraq. During the Gulf War, Bush expertly held together this tenuous and diverse coalition against the Eight Saddam Hussein, largely through emphasizing the need *to act in concert against* Hussein; rallying under the leadership banner of George Bush was not central. The coalescing focus was the enemy. (Compare with a One leader like Margaret Thatcher, who emphasized "right and wrong" to justify the Falklands war; compare with a Three like George Washington, whose banner everyone *could* rally around.)

Sixes tend to be parriers of what's in front of them. They *manage*. But they may struggle to lead by inspiration. Once the Gulf War was over, Bush was unable to articulate a leader's proactive, positive vision. Bush always felt he was unduly saddled by the press with what he called "the vision thing," a criticism he never understood.

Given their issues with their own authority, many Sixes tend to be uncomfortable in the public role of boss. As a result, a Six in authority may act like a martinet who barks orders and brooks no dissent in the hope that his ever-present sense of doubt will disappear. Or he may be a coconspirator who colludes with his employees against a bigger boss or outsiders, abdicating his role as boss and avoiding exercising authority.

Six bosses want to avoid blame. They may diffuse attack by being "nice." They may blame any unpleasantness on pressure from colleagues, clients, the press, their own boss, or company procedures. Says a Six attorney who is the managing partner of a medium-sized law firm, "I want company guidelines to be so clear, so explicit, that when I have to do something negative—reprimand someone, fire someone—I'm virtually forced to do it. Without rules, you get people mad. Then anything can happen."

In her continuing effort to avoid blame, a Six boss may issue verbal but not written orders, make commitments that are fuzzy and negotiable, and even praise employees verbally while protecting herself with more stringently written performance appraisals.

At the moment when a Six boss decides that he is willing be in the market and take the hit—the responsibility and the blame—he becomes among the most thoughtful and determined leaders on the Enneagram. *No one has pondered more the nature and issues of authority or worried more about abuses of those in power than has the Six.* No one strives more than the best Sixes to be loyal and considerate to colleagues and employees. My friend Chris, the director of a large community services agency, is very clear about the reasons for his personnel actions; his hirings and firings are well reasoned but a long time coming. The best Sixes are by temperament mindful philosophers and practitioners of leadership.

The Six Work Style

Six employees work best when they understand the rules, their responsibilities, their role, and especially where they stand with you. Help them feel safe, be sensitive to unspoken concerns, and you'll find they work much more creatively and effectively.

But Sixes won't necessarily be grateful for your efforts on their behalf. Gratitude does not flow easily for many Sixes. Their attention goes more to the ways they may be being taken advantage of, and they will look to indicators like project assignments or office location and perquisites. While Threes see their prerogatives as evidence of their hard work, Sixes see them as clues to what's *really* happening and where they *really* stand.

If mobilizing to quick action is the task, Sixes can focus quickly if they understand the urgency. Many Sixes work well when there is no time to worry but time only to act in concert with colleagues in the same boat.

Sixes naturally find enemies to align against (these may be the company's competitors as easily as a colleague) as well as allies to team up with.

The Six Learning Style

Sixes learn best when they can trust the teacher and the information. If you're teaching a Six, she will want to know who you are and where you have come from. What is your authority to teach? Is it your experience? Your abilities? Your position? How do you know what you know? Who sent you? Will you be judging her?

Sixes are excited by the difference between surface appearances and the hidden truth. You can snare their attention by promising to tell them the straight dope, "how things really work," the unconventional or hidden wisdom.

Sixes like an overview of any new task and then like to closely examine the component parts. Spend time on the details, not just the overview. *What kinds of problems should they expect?* How might they be solved? Sixes value most how your teaching will help them be "more prepared for whatever's down the pike."

The Six Organization

The Central Intelligence Agency is the Six organization *par excellence*, always on the lookout for hidden intentions and dangerous activities. Everyone at the CIA—whatever their personal fixation—is immersed in this Six culture. Periodic lie detector tests, background checks for clearances, and the way classified and sensitive materials are handled all nurture caution and paranoia. At the agency, offices are called vaults because of the combination locks on every door, and offices are searched every day for security violations (which generate demerits). Visitors must be escorted everywhere, even for the most personal of functions.

Authority issues are legion at the CIA. Uncovering intrigue by asking "Who's really in charge here?" and "Who's really on our side?" is always a favorite activity, whether the authorities are abroad or within the agency itself.

Six organizations generally are distinguished by lots of intelligence gathering—by feedback forms and surveys and focus groups of customers. The CIA generates enormous amounts of data on its people. CIA managers regularly and frequently appraise their employees' performance in detail. But these managers are also graded by those who work for them and by their bosses (more frequently that anywhere else I have consulted). Six organizations are obsessed with control through finding out things.

At the CIA, internal authority is further suspect for being "political." The charge is that senior managers (or the policy makers who are their clients), grown cynical or cautious, reek of ulterior "political" motives—that they shape the material to fit preconceived notions—and will corrupt the "truthful" analysis. For example, the CIA was charged with missing the impending collapse of the Soviet Union by misconstruing that country's level of economic and military strength and political coherence so as to meet the preconceived political notions of the Reagan administration. Such is the Six way of thinking: an idea is hatched and evidence is sought, relentlessly, to back it up.

Getting the Best from a Six

When cautious, nearsighted Sixes move to High Performance Point Nine, they take their blinders off and see the big picture: where they fit in and how they can trust that others will do their part. At Stress Point Three, Sixes feel pressure to produce work without having enough time to think and review and prepare appropriate cautions. Instead of driving with one foot on the brake, they push the accelerator to the floor.

Seven is Six's Ally Point. Sevens and Sixes are both possibility thinkers; Sevens are wedded to the upside and Sixes to the downside possibilities. Sixes are energized and transformed when they include the positive options. Five is Six's Shadow Point. Sixes are grounded by an objective, nonpartisan, detached look and by getting all the information they need, the perspective of Five.

Bonnie's Story

Bonnie, a high-powered executive for a major studio, was having a problem with her new boss.

Bonnie knew the Enneagram and knew that she was a Seven: an enthusiastic high flyer, with lots of ideas, lots of projects, and boundless energy. She traveled to Europe and Asia frequently, first class of course, and sealed important deals with a handshake. A rising star, widely admired as brilliant and well connected in Hollywood, she seemed to know everybody. Virtually singlehandedly she created—out of bravado and air—the important, profitable division she now controlled.

Then her studio was purchased by a large nonentertainment company. Although senior management was still in place, the studio's culture was undergoing a sea change. As part of a tight overseeing process, a member of the new management team was assigned to evaluate each of the studio's senior executives, "participating" in that executive's decision making and planning.

Mori, head of the management review team, assigned himself to Bonnie. When she came to me, the relationship was not going well. What seemed like an intractable personality conflict had Bonnie worried about her job.

"I go to these meetings with Mori with as much enthusiasm and goodwill as I can," Bonnie reported. "I am not without a certain charm. I give him a full plate of opportunities, and I explain that I'm ready to move very quickly. I convey my enthusiasm, but he just sits there stone-faced. The more excited I get, the cooler he gets."

Of course, Mori had legitimate reasons to move prudently with his company's investment. They were in an unconventional business, with which they were unfamiliar, and their new employees did not welcome them with open arms.

But Mori worried over even the slightest decision, particularly how he would explain it to his boss. This Bonnie found incomprehensible. Surely the new management should be mainly concerned with results and not worry too much about how she got them. Also frustrating to her were the long meetings Mori held to review the deals that were not going well and to try to limit the studio's exposure. He took great pride in his own rational approach, continually emphasizing the need to do things with prudence and foresight. For Bonnie, these encounters were excruciating; she felt imprisoned. "My real job is to meet with people and create opportunities," she said.

The predicament became clear: Bonnie's scattershot, seat-of-the-pants approach was impossible for prudent Mori, the quintessential Six, to have faith in.

Bonnie and I noted Mori's caution and ambivalence and especially his inclination not to trust what the staff told him. When the staff screwed up, he took it as an intentional effort to embarrass him personally. When dealing with Bonnie, he seemed to have no feel for the transient, high-energy, high-risk, high-gain flux that was the nature of deal making in Hollywood. Bonnie could not believe he did not trust her in an area where she had perhaps the best track record in the entire industry.

"You'll have to land the Seven spacecraft," I said. "If you want to communicate with a Six who has put himself on the line, you have to show him how you're going to protect him and the company. Sixes are deliberative. You need to walk him through each potential deal and explain where you are, not merely where you'd like to be, and where you're committed and where you're not. He needs a predictable course of action. And also a predictable, reliable, sober person."

Over time Bonnie learned that the enthusiasm for new projects and the pleasure in the game that were natural for her were extremely hard won for Mori. With each new venture or possibility, he had to resist the tendency to be anxious and immobilized. Bonnie learned something about herself too: that while *she* knew most of her projects wouldn't pan out, other people took her extraordinary enthusiasm at face value and misjudged what was happening. Without decreasing her excitement, she would say to Mori, "I'm just exploring the possibilities of this one." "Fine," Mori would say. "Let me know if it gets serious."

Over time, Bonnie learned to deemphasize her impulsive decision-making style when explaining her choices to Mori. She learned to take the time to parse out the downside exposure with him, even when to her the choice to go ahead was clear.

Stress Point: Three

Under stress, Sixes go into overdrive at Three. When Mori was stressed, he became an overcontrolling, frenzied workaholic who maniacally focused on production. He uncharacteristically pushed for closure on deals so that he would have substantive projects to report. His main goal was to create a balance sheet that showed profit. He pushed everyone to work harder, and after Bonnie had put in a seventy-five-hour week, he urged her to work even harder.

Fortunately, Bonnie was beginning to understand her Six boss. She reminded Mori of the hours she had put in. She noted their projects were precisely on schedule and reassured him that the reports he was awaiting would be done on time. When Sixes are in Three, the trick is to align with their goals (Three) rather than their fears (Six). Reality feedback, served up without frustration or agitation, is very helpful and effective for a Six.

"Actually, I don't mind him that much at Three," said Bonnie. "At least he's focused on movement and activity."

High Performance Point: Nine

As Bonnie discovered, Sixes normally hold tightly to their position and their narrow focus. What the Six fears most yet needs most is "giving in," trusting that others can and will do their jobs. Such trust in the process is the specialty of their High Performance Point Nine.

At his best, Mori built consensus by involving colleagues from other departments in major decisions, listening to their comments and criticism without acting defensive, thus gluing together the work team, a special gift of

Nines. Bonnie could always tell when Mori was in his high performance mode, because people just seemed to gather in the conference room next to his office, which never much happened otherwise. (Compare this with Bonnie, a normally chatty and social Seven, who, at her High Performance Point Five wants to "be alone.") Once, when a promising deal fell through, Mori said with a warm smile, to her shock, "Well, Bonnie, at least we learned a lot on this one." Nines see the big picture and trust the course of events.

Wings

Shadow Point: Five

Sixes are rarely neutral; they inhabit a world of enemies and allies. For that reason they are stabilized and grounded by their Five wing. Fives are neutral observers who are not emotionally engaged like Sixes. Sixes want to know all about the players, particularly the (hidden) alliances, and the real scoop on the issues. Data of all kinds is ground for a Six. (This is not centrally true for a Two or a Nine, for example.) Sixes ground as they acknowledge the part of themselves that is the disengaged observer.

Bonnie learned to serve Mori's Shadow wing with the best possible market, industry, and product information. He loved it. So armed, he could stand above the fray and act confidently on his own authority, an evolved Six position.

Ally Point: Seven

Sixes are energized and invigorated by their Seven wing. Seven is the place of upbeat spontaneity, fun, endless possibilities, and networking of ideas and people. Mori was truly fascinated by the film business: the fast pace, the kaleidoscope of opportunity, the deal makers, the screenings, the fun, and the glitz.

A Six appreciates projects that offer opportunities for imaginative or interdisciplinary expansion while maintaining the Six requisites for safety, control, and low downside exposure. The Six chef who headed a culinary school in Washington, D.C., planned for several years to establish a catering service using senior students. After much stewing, he started the catering business, which became an immediate success. In his role as head caterer, the Six chef was able to attend embassy and political affairs, a Seven milieu. Of course, he did it as a Six, worrying about all the catering details, and yet he was energized by the scene, the socializing, the contact, and the publicity. To those who did not know him, he seemed like a Seven.

Sixes with a strong access to their Ally Seven learn optimism. They are more extroverted, sociable, and charismatic. They may be playful, with a good sense of humor and an epicure's enjoyment of worldly things. They confidently rely on their skills and perseverance to handle problems.

Cardinal Rules

If You Work with a Six

- Keep your word. Nothing helps a relationship with a Six more than the sense that you mean what you say, that you have integrity, and that you can be trusted. Be cautious about what you commit to, and then meticulously comply with all aspects of the commitment. Sixes are looking most of all for *congruence* between what you say and what you do.
- Don't assume you can gain the Six's trust immediately. Almost always trust is established over time. The Six is watching to see if you keep your agreements, even the small ones.
- Don't engage in a win-lose argument with a Six about something over which his mind is made up. You can't win. He doesn't want to be confused with the inconsistent facts. Better to expand the discussion to include alternate ideas (Ally Point Seven) and additional people (High Performance Point Nine).
- Don't exaggerate. Don't overplay or underplay your project or your opponent's position. Just tell the story straight. Sixes have a terrific fear of being conned in any way.
- Make your allegiances clear. In the Six unconscious, the world is clearly split into good (us) and bad (them). Once the Six accepts you as part of the team, she will see your battles as her own. If she suspects disloyalty, she can be brutal.
- Disclose your self-interest. Sixes like to know what's in it for you. It clears their head. But never count on a Six to disclose her own private motives; that would be foolhardy.
- Salt the positives with negatives. Unchecked enthusiasm is scary for Sixes, no matter whom or what it is about. This especially includes full frontal compliments. A Six will wonder why you're trying to butter him up.
- Don't pooh-pooh a Six's fears or offer reassurance. Never say to a Six, "Don't worry about that!" Sixes particularly mistrust anyone who suggests their suspicions are unwarranted or who tries to provide comfort. They will question your sincerity or your good sense. Much better to say to a worrywart Six employee, for example, "You're right. That's a legitimate concern. What do you think we should do about that?"
- Don't order a Six around. The worst thing to say to a Six is, "Because I'm the boss, that's why." If you want a Six to do something, share your

thought processes and give reasons. A good thing to say to a Six is, "I trust you with . . . " And then say why.

- Restate reality. If you work with a Six, be prepared to function as her memory and reality checker during her inevitable doubt attacks. Whatever the issue, calmly remind her how you got there, restating the agreements on the table, the nature of the risks, the motives of the principals.

- You can widen the Six field of vision without negating his assumptions: "Yes, those are certainly legitimate concerns. Just to be safe, shouldn't we also consider that the deal might go through?" And, "Yes, that is possibly what he meant. But, you know, in his business, that answer also can mean he's ready to put his money down."

- Lay out a clear plan, with fall-back positions. Sixes don't like surprises. Sixes want security and predictability. They want backup data and specifications.

- Even if a Six has a problem with you, understand that the Six is at odds with herself. Can she trust herself or you? How can she survive in a dangerous or disappointing universe? This is her internal battle. Her tortures are self-inflicted. The problem becomes yours when the Six tries to blame you for her bad feelings about herself. When things get really bad, you'll find yourself actually feeling the way Sixes feel: self-doubting, beleaguered, misunderstood, and angry. Don't buy into this.

- When the Six's considerations are out on the table, this is a good time for action. Acknowledge that the mistakes you are being blamed for are mistakes, without taking blame for what is not your fault. "Yes, boss, that looks terrible. I agree." Then you can move to, "Here's what we can do to fix it."

- Be straightforward about admitting when you're in trouble. Sixes understand trouble; that's where they live. Most healthy Sixes will want to help, especially if the trouble is even partly due to the fact that you're in a one-down position vis-à-vis some outsider or authority.

If You Are a Six

- *If you meet the Buddha on the road, kill him.* Some Sixes avoid the anguish of constant doubting by assuming their leader has all the answers and they have none. Sixes have to find their own inner authority.

- Practice faith. When Sixes look for ways to trust (rather than not trust) others, they find them. *The "process of trusting" makes the most important changes in a Six, not the reality of whether the world is trustworthy.*

- Don't be afraid to play devil's advocate. It's your strong suit. Use your skills at cutting through pretense and exposing what won't work. Show where the problems and pitfalls are. But do it consciously, with the intention of helping, not compulsively or fearfully.
- Learn to give compliments. Sixes have problems with gratitude. Stuck Sixes think that if they give a compliment they will be one down.
- Define your positive goals; don't get lost in just defending against what can go wrong.
- Use *and* rather than *but*, as in, "I see your idea, *and* have you also considered this possibility?" This brings your Seven Ally Point *and* Nine High Performance Point into play.
- To avoid laying blame so frequently, focus on the problem rather than on who may be at fault.
- Remember, as Samuel Johnson said, "Nothing will ever be attempted if all possible objections must first be overcome."

1. Cited in "Richard M. Nixon" by Tom Wicker in *Character Above All*, Robert A. Wilson, ed. (New York: Simon & Schuster, 1995), 137.

SEVEN

The Visionary

AKA	The Imagineer, the Planner, the Epicure, the Optimist
Worldview	"To explore strange new worlds . . . to boldly go where no one has gone before." The world is full of exciting possibilities, concepts, and experiences. My mission is to explore them.
High Side	Innovative, optimistic, enthusiastic, funny, witty, inspirational, big-picture planners
Low Side	Irresponsible, shallow, intellectually promiscuous; dilettantes with a short attention span and poor follow-through
Leadership Style	Cheerleaders for *ideas*; management by juggling, plate spinning, walking around, storytelling, and net-working
Credo	Let's take a flyer.
Appeal to	Fun, impact, adventure, novelty, idealism
Don't Appeal to	Duty, stability, the way we do things around here, the norms of the industry, prudence
Talk/Communication Style	Brainstorming, tripping on ideas, hypothesizing, tall stories
Makes You Feel	Entertained, dazzled, and inspired; and—sometimes—earthbound, slow, unimaginative, exhausted
Appearance	Bright colors, bright eyes, hard-wired smile
Good Work Setting	Creative, flexible, informal, interactive, like to be "consultants": independent members of a team without line responsibility

Difficult Work Setting	Machine bureaucracies, routines, tight, formal performance evaluations
Books	*Thriving on Chaos* by Tom Peters *Body and Soul* by Anita Roddick *The Republic of Tea* by Mel Ziegler, Patricia Ziegler, and Bill Rosenzweig
Sayings	"I gotta crow." —Peter Pan "Everything is for the best in this best of all possible worlds." —Dr. Pangloss in Voltaire's *Candide* "Deep down inside me I'm four years old, and I wake up and I think, 'Out there, there's a cookie.' Every morning I'm going, you know, either it can be baked or it's already been bought. . . . And so that means when you open up the cupboard and the cookie isn't there, I don't say, 'Gee, there's no cookie.' I say, 'I wonder where it is!'" —Newton Leroy Gingrich "Promise Yourself—To be so strong that nothing can disturb your peace of mind. —To talk health, happiness and prosperity to every person you meet. —To make all your friends feel that there is something in them. —To look at the sunny side of everything and make your optimism come true. —To think only of the best, to work only for the best and expect only the best. —To be just as enthusiastic about the success of others as you are about your own. —To forget the mistakes of the past and press on to the greater achievements of the future. —To wear a cheerful countenance at all times and give every living creature you meet a smile. —To give so much time to the improvement of yourself that you have no time to criticize others. —To be too large for worry, too noble for anger, too strong for fear, and too happy to permit the presence of trouble." 　　　—From the Optimist Creed, Optimist International

Of the Seven Persuasion	John F. Kennedy, Richard Feynman, Bill Lear, Anita Roddick (The Body Shop), Tom Peters, Peter Pan, Cosmo Kramer (*Seinfeld*), Ram Dass, Richard Branson (Virgin), Andre Gregory, Regis Philbin, Timothy Leary, Charlie Rose, Goldie Hawn, Zonker Harris, Malcolm Forbes, Larry King, Robin Williams, W. L. Gore (Gore-Tex), Ben and Jerry's, 3M, Brazil
High Performance	5 Self-contained, scrupulous, detail-oriented observer
Stress	1 Autocratic, brittle, rigid, demanding
Ally	8 *Energized* by committed exercise of power
Shadow	6 *Grounded* by fidelity, by dealing honestly with fears
Virtue	Sobriety
Vice	Gluttony (for ideas and experiences)

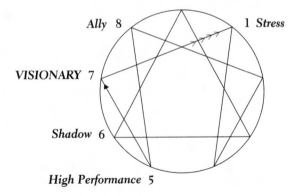

Getting to Know a Seven

Merle's Story

Merle runs a direct marketing company that sells unusual products to consumers through cable television and print advertising. His main home is in Taos, New Mexico, flush up against the Taos Indian Pueblo, and he is a discriminating collector of the pueblo crafts. For a few days every week he commutes to Los Angeles, flying his own plane. He uses all the latest computing and telecommunications technology to run his business from home or, more frequently, while on the road. He has additional homes on Portobello Road in London and on the north shore of Maui and travels to them frequently.

Merle loves the marketing business. He loves going from project to project. He loves the fun in getting behind a new product. Most of all, he loves living by his wits and being successful.

There is a single round table in the center of Merle's office in Los Angeles. Meetings take place all day long, each running into the next, as people arrive with their papers, pitches, and concerns. The atmosphere is social and informal. Various people bring food and drinks, so that the whole operation seems like a continuous, dizzying feast.

Merle is delighted when someone approaches him with an unusual or clever product for a potential campaign. Within minutes he'll decide whether it's for him, based on his intuition. If he says yes—which would mean a substantial commitment for his small company—he quickly has lots of ideas about how to package and market the product.

In such a meeting with the new client and project team he will speculate on a marketing strategy; he may rattle off a list of ancillary products that could be sold together with the product, no matter what its subject—cosmetics, electronics, a touchy-feely pop psychology program. Perhaps there should be audio or video tapes. Perhaps there should be a book.

Merle's deputy is a Three, and she takes down (and shakes down) all his ideas and immediately prioritizes and costs them out. Within days, at most, she will have a contract or a memo out to a client.

The company is run as a completely ad hoc operation. Job descriptions are fuzzy and overlapping. This arrangement generally serves the current project well because all resources and enthusiasm are focused on it; but there is no administrative structure to serve ongoing needs such as human resources. The health insurance program seems to fail every so often, and newly hired staff creates their own jobs within certain limits, adjusting to the company's or Merle's needs. For example, the company administrator's job has varied from being an executive secretary to being an industry heavyweight, depending on who held the position.

In lieu of management training, Merle likes to "get everybody to play together." He'll take the whole company hang gliding, and he has sent his senior executives to the Bondurant race car driving school and the Dodgers' fantasy baseball camp. "Lighten up and fly right," he tells his team.

"The main thing I bring to the party," he says, "is that I share my enthusiasm. I turn people on, and they get to try new things. This is good for the soul. You may think this is some flaky, manipulative, opportunistic sales organization, but you would be wrong. What we do is put customers in touch with their aspirations and then fulfill them."

If a product doesn't work out in the test campaign, Merle will terminate it quickly, regardless of his expectations or the effort the company has put into the project. There is no real attempt to fix anything because so many new projects are lined up awaiting their turn. Sometimes the hopes of those who had invented products or written books were dashed before they even realized what was happening, but Merle's empathy for their concerns is not immobilizing. "I get terribly disappointed, sure," he says. "Until we get started on the next project. There are plenty more possibilities where those came from.

"I generate lots of ideas. I make lots of suggestions. If the people watching say no, and it won't fly, I go on to other things. Why not? Anything else is wasteful."

Do you recognize Merle? Merle is a Seven.

The Basic Premise

Sevens are articulate, witty, and charming connoisseurs of a makeshift, provisional life. They juggle prospects and opportunities in order to *keep their options perpetually open.* Flashy Sevens are upbeat futurists, playful romancers, quirky visionaries, and *masterminds of grand schemes and plans.* "I am a possibility-creating machine," says my colleague Jack, a strategic planning consultant to very large organizations. "I generate more ideas than I could possibly handle." Or, as Suzanne, an artist's agent in Los Angeles, puts it, "I'm a cosmic cheerleader."

Sevens are dream merchants and big-picture grand planners, like Don Quixote or Joseph in the Bible, who interpreted Pharaoh's dreams and planned for the fat and lean future ahead. And Joseph certainly dressed like a Seven, in a coat of many colors.

The entertaining champions of what-could-be, Sevens are the best on the Enneagram at seeing a new angle on something. Stan, a management consultant who is a Seven, says, "What I like to do is go into a company, flush out the conventional wisdom, and then turn it on its head. That gets them out of their rut!"[1]

Sevens send up trial balloons. If one doesn't fly, surely another will! The dizzying books and spellbinding idea-a-minute lectures of management guru Tom Peters are filled with completely genuine, highly infectious enthusiasm for excellence and knock-your-socks-off service. Sometimes the opinions are contradictory, the advice is impractical, and the facts are not quite factual. So what if the "excellent" companies upon which he based his reputation and his famous book, *In Search of Excellence*, seem in retrospect to have feet of clay. No problem! In his subsequent *Thriving on Chaos* he begins, "There are no excellent companies." If you think you've found one, "you just haven't looked hard enough."[2]

Sevens are *multifocal*, doing lots of things at the same time, and *multioptional*, following lots of paths simultaneously. "Going off in several directions at once helps me keep my balance," says Merle. Sevens can be known as dabblers and dilettantes, eternal children who, as they evolve, become renaissance men and women, able to see the true connections among all things and able to inspire us all to see what could be.

Until they reach this point, however, they are dashing and innovative but fairly superficial. Scratching the surface would mean confronting one's inner life and psychic strengths, not an engaging prospect for most Sevens.

To stay on the surface you need to keep moving (like Threes), and Sevens do well in uncertain, fast-paced, information-laden settings where the basic premises change quickly and often. Sevens can be hard to pin down. They like intense, exciting projects with built-in time limits or other limits. With an escape hatch there is always the possibility of moving on.

Naturally, Sevens tend to avoid the nine-to-five workaday grind. ("Why commit to a career? My life is my career!") Typically, they have had unusual nonlinear career paths. They freelance and consult. If they are in a big organization they intra-preneur. They like living by their skills and wits; they like outwitting convention and the ponderous system, and they enjoy flaunting their ability to do so.

Roger, a Seven, is the head of charter marketing for a global airline. He loves flying around the world, holding seminars, meeting clients, then going on to the next city. "I enjoy bringing the business in, but once we have it I don't want to do the grunt work. So I have self-starters working for me."

Sevens may give the impression that they have taken on their day job as a lark on their way to their great destiny. "I'm just visiting this planet," says the Seven. (Fours, who also feel destiny calling, instead wear their workaday job like a lodestone, waiting to be recognized for their True Self.)

Sevens are interested in the alien, the inaccessible, the eccentric. As paranoid as Sixes, they are continually looking for secret meanings. But where the Six looks for and finds conspiracies that are negative, the Seven usually suspects hidden intrigues that are positive. "The world is secretly conspiring to do me good. The universe is on a path of conscious evolution," says Seven. Alas, the Seven's *fixation on the upside* is as limiting as the Six's fixation on the downside.

Sevens are the mental version of feeling-oriented Twos. These are the two Enneagram points most delighted with themselves—Twos for how good a friend and support system they offer, and Sevens for how conceptually clever they are. ("Oh, the cleverness of me!" says Peter Pan.)

Psychology

Sevens almost always report happy childhoods that are revealed as painfully troubled when the surface is scratched. Generally, there came a point in Sevens' childhood—divorce, abandonment, shuffling among relatives, or just being ignored—when they realized the world was scary and painful. In that instant Sevens simply denied that this could be so, turned around, and went back to their play. They've been pretending ever since.

In order to keep up their pretense that everything is fine, Sevens avoid real engagement with the psychological underbelly of life, with longing, loss, and tragedy. Though they have spirit—and are frequently inspirational as well as aspirational—they tend to lack interiority, the sense of the soulful self (where Fours live). Instead, Sevens generate alternatives as a way of avoiding responsibility and commitment.

Sevens are golden children who believe they are specially blessed and largely exempt—because of their cleverness—from the trials and tribulations of everyday life. But just as Eights overvalue their own power and underestimate the strength of others, Sevens overfocus on their own brilliance while undervaluing that of others.

The Good News

Sevens are the big conceptual innovators on the Enneagram (unlike Threes, who do wonders with existing ideas). They like to try new forms, to experiment without being chained to the bottom line. They come up with ingenious or playful proposals and network outside their organization or their field to find parallel, synergistic, similarly enthusiastic thinkers. At their best, Sevens have no trouble seeing the forest for the trees.

"My nickname is Mr. Methods," says Warren, a Seven partner at one of the country's largest management consulting firms. "I have a reputation for being a process maven, for always bringing in new ideas, new ways of doing things."

Sevens don't hold grudges and don't keep score. (But they are also unlikely to stay around until the end of the game, when the score is tallied.)

Idealistic

Sevens are idealists. At their best they are genuinely in service to the community and the planet. Anita Roddick, founder and CEO of The Body Shop, says, "Working for The Body Shop should be not just selling bars of soap, but working for the community, lobbying for social change, campaigning for the environment . . . working, in fact, for the greater good."[3]

Doug Ingoldsby, a Seven, is the founder and president of Nutritech, which designs and sells the phenomenally successful All One vitamins. Ingoldsby's logo is the ultimate in high concept: the words *All One People* superimposed on a picture of the planet Earth taken from space. Famous far beyond the marketplace, the logo has been seen at political conventions, on television shows, and in films. Most people have no idea it's connected to vitamins. "I want to get the logo to as many people as possible," Doug says. "I own the copyright, but I hope everybody knocks it off."

Nutritech has offices in Santa Barbara, but Ingoldsby begins his day at his studio high in the mountains above town, overlooking the ocean. "I keep the finances, the numbers, the details down at the office. The studio is for conceptualizing, for imagining, for playing music," he says.

"What I'm good at is initiating marketing strategies, concepts, new ideas to get exposure for our products. But a business has to be systematized; it has to function in a linear manner. Tasks need to be performed on a daily basis. In order to accomplish anything you have to embrace linear people. Or I'd just be having great ideas that didn't go anywhere.

"When I go down to the office I know that I'm moving into a linear world, which I have created and which other people are implementing for me. I try not to disrupt that, but at the same time I want to expose the company to the inspiration that comes out of my early morning meetings with my design people and my copy people. These two tracks operate simultaneously."

Ingoldsby says his company has "a dual bottom line," where viable humanitarian projects are incorporated directly into the company's master plan. For example, he organized the industry-wide Vitamin Angel Alliance to donate vitamins to the poor and malnourished around the world.[4]

Fun Loving

Richard Branson, the iconoclastic British founder of Virgin Atlantic Airways and Virgin Records, is a hierarchy-busting Seven. Each of the six thousand Virgin employees has Branson's home phone number and calls him by his first name.

Branson wanted Virgin Airways to offer the best service at the best price and for the whole thing to be fun. "If I invite you to my home," Branson has said, "I'd try to entertain you, not put a chicken in front of you and leave you staring at a blank wall." Some Virgin flights have live entertainers—musicians, magicians, a comedian—along with manicurists and massage therapists, which makes the festive atmosphere dizzyingly Seven.[5]

Sevens are experts at making the best of a bad situation, at making lemonade out of lemons. Sevens may not even recognize failure as a concept, since they are not so much goal oriented as experience oriented. "Well, we had a nice run as long as it lasted. What more could we ask?"

Creative, Offbeat Thinkers

For all their puppylike needs for immediate gratification, Sevens are natural long-term, big-picture planners. Setting off simultaneously in all directions (unlike Threes, who rarely stray from the clear path to their goal), Sevens are gifted at finding the common rule or crucial fact in a mass of unorganized data.

A week after the Challenger explosion in which seven astronauts were killed, the brilliant and quirky physicist Richard Feynman was asked to join the presidential commission of inquiry into the accident. His health was not good, and he was hoping to find a way of turning down the invitation. He described his quandary this way:

> I'm still trying to get out of it, and I'm talking to my wife, and I asked her. I have to be immodest here to explain the effect. Gweneth said, "If you're not on the commission, there'll be twelve members in a little knot which will go from one place to another, figure it all out, and write a report. If you are on this thing, there'll be eleven guys in a knot, going around, writing a report, and one guy like a mosquito running all over the place. You probably won't find anything, but if there is something interesting, if there's something strange, then you'll find it and it wouldn't have been found otherwise."
>
> Well, I had to believe her, because I know how I act. I'm an explorer, okay? I get curious about everything, and I want to investigate all kinds of stuff. So I knew she was right, and I had no further excuse. I could make a contribution

that not everybody could make. Could be true, or be untrue. Anyway, she used my lack of modesty to convince me to do it. And I did it.[6]

In the public hearing, Feynman dramatically demonstrated the fatal problem of the O-rings by immersing one in a glass of ice water. Said General Donald Kutyna, a fellow member of the commission,

> I don't think any of us could have done the experiment. It just would not have been fitting for a two-star general, or a former Secretary of State, or the first man on the moon, to pull out his beaker of water and do that kind of a thing. But Feynman was able to do that. I guess if he had a weakness, it was for showmanship. He was a superb showman.[7]

Motivators

Sevens are inspired motivators. They conceptualize new projects and get people on board through their excitement and vision. "I'm often amazed at how frequently people get behind my half-assed ideas if I offer them with enough enthusiasm," says Ivan, a Seven public relations executive.

In true Tom Sawyer fashion, Jason, the Seven editor of a trendy West Coast design magazine, enlisted friends who were writers to proofread the galleys of his first issue for free. "You know proofreading is something I'm not very good at," he told them. "As a matter of fact, I'm dyslexic. But this issue is going to be terrific—the pictures are sensational. A lot of writers I know are coming over. Why don't you come, too—it'll be fun!"

The Bad News

Elusive

Sevens dread being pinned down. If you doubt that optimistic, fun-loving Sevens are secretly driven by fear, try pressing them for a commitment. Directly calling their game causes anxiety, and they'll come up with imaginative reasons—rationalizations—that support their position. They avoid the painful feelings of loss by shifting focus—having lots of possibilities (in contrast to Fives, also members of the mental triad, who avoid the same feelings by minimizing connections).

As a result, Sevens are exceptionally fluid about appointments and other obligations. In fact, Sevens are famous for double-booking. I had a lunch date with my friend Danny, a well-known human rights activist. Knowing he was a Seven, I called to confirm at 10 A.M., before I had to fight my way across town. "Sure, Mike, I'm looking forward to it," he said. I showed up at noon.

His secretary greeted me. "Oh, Danny's on his way to the airport. He had to go to Bolivia!"

Lack of Staying Power

It's not uncommon for Sevens to be impulsive and to lack the staying power to complete a long-term project. They are restless and easily bored; everything emerges from their heads full-blown. Though imaginative, they are not necessarily thoughtful, and their inability to deal with the negative aspects of their job may lead to serious problems. Calvin, a hugely successful salesman of recreational equipment, left a trail of unhappy customers because of his failure to follow up as promised on defective products and credit problems.

Great starters, Sevens have trouble with the end game. Of course, they rarely stick around to pick up the pieces. Charlie, former director of research and development for a computer firm, describes a typical scenario: "I remember this critical research and development project going down to the wire. Our company's technology was due to be shown at an international trade show in less than a week. We were scrambling to build a prototype, but it kept crashing. It was our last possible chance to make a niche for this technology. The company was basically out of money.

"I had done many impossible things before. The research lab loved me. They believed in my magic.

"In spite of the massive reengineering required, I could not bring myself to admit that we wouldn't make it. There was just too much riding on the show. With less than a two days to go, I still believed that the old magic would be there for me one more time. Well, it wasn't.

"Everyone in the company blamed me. I just turned and walked away from the whole mess. I didn't even negotiate my good-bye. Too painful. And besides, something else was already calling."

Commitment or loyalty is hard for Sevens, who usually have more job changes—even career changes—than other Enneagram types. Consider Jason, the dyslexic editor discussed earlier. Before embarking on his magazine venture, Jason ran an art gallery in St. Louis, formed a real estate partnership in Los Angeles, took six months to go around the world (taking hundreds of excellent photographs along the way), and spent a year in India studying yoga.

Pie in the Sky

It's no accident that many airline pilots and flight attendants are Sevens. Malcolm Forbes, the late publisher of *Forbes* and a Seven, liked to balloon.

From an airborne vantage point, Sevens have a great overview, but they also find themselves "above it all"—oblivious to the concerns of the rest of the Enneagram. They "get high" dealing with "high-level" people and selling "high concepts."

Like Peter Pan, the preeminent Seven, they think wonderful thoughts and focus on imaginative possibilities that excite them and others. They take flights of fancy. They avoid getting "heavy," which might "bring them down." Without a real strategy, Sevens "wing it." They throw out all kinds of possibilities and see what will "fly."

One version of their lack of groundedness is a tendency to become instant masters without laying the groundwork. From time to time a Seven getting his first exposure to the Enneagram in a workshop will tell me afterward with great sincerity where I properly explained the Enneagram and where I got off base. This from someone who has just learned it. From me.

Change for Change's Sake

Sevens, fascinated with variety, want to do things differently each time. They are consistent only in their inconsistency, in their impulse to stir things up.

Tom Peters asks, "Are sales consistent with your forecast? Did you exceed budget? These are reasonable and important questions. They are standard fare for performance appraisals or quarterly or monthly reviews. They deal, as the experts say they should, with results that presumably are more or less under the manager's control.

"But I believe these are the wrong questions for the times. They are tangential to the main event. We should be asking something more fundamental: 'What, precisely, exactly, unequivocally, have you changed today?' And: 'Are you sure?' And 'What's next?' And: 'Exactly what bold goal does the change support?'"[8]

Of course, this thirst for change can be hard on other people who are just trying to get through the day.

Dabblers

Gluttony is the Seven's vice—gluttony for ideas and mental experiences. They devour ideas but do not digest them. Like Eights, the rapacious physical counterpart of the mental Sevens, they are not nourished by the enormous amounts they consume. "Producing came out of a feeling of impatience and ambition," said Steven Spielberg, a Seven. "Wanting to have more on my plate than I could possibly digest."[9]

High concepts are the coin of the realm, but because the idea mint runs nonstop, the value of each individual new idea is somewhat degraded and may be easily dropped for a new fascination. In a way, Sevens believe that having and appreciating a good idea is the same as actually implementing it. But when ideas and thinking are more central than doing, problems can arise because the gears haven't engaged.

Sevens tend to live in a preternatural part of life, the magical realm between an idea's generation and its testing by reality. The Seven is most potent in this land of potential. The best part is right before it happens.

By the same token, Sevens know what's happening now: they dabble in the latest movies, restaurants, trends. They may have a "been there, done that" attitude; when pressed, they turn out to have only "read this and thought that." While they may seem to know a lot about other people (and their own inner workings), their knowledge tends toward the theoretical. Many Sevens haven't done the tough emotional spadework.

Working with a Seven

Influencing a Seven

It's easy to influence a suggestible Seven; you'll be flying high if you can suggest an idea that appeals to her sense of adventure and then offer to put it into operation yourself. Remember, though, that Seven is the most insistent on the Enneagram that you (not she) be the responsible one. Ones and Sixes probably have the easiest time of it; they appreciate Seven's originality and, as long as their own concerns are addressed, don't necessarily mind taking on the mundane tasks that Seven shuns.

The fastest way to turn a Seven off is to wield deadline pressure like a club. Sevens are frightened of finality and closure, when potentials and possibilities come to an end. When it's possible, assure the Seven he'll have the opportunity to revisit the question in the future.

How a Seven Makes Decisions

For a Seven, there are no final decisions in the game of life. What may seem like a final decision is simply the most interesting idea at the moment, the foreground idea among many in an ever-changing kaleidoscope of ideas and people and events.

Like Twos, Sevens are impulsive and apt to decide too quickly. Sevens tend to have lots of plans and goals, but they are not attached to them; they may fail to follow through. ("There are plenty more where those came from.")

They're already focused on the next problem, the next set of possibilities. They have trouble taking a stand.

Given how foreign the idea of a final decision is to a Seven, it's not surprising that they make excellent brainstormers. They love being asked questions and hypothesizing responses. Then they listen to themselves (with pleasure) in order to hear the impressive range of their thinking.

The Seven Leadership Style

Visionary Sevens manage by wandering around. Like Twos, they think in terms of people networks, not hierarchies or organizational pyramids. But Twos network emotional exchange, while Sevens network ideas.

Sevens are decentralizing egalitarians. "I wreak havoc around here as a manager," says Elliott, the managing partner of a consulting firm. "And here's how I do it: I push power and responsibility out." Sevens are terrific as empowerers of others, but they have as much trouble with authority (their own and others') as do Sixes. Sevens' solution is to diffuse authority by decentralizing power and flattening hierarchy, which coincidentally minimizes their own accountability. But being a real authority means being accountable, and many Sevens don't like being called to account. "I'll work with anyone, but I work for no one," says Elliott.

Seven managers may be gracious or subtly patronizing rather than oppositional. Consider the brassy habit of CNN television interviewer Larry King, a Seven, who calls everyone, including presidents and other heads of state, by their first names.

Sevens often resist such mundane measures of their achievement as the conventional bottom line. Anita Roddick says, "Such figures got to mean less and less to me. I often wished that our success could be measured in quite different ways. . . . Where did we stand on the quirkiness scale?"[10]

The Seven Work Style

Most Sevens enjoy working intensely in spurts. They resist being pinned down in drudgery without a way out.

As Anita Roddick puts it, "I can't bear to be around people who are bland or bored or uninterested (or to employ them). The kind of brain-dead, gum-chewing assistants you find in so many shops drive me wild. I want everyone who works for us to feel the same excitement that I feel; to share my passion for education and customer care and communication and motivation and to put it into place." She says, "First you have to have fun and then you have to go in the opposite direction to everyone else."[11]

Seven bosses as well as Seven employees are allergic to hierarchies. Says Peggy, a Seven who works as a flight attendant, "We're all equal. There's plenty to do. Let's just work together as a team and enjoy ourselves! Why get hung up on reporting relationships?"

"I never lose sight of who the boss is," says Mel, a Seven who does development work for a record company. "But I don't like constant reminders of who's in charge."

Anyone who has worked with a Seven knows they need help with

- commitment ("Can we write it down?")
- follow-through ("Do you agree on these procedures?")
- pacing ("Will this schedule work for you?") and
- the reasons for a particular decision ("Do you understand the consequences of failure here?").

The Seven Learning Style

Sevens can assimilate a lot of information quickly. They like an interactive, multimedia approach with lots of opportunity to be a clever cock-of-the-walk in front of others. But they hate the one-down role of student. They'd much prefer to teach someone else whatever it is they've figured out about what you just taught them.

The Seven Organization: The Adhocracy

When NBC televised the 1988 Olympics from Seoul, the project was enormously complex. Sixty million dollars' worth of broadcasting equipment was shipped to South Korea, along with over a thousand NBC employees. Most important, televising the Olympic Games required extreme flexibility because several hundred events were happening in dozens of locations, many concurrently. NBC needed to switch suddenly and unexpectedly between equally important and exciting ongoing events. The network was required to be imaginative and energetic and to keep its options always open. NBC devised an adhocracy, the basic Seven organizational structure, ideal for flexibility and innovation.[12]

(By the time NBC televised the 1996 Olympics from Atlanta, the structure was far more instrumentally controlled. Every minute of prime time was accounted for well in advance. The general rule was that when important events were happening simultaneously, the network would stay with one and videotape the others for later broadcast. Such a structure was more tightly organized than an adhocracy but left far less room for Seven-ish flexibility, imagination, and seat-of-the-pants creativity.)

The adhocracy consists of specialists who work on ad hoc interdisciplinary teams led by project leaders. Everybody's on the team and everybody contributes. Supervision is minimal because professionals know what is expected. The system has little bureaucracy so that it can adapt quickly.

Employees might report to several ad hoc bosses. For example, one engineer might report to both the chief of engineers and the boss of the project she's working on, as well as keeping a staff function manager fully informed. Overlapping authority and responsibilities of a Seven structure naturally create ambiguities. For Seven employees, multiple bosses take the pressure off. Decision making is thus decentralized, or multicentered. You might ask a Seven at work, "Who reports to whom?" and she would respond, "We all report to each other!"

At meetings in a Seven culture—which might seem like a work session of comedy writers, where each idea is meant to top the last—people will freely interrupt one another in competitive intellectual jousting, each trying to get the final punch line. Staying on track to the purpose of the meeting may be hard, but the meetings will be full of energy and imagination.

The company 3M, radically decentralized and famous for supporting innovation, has had a successful Seven culture. 3M manufactures more than 55,000 products, with over 100 new products a year. The "Eleventh Commandment" at 3M is "Thou shalt not kill a new product idea."

When 3M decides to support a new product, an interdisciplinary task force—pure Seven—is created, drawing together people from the technical area, manufacturing, marketing, sales, and finance, whether or not they are needed right away.

As in all true adhocracies, intense informal communications are the norm at 3M. People meet randomly and regularly to get things done. Issues of position and authority, which can stifle innovation and communication at other companies, tend not to impede the free flow of ideas in a functioning Seven system.

Seven systems have a natural affinity for individuality, experimentation, and creativity, all of which are supported at 3M by the single most helpful intervention for a Seven system: commitment. "What keeps them satisfied in St. Paul," according to *Fortune*, "is the knowledge that anyone who invests in a new product, or promotes it when others lose faith, or figures out how to mass produce it economically, has a chance to manage that product as though it were his or her own business and to do so with a minimum of interference from above."[13] More recently, 3M has run into some problems that have led to divestitures and downsizing. The conventional charge from analysts is that "they have no strategy," a problem that is endemic in the Seven position.

Seven structures work best when the business calls for

- flexibility
- rapid change
- high professionalism with little supervision
- interdependent experts
- cross-disciplinary ideas
- innovation
- complexity
- advance planning
- optimism about the future.

Getting the Best from a Seven

Sevens evolve when they treasure their ideas enough to act on them instead of thinking, "There's plenty more where those came from." This is the perspective of Seven's High Performance Point Five. When Sevens are stressed they see only one right way, like a brittle and rigid One, instead of a multiplicity of options.

Sevens run from their fears (at Shadow Point Six). When they own their fears, they no longer need to run from them. But no point on the Enneagram is more surprised to discover its shadow. The key intervention for a Seven is landing on the planet at earthy Ally Eight: How do I get from here to there? With power, I engage with commitment.

Oliver's Story

Brilliant and oozing good-humored charm, Oliver, an engaging, nonstop talker, landed a series of progressively more important jobs at one of the defense agencies for which he had little or no substantive expertise. With only a B.A. in classical mythology, he has led teams of "bomb jocks" who are experts in thermonuclear hardware and groups of Ph.D.s in international and strategic studies. He is one of the few people whose career has taken him back and forth between substantive operations and analysis.

As he sees it, his ease in inspiring people and in handling information—regardless of what he really feels or knows—have been the main factors in his rapid advancement. ("Tell your readers," he said, "that my favorite movie is *The Great Impostor* with Tony Curtis.") In my visits to his office, I discovered that he is a "famous character"; there are funny yarns about him, and a number of people have told me that he has personally inspired them or helped their careers in important ways.

But when he was made head of an important overseas administrative unit, he was forced out after a year. "One trap I did get into was reassuring people about downsizing. Instead of being real and just laying out what we needed to do, I was a little too protective of my people. I tended to put a positive spin on things and indicate that everything would be okay. When the truth came out, it made me noncredible. When my employees did upward evaluations, they killed me."

After this temporary setback, he landed on his feet with a prominent defense contractor. I asked what made him so resilient. "Well, I'll tell you, and — although it may sound strange or arrogant to some — this is my true private view," he said. "When I find someone who dislikes me, I am genuinely shocked. I can't imagine why. I figure it's their problem, and I move on."

Oliver's current boss at the defense contractor is Ted, a Three. "He's one of the few people I know who can match my energy," Ted says. "But we are very different. He is all ideas, but you can't rely on his follow-through. I say to him, 'Let's get this done. Let's get so-and-so on it.' Sometimes I feel like a nag. But he can be bloody brilliant. I need to find a way to harness his contribution, or he will self-destruct for the last time."

Sevens do best when they have strong boundaries that they can rely on. Then they can do their high-wire act with a net. But you must have certain, agreed-upon consequences if the Seven fails to measure up to what he has agreed. Interim reporting is very helpful for Sevens; it pushes them to organize, evaluate, and reflect (High Performance is Five). Otherwise, they just float on to the next fun experience.

Stress Point: One

Normally Sevens hide their rigidity and criticality in their *insistence* on playfulness. But when they move, under stress, to One, these easygoing folk become autocratic and directly insist on the one right way to do things. They may also feel themselves the victims of critical, demanding ideologues or rulemongers. Visionaries wilt under such routine tasks as filling out sales reports or supervising routine details. The resulting funk brings out their own critical, judgmental, and rigid side.

But One can be useful to a Seven. "When I go to One," says Oliver, "it's no more Mr. Nice Guy. I prefer keeping it light, but when something's not quality, I want to find out who's responsible. Then I have to be the judge based on my experience and my standards. There's no one else."

High Performance Point: Five

Sevens are jacks of all trades; Fives are masters of one.

By keeping the door always open, as Sevens do, opportunity can't knock. Opportunity can only drift in and may just as easily drift out. Stuck Sevens don't have the closed door—the mechanism for considering, evaluating, and accepting or rejecting opportunities.

When Sevens feel secure enough to move to Five, their leaky sieve becomes a solid container. The public, exhibitionist path becomes a private one. "I go off by myself," says Oliver. "I read. I think. I ask myself, 'How can I keep it simple and spare?'"

Unevolved Sevens assume that there will always be an abundance of ideas, energy, and people available. They spew. When Sevens gain access to Five, they learn what is worth treasuring.

By observing, like a Five, they learn patience and discipline. These "big picture" people learn to honor themselves and others by honoring the details. (Five, Seven's mirror, must learn in turn to honor the flow of high concepts.) Sevens at Five give context and meaning to their experience. Five gives Sevens a vantage point off the playing field, where they can analyze and observe.

When Carl Jung addressed the problem of the *puer* (the "eternal child"), he had but one answer: "Work."[14] Sevens finally land on the planet when they see the value of sticking it out and owning the consequences. So projects that require patience, commitment, and long, focused effort are not the natural draw for Seven, but they can be Seven's salvation.

For some Sevens, the grounding element is not their work but a committed relationship. Says Emily, a Seven musician who plays and records both classical and country music, "My work is constant change. I travel all over. If I didn't have my twenty-year marriage, I would be done in."

Wings

Shadow Point: Six

Whenever I feel afraid
I strike a careless pose
And whistle a happy tune
So no one ever knows
I'm afraid.

—Oscar Hammerstein, from The King and I

Sevens are narcissists who, like Peter Pan, have lost touch with their own shadow. (They need to find a nice Two, like Wendy Darling, to sew it back on.) The shadow provides the depth that Sevens crave but flee from.

Without a shadow, Sevens are promiscuous Pollyannas. Under the guise of being positive thinkers, they are wishful thinkers. Pretending to be visionary leaders, they are pied pipers. They escape the real concerns and problems that are in front of them by imagining what wonders might be in the future. Filled with possibilities but capricious, they are fly-by-night operators.

Sixes, by contrast, are consistent and reliable. Once they're in, they're in for the long haul. But most Sixes are far more conscious of what worries them than are Sevens. Deep into denial that anything (especially themselves) could be less than positive, Sevens are reluctant to scrutinize their own processes and motives. Though Sixes often blame others, they also do a lot of self-examination, and they recognize that the best way past trouble is through it. When Sevens own Shadow Six, the change is obvious: Sevens know what they are running from. They can choose to stop.

Sixes reject detachment, while Sevens reject fidelity. Sixes are cautiously strategic, while Sevens thrive on chaos. When Seven owns his shadow, the fear stops running him. For the paranoids (Five, Six, and Seven) their apprehension looms too large. Acknowledging it allows them to put it in perspective.

Ally Point: Eight

Eights are master builders, comfortable with power and aggression. When Sevens move to Eight, the word becomes flesh.

At Eight, instead of being dilettantes, Sevens learn what every Eight knows: how to build and follow through with power and impact. Eights have intention and staying power that Sevens don't. Intention for Seven is evanescent. The next possibility is always as good as the present one, so a loss doesn't really matter. But Eights want what they want when they want it, and they act on their wants.

When Sevens, normally reluctant to commit, move to Eight, they move ahead in real (not imaginary) time and are not afraid to ruffle feathers in pursuit of their goals. They are concerned for and protective of their people in a way that Sevens tend not to be. Oliver learned something from his experience. More like a top-dog Eight than a "consulting" Seven, he says, "For the first time in my life I am the backstop, the responsible official."

Cardinal Rules

If You Work with a Seven

- Be prepared for rapid give and take. Sevens talk fast and think circles around everybody. Recognize that this is just possibility talk, not commitment. If you want commitment, get it in writing. A handshake and that big Seven grin is not enough.
- Align with the dream. Let the Seven share her vision and enthusiasm. Sevens receive support from others' commitment to their individuality, experimentation, and creativity. Don't clip their wings too soon by judging or focusing on picky details.
- Probably the best way to get the best from a Seven is to ask lots of questions. Sevens love hypothesizing and answering them.
- Show Sevens how their dreams can work. They won't want to do the grunt work themselves; if at all possible, give them permission to find someone to do it for them.
- Help the Seven be a container rather than a sieve by enforcing boundaries and deadlines and setting limits with teeth. But resist the temptation to play the authoritarian heavy, which will scare Seven away. Cocreate agreements.
- Share your problem with the Seven rather than secretly stewing or judging. Sevens like being part of the process; what you see as a problem they may see as interesting opportunity.
- Recognize that for a Seven job descriptions may be vague or overlapping. If you want a Seven to be the buck-stopping responsible official, duties, responsibilities, and consequences must be crystal clear.

If You Are a Seven

- Ask yourself, what are the plausible negatives on this project? Then find ways of dealing with them.
- Underpromise. Sevens tend to overpromise because they don't want to disappoint in the moment.
- Get a stable place in your life from which you can observe. In order to do your soaring, you need a tether to connect you with the planet. For some Sevens this is a family or the routine demands of work.
- Learn to ride out the consequences of your choices rather than simply switching horses in midstream.
- Every idea that comes into your head does not need to be expressed.

- Curb your tendency to make fun of people, to treat them carelessly, and to tell them to lighten up. When you catch yourself doing this, consider it an indication that your paranoia is cooking. What exactly are you afraid of?
- Think about closure in advance. If you're trying to make a sale, you may have to limit your options.
- Be aware of your tendency to rationalize, to explain away failure and ethical violations.
- Learn to listen without thinking about what clever thing you are going to say next. The name of the game is not one-upmanship but empathy.
- Work! Hunker down and finish what you've committed to doing. Develop habits of self-discipline. Stay organized. Prioritize what you are doing.
- Use your splendid Seven gifts: raise lots of questions; generate alternatives; visualize how the scheme will look in the future. Keep everyone's energy up.
- Practice mental sobriety, the virtue of Seven. Don't get drunk on ideas. Sip them slowly with a dinner of practicality.

1. Danny Hillis, quoted in Christopher Sykes, *No Ordinary Genius: The Illustrated Richard Feynman* (New York: W. W. Norton, 1994), 180.
2. Tom Peters, *Thriving on Chaos* (New York: Alfred A Knopf, 1987), 3.
3. Anita Roddick, *Body and Soul* (New York: Crown Publishers, 1991), 111.
4. Interview with the author, April 4, 1995.
5. Michael Adams, "Fly By," *Successful Meetings* (August 1992), 38.
6. Sykes, *No Ordinary Genius*, 192–93.
7. Sykes, *No Ordinary Genius*, 210.
8. Tom Peters, *Thriving on Chaos* (New York: Harper & Row, 1987), 561.
9. Randall Lane, "I Want Gross," *Forbes* 154, no. 7 (September 26, 1994): 107.
10. Roddick, *Body and Soul*, 114.
11. Roddick, *Body and Soul*, 118, 218.
12. The term *adhocracy* is from Henry Mintzberg, *The Structuring of Organizations* (Englewood Cliffs, NJ: Prentice-Hall, 1979). For Olympic broadcasting as an adhocracy, see Stephen Robbins, *Organization Theory* (Englewood Cliffs, NJ: Prentice-Hall, 1983), 329.
13. Lee Smith, "The Lures and Limits of Innovation: 3M," *Fortune* (October 20, 1980), 86.
14. Carl Gustav Jung, *Symbols of Transformation*, vol. 5, *Collected Works*, 2d ed. (Princeton: Princeton Univ. Press, 1967).

EIGHT

The Top Dog

AKA	Alpha Dog, Chief, Leader, Boss, Potentate, the Kingfish, the Challenger, the Champion
Worldview	I am strong. I avenge the weak and expose the power abusers, the pretenders, and the fools.
High Side	"The buck stops here"; a take-charge doer; a powerful, responsible, high-energy sovereign; a paladin
Low Side	Loud, excessive, confrontational, dissipated, bossy, unsubtle, reckless; a raging bully
Leadership Style	Autocratic, a paterfamilias; blunt, confrontational, sometimes harsh power brokers
Credo	Truth and justice; my way or the highway.
Appeal to	Their power and influence; justice, their desire to help the underdog; their taste for immediate engagement ("Saddle up!")
Don't Appeal to	Sympathy, diplomacy, the rules
Talk/Communication Style	Diatribes, harangues, threats, all unmediated and uncensored, blunt
Makes You Feel	Well protected, part of the action; and—sometimes—steamrolled and assaulted
Appearance	Brash, commanding
Good Work Setting	High risk, high engagement, high energy, big impact
Difficult Work Setting	Quiet, austere, formal, rule or tradition bound

Books	*Leadership Secrets of Attila the Hun* by Wes Roberts *The Godfather* by Mario Puzo *The Power Broker* by Robert Caro
Sayings	*Veni, vidi, vici* (I came, I saw, I conquered) —Julius Caesar "L'état c'est moi." —Louis XIV "I am in charge." —Alexander Haig "Political power grows out of the barrel of a gun." —Mao Zedong "Our basic plan of operation is to advance and keep on advancing, regardless of whether we have to go over, under, or through the enemy. We have one motto, 'Audacious, audacious, always audacious.'" —George Patton "You can get a lot more with a kind word and a gun than you can get with a kind word." —Alphonse Capone
Of the Eight Persuasion	George Steinbrenner, Marge Schott, Jimmy Hoffa, Saddam Hussein, Carl Reichardt (Wells Fargo), Armand Hammer, John Gotti, Robert Maxwell, Fritz Perls, Bella Abzug, John Sununu, Pat Buchanan, Don Vito Corleone (*The Godfather*), Boris Yeltsin, Golda Meir, Mao Zedong, Charles de Gaulle, Slobodan Milosevic, Ann Richards, Mike Tyson, John Wayne, Lyndon Baines Johnson, Dixie Lee Ray, Robert Bork, Mike Ditka, Sam Donaldson, the Hell's Angels, the Mafia, Serbia
High Performance	2 Protector of the weak; generous, helpful, charming, wears heart on sleeve
Stress	5 Retreats into the cave; avoids people; observes and thinks; consolidates plans (focused by analyzing)
Ally	9 *Energized* by the peaceable kingdom, empathy, and humility (like Nines), by considering alternatives instead of blazing straight ahead

Shadow	7 *Grounded* by taking themselves lightly, by alternative ideas, by a bird's-eye view, and by flexibility
Virtue	Innocence
Vice	Lust

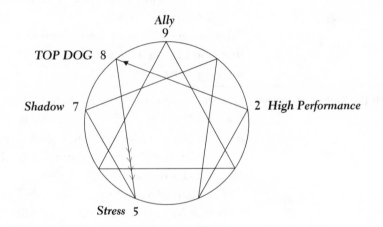

Getting to Know an Eight

Sam's Story

A big bear of a man, six feet tall with an ever-present cigar, Sam is the burly, gruff, barrel-chested head of his own production company specializing in television commercials. He's fifty-five, with a large smile and big, meaty hands that envelop your own when he greets you.

Thirty-five years and seventy pounds ago he was a dancer for Martha Graham. "I was a little crude," says Sam. "She liked that. She used to say to me, 'You're a street dancer, an animal.' She meant I had no technique, but I had charisma, energy. It was the way I moved and filled up space. I relied on that. I was direct. That's my battle plan still."

On the set, no one doubts Sam is in charge. His energy and his voice fill the room. Those who work for him hesitate to get in his way. "But Sam is definitely not a tyrant, like some other famous commercial directors," says his assistant, Carla. "He takes extremely good care of the crew. He makes sure his people have very high-quality catering. He doesn't make people stand around when they could be on break. He keeps everybody in a fairly good mood. But when he works, he's very intense. The volume is up. He doesn't screw around with a lot of takes. It's 'Bam! Bam! And in the can.' Your equipment better be working or he'll have your head."

Once, during a commercial shoot, the producer from the ad agency told Sam, "I don't like where you have the camera." Everyone got very quiet. Sam nodded. Then she said, "You know, you really ought to shoot more film. We may need it." Finally, when she criticized the animation guy directly, Sam exploded and kicked her off the set. "Get out now!" he roared. Later, the producer apologized. Sam accepted her apology right away. "Because I felt she learned her lesson," he says.

Sam says, "I'm a reasonable person. I speak up when I'm forced to. Sometimes I blow off steam. What you see is that I care about my people and my product. I run the shoot by consensus."

"Consensus?" I ask, incredulous.

"I mean that I take pains so that everyone knows what I am up to," he says, laughing at himself.

Sam tends to act first and think later. Says another longtime employee, "He's too loud. He likes to talk and to hear himself talk. He's never subtle. Everything's always in your face. He uses a sledgehammer when a flyswatter would do. This makes him a bully sometimes. He definitely holds grudges and takes revenge."

"But I have to admit that he can be incredibly great fun to work with. You feel like you're working on something big. You never worry that the action is happening somewhere else. Yes, he's demanding, but I don't doubt for a second that he stretches me to do my best work. He rips me up like he rips up everybody else, but I love him. I really do. Sam's a great boss."

Do you recognize Sam? Sam is an Eight.

The Basic Premise

Bursting with what used to be called "animal magnetism," Eights can be enormously attractive, *flamboyant*, larger-than-life characters with a lust for worldly pleasures and sensual indulgences. Built to run the show, not squeamish about giving orders, they are the *paterfamilias*, the king of the mountain, the top dogs of the Enneagram. Eights are more than willing to have an impact on people, on the market, on their environment, and on events. They are not afraid to take the heat and the responsibility. They feel little restraint at the beginning and little remorse after the fact. "It's much easier to ask for forgiveness than permission," says Ed, an Eight who is chief of material acquisitions for a large manufacturer.

In the film *Raiders of the Lost Ark*, a desert bad guy threatens Indiana Jones with elaborate, masterful swordplay, demonstrating considerable power, skill, and evil intent. Jones seems overmatched, but when the poor hoodlum is done with his threatening exhibition, Jones simply takes out his pistol and shoots him dead. That's how Eights act—direct, powerful, no frills, final.

For Eights, the world is a power game, plain and simple. "Have lunch or be lunch," says Sandy, an electronics manufacturer. What matters is who has the power. If the Eight doesn't have it, he pursues it. "When I'm not in charge, it's not a problem at all," says Richard, a former gang member who now directs a city program for gangsters. "I just figure out a way to become the person in charge. And then I do. No problem at all." When the Eight does have power, he enjoys exercising it in pursuit of his appetites or in defense of his people or to support the weak or downtrodden. Although capable of accomplishment on a grand scale, Eights are driven not so much by goals or achievements (like Threes) as by *potency*. Eights build a power base—a political machine, a multinational media conglomerate, an army—that can perform for good or for ill, but its driving force is the organization and effective use of power. As Lord Beaverbrook said of Lloyd George, "He did not seem to care which way he traveled, providing he was in the driver's seat."

In his best-seller, *Leadership Secrets of Attila the Hun*, Wes Roberts describes his version of Attila, "a determined, tough, rugged and intriguing leader who dared to accomplish difficult tasks and performed challenging feats against 'seemingly' insurmountable odds." Attila had "an inherent commitment to influencing people, processes and outcomes," but more than that he had "the lust for leadership." "You've got to want to be in charge," says Roberts's Attila, a true Eight.

Psychology

Eight maintains power and control in order to combat those who abuse power, to protect those who can't protect themselves, and to fight for worthy projects and causes while denying their own mortality and vulnerability. Eights typically tell a childhood story of struggling against injustice or long odds or being left to their own devices. The Eight may have been physically beaten or abused. Or the abuse may have been psychological: an older sibling who systematically put down the Eight, parents who derided the Eight's tender feelings or desires, a teacher who razzed the Eight for underachieving, a neighborhood bully who singled out the Eight for target practice. Sometimes the Eight's whole family had to fight against an injustice like racism or poverty or difficult circumstances. There may have been an early illness that the Eight battled, like cancer or polio. Whatever the circumstances, the Eight got the message: fight back or die. Eights decided to fight back.

The young Eight resolved that to survive she would have to move from being powerless and a victim to being potent and in charge. The sense of being shamed or deprived led to the conviction that standing up for yourself and your position is central in life and that being weak or sensitive can get you in trouble. Very early in life, most Eights vowed not to be humiliated again. Winston Churchill remembered the very moment when, under a rock-throwing attack by some classmates, he resolved never to be a victim. "Never give in," he said some years later to great effect. "I don't do weakness," says my friend Sister Rose, a Catholic nun of the tough-and-tender Eight variety who is a recovering alcoholic.

Steve, a successful filmmaker, tells a story of his father, an Eight. When Steve was eight years old and out with his father in Brooklyn, his father got into a dispute with a stranger, a street tough, over a parking space. Words came to blows, and Steve's father pulled the stranger from his car and whipped him. Steve watched with big eyes. Then, the fight over, Steve remembers his father's big face in his. "Where were *you?*" his father asked. Steve, an Eight himself, says, "I never wanted to feel that small again."

In the Eight's rough-and-tumble world, only the strong survived. Forced by circumstances to hone their fighting skills, many Eights were difficult or rambunctious kids who got into scrapes and were sent to the principal's office. Some Eights joined gangs under the guise of fighting for justice. Others did well in school; some went on to become powerful fat cats, while others went on to fight for the underdog against the fat cats' abuse of power in all fields of endeavor—in business or as teachers or politicians or activists for a cause.

Because they learned so young to steel themselves against any feelings of vulnerability, Eights as adults need a bigger jolt of experience than most to feel alive. But scratch the surface of an Eight (do this carefully), and you'll find the Eight sees himself not necessarily as the king of the jungle but as a big-hearted, playful pussycat, an uncomplicated innocent. Thus Eights can be easily wounded, not so much by a punch in the nose as by an offhand comment regarding their insensitivity or bullishness. Eights, more than any other type by far, object to what they feel is unfair stereotyping at the hands of the Enneagram. "I'm more vulnerable than people know and very sensitive," insists the Eight loudly, pounding his fist again and again, until you get it. (And it is surely true.)

The Good News

Eights are the epic heroes of the Enneagram. Life for them is a series of show-downs where they use their power to crush the ruthless and the unkind, the dunderheads and the pretenders to the throne, while protecting the worthy who cannot protect themselves. (Compare with Threes, who value mastery and success but generally are not motivated by *vindictiveness* or *vindication*.)

The Guardian Angels are a typical Eight outfit, vigilantes who take the law into their own hands in order to protect citizens. Eights champion whatever people and causes are put in their care, whether it is their team at work, their customers, their clients, or their caseload.

Eights *enjoy* exercising their power. This is a good way to tell an Eight from others who happen to hold power: Eights rule without worrying about being judged (like a One) or fearing retribution (like a Six) or obsessing about unintended consequences (like a Nine). Power expressed so directly and naturally, without the ambiguity that comes from second thoughts, is simply grace-ful and elegant.

Most of us admire Eights for their direct engagement with life and their innocent sensate enjoyment of experiences and of events. Leo Rosten wrote of Winston Churchill,

> He looked like a Toby jug, a character out of Dickens, but he was born to command, to fight, to inspire, to prevail. He lived with unquenchable gusto, sipping massive quantities of champagne, brandy, whisky, wine; fondling long cigars all

day long; working in bed until noon, lunching at three, taking a siesta — one hour, two hours, unclothed in bed — then working again, and again after dinner until three or four or dawn. He loved . . . the posture of chivalry, the panoply of kings.[1]

Tough and Tender

Eights have a full-bodied, earthy charm, superabundant drive and energy, and often a broad sense of humor, which makes them among the most popular of the Enneagram types. The rest of us, caught up in our ambivalence and insecurity, can only marvel at their apparently guilt-free delight in life. It's easy to want to hitch your star to an Eight.

But for all their enormous resources of strength, energy, and drive, Eights are a surprising combination of tough and tender. They like to see themselves the way native-born Israelis do: as *sabras*, a desert cactus that is prickly on the outside but soft and sweet on the inside. An Eight may concede a gruff exterior, but he knows he has a big heart.

Eights are outraged when they see defenseless people being mistreated, and they will not hesitate to confront the offenders. "Penny always takes care of us, " says Rich, a staffer in her department at a startup high-tech company. "As aggressive as she is in her work, that's how aggressive she is in her nurturing. She's always taking on battles for me.

"We have company credit cards. This is a volatile business, and at one point the money got really tight. The credit card company called up and said, 'Your company is not paying the bills. You're personally responsible for what's on the card.' I freaked. These were business expenses. I couldn't see any way I was responsible, but the woman was pretty brutal. Penny was listening and grabbed the phone from me. She just tore the poor woman apart. The next thing I know I get an apologetic call from a vice president at the credit card company, and that was the end of it."

Straight for Truth and Justice

Eights are powerful, straightforward, tough-minded bulldozers. They can be bullies, but at their best they are bullfighters who take the bull by the horns (and countenance no bull: pretension or fancy theories, sometimes including the Enneagram).

"I always laugh when people ask me about rebounding techniques," says basketball player Charles Barkley, the Phoenix Suns' power forward [the basic Eight position]. "They want to know my secrets when it comes to rebounding. Most young players have been told that they should concentrate first on boxing out underneath the boards; 'find a man and put a body on him,' is what most coaches say. Then the players are told to read the spin and trajectory of the basketball so they can anticipate in which direction it will come off the rim and how far. Well, all that is garbage.

"'Yeah, I've got a technique,' I always say. 'It's called, Just Go Get the Damn Ball!'"[2]

Blunt and unceremonious, Eight's unvarnished directness can be overwhelming, but it also can be a powerful force for good. Says Meg, a former mayor who is an Eight, "Eight energy is raw. Raw is direct and powerful. Raw can save the day." Meg naturally used her powerful personal presence to calm unruly city council meetings, and she also ensured that citizens who might not normally have the courage to speak at a council meeting felt safe to approach the microphone and do so. When timid citizens approached the microphone, Meg made sure they got their say.

Richard, an Eight, is the head of a program that teaches the building trades to gang members in the Midwest. The most important part of the program, according to Richard, is learning the skills involved in holding a job: organizing your life so that you show up on time and learning to deal with a boss and work within a company structure. "It's discipline," he says. "I get them ready to enter a workforce that really doesn't want them.

"One way I find out about these guys is to *push them physically*. That's how I find out what they're about, who I can rely on and who I can't. Sometimes they come back at me. My job is to make sure they know I can take whatever they dish out. I try to civilize them without breaking their spirits. When I'm finished with them, they're definitely ready for the workforce.

"My other problem," says Richard, "is making sure the building trades are fair to these guys."

"How do you do it?" I asked.

"I *convince* them. I make them an offer they can't refuse. I explain how when they are building buildings in the community where our graduates live they are helped by employing our graduates."

Shameless and direct, Eights like to do as they please. They aren't afraid to bully other people into shape. They press hard against the restrictive conventions of business and society. And they see the resulting controversy as simply the result of telling the truth—unmasking pretense and injustice—in a world where uptight people aren't used to it. Says basketball player Charles Barkley, "*Controversial* is the word I often hear associated with me and quite frankly, it offends me. What some might call controversial, I call telling the truth. I don't create controversies; they're there long before I open my mouth. I just bring them to your attention. If that's controversial, then so be it."[3]

Eights believe that the truth will set you free. Says Meg, the former mayor, "I believe that as a culture we've just quashed Eight energy. We've equated directness with conflict. Well, there's nothing so devastating in our society as the fact that we've 'made nice' for so long that we haven't solved a damn thing. If you get people's honesty out on the table, you'll find the best solutions will be on that table."

Unlike Sixes, who can be tactical and hidden, Eights are without guile: what you see is what you get. Although they can be vindictive, their vengefulness is not particularly subtle or manipulative. They hold grudges and they act on them. And then, generally, they are done. (Compare with Fours, who keep holding on.)

The Bad News

Polyphemus, the Cyclops who captured Odysseus and gobbled up most of his crew, was a classic Eight. With one huge eye in the center of his forehead, Cyclops could see only straight ahead. There's not much "perspective." Eights don't have much of a flair for lateral thinking or for finessing around a problem. Eight General Norman Schwartzkopf's original plan for Operation Desert Storm was simply to head straight in, guns ablaze, directly at the Iraqi forces, but military strategists insisted on a more sophisticated flanking action.

Eights deny complexity. These are not people who dance the dance of ambiguity. Their world is black or white; you're either friend or foe, strong or weak, likable or not.

A Passion for Anger

Eights are, with Ones and Nines, members of the anger triad. Anger is Eight's signature expression. Certain that everyone else around them is as concerned as they are about power and control, Eights can be domineering, intimidating, and arrogant. Unconcerned with propriety, they believe "the truth comes out in a fight." To them, a good fight is something like a conversation, a useful exchange of information. "I like a guy who will pound his fist back at me," says Henry, an Eight divorce attorney. "Someone I can have a discussion with."

Eights don't merely want to fight. They want to win. And not just win but pulverize the opponent. (If Ones cauterize their colleagues neatly and effectively, Eights prefer to eviscerate them, leaving messy carnage and destruction in their wake.) A colleague said of Disney's CEO, Michael Eisner, "There is an excessiveness that has always bothered me. Disney makes deals that are too tough, and when a deal's too tough, it never works out in the end."[4]

In an article in the *New York Observer*, Robert Sam Anson rather brazenly describes Eisner as a person "who tells the likes of Dustin Hoffman, 'My job is to fuck you,' who has been quoted as saying that lying is part of the 'business,' who plots revenge against his enemies, and whose company pursues adversaries with no fewer than 800 lawsuits a year." Eisner, he says, "prized ferociousness in his executives. . . . *He reveled in contention, indeed, encouraged aides to battle him believing that out of the cauldron of Fuck you's and You're crazy's a purer truth emerges*" (my emphasis).[5] Eights believe that the truth comes out in combat.

From the point of view of the Eight, what anger she feels is justified. But for all her explosiveness, her internal experience is actually one of restraint and frustration, of being pushed to the limit by fools. Much like Fours, Eights ask, "Why me?" But instead of making themselves miserable, like Fours, searching for the reasons why, Eights simply eliminate the offender. Constraint is not their strong suit.

While apparently at home in a sea of contentiousness, power plays, and even lawsuits, Eights actually tend to avoid *real* engagement. I once watched Rita, the Eight manager of a clothing store, say to two subordinates, "Okay, you two ladies have a problem? Well, not anymore, because this is how it's going be." Rita was disinclined to address the real issues between the two or to set forth any workable procedures for resolving future difficulties. Yet Rita thought herself "good with conflict" because she dived right in.

For all their vitriol, Eights are as out of touch with their real anger as are Nines and Ones. Unevolved Eights don't own their anger, they just display it. Although they may characterize it as "letting off steam," in fact their anger never discharges. Rather, Eights get angry as a defensive habit, to scare others off, and as a ruse to cover up their real feelings, vulnerabilities, and issues.

When you have been wronged by an Eight, don't wait around thinking the Eight will surely see the error of his ways. It's not likely to happen. Eights have what the family therapist Ivan Boszormenyi-Nagy calls "destructive entitlement." As a result of the abuse they've taken, the good fights they've fought, Eights feel they have accumulated a credit balance in their moral account that entitles them to take revenge and not feel remorse. Astonishingly, they feel as *justified* as Ones.

Provocative and Vengeful

Like adolescents drawn to applied entomology, Eights like to poke at their target with a stick to see how he will react. Will he run? Will she struggle? Will he give up? How far can I push? You won't find anyone on the Enneagram who likes to push your buttons or stir things up more than an Eight.

A favorite technique is to cover up a blunder or a change in direction by creating chaos and then blaming others for it. Writes Roy Greenslade about his former boss, Robert Maxwell, the British publishing magnate, "A typical Maxwellian panic began with an out-of-the-blue phone call in which he ranted. It was followed by a burst of calls—as many as a dozen within an hour—and many calls to other executives who then began to ring each other. Having stirred everyone else into hysteria by urging several people to carry out the same order . . . he then called a meeting. 'Why are you all running around like chopped worms?' he would scream."[6]

When they feel wronged, angry Eights don't hesitate to seek their version of appropriate revenge. For example, when Doug, an Eight, was fired from a consulting firm for not respecting lines of authority, he sent a letter purporting to be a legitimate informational letter on company letterhead to clients and colleagues that went into minute detail about how power really flowed in the firm. It was a terrific embarrassment for the firm, "just the lesson they needed," Doug later claimed. "I knew where power was in the firm, and now so does everybody else."

In fact, Eights are the Enneagram's connoisseurs of revenge, one area in which they can legitimately claim a certain subtlety. Remember the scene in *The Godfather* when a neighbor whose daughter was beaten comes to Don Corleone (an Eight from the original mold) to ask the Godfather to murder the attackers? "That I cannot do," Corleone replies. "That is not justice. Your daughter is still alive . . . We are not murderers, despite what the undertaker says." He sends his soldiers to beat the attackers instead, as they had beat the young woman. For Eights, the punishment must fit the crime. But make no mistake: there *will* be punishment.

Excessive

"The road of excess leads to the palace of wisdom," wrote William Blake. Eights are people of enormous physical and energetic appetites; whatever it is—food, sex, work—they can't get enough.

If Fives are minimalists, Eights are maximalists. Like Ones, Eights lack a rheostat. Their switch is either on or off. Whatever the game, Eights want to take it to the limit one more time. Eights feel that more—larger, longer, louder, stronger—will satisfy, but it does not. Says Marvin, an Eight television producer, "Anything worth doing is worth overdoing."

Fidel Castro, an Eight, gave speeches for four, six, eight hours or longer, until he ran out of steam. Andrea, an Eight writer, says, "I'm totally mystified when I hear about writers who work between eight and twelve every day. I could never do that. Never! I write from six in the morning until twelve at night until a project is done or until I keel over. Then I screw off until I need to do it again."

In practice this means Eights find it difficult (if not impossible) to moderate their behavior. Darla, a dynamic, bossy, hyperkinetic bulldog, runs a women's sports apparel manufacturer. She barks orders. She is loud and profane. She goes nonstop and full tilt. She has tantrums. She denigrates other people's opinions. She has her way. She takes up all the space. Everything is full speed ahead. She is, in many ways, the classic steamroller boss from hell, and her employees feel flattened by her.

Employees of an Eight may get burned out quickly from full-throttled management.

Lord of the Domain

"L'état, c'est moi," said Louis XIV. Eights are territorial. They are sovereign in their domain. When Lyndon Johnson was president, he was bounding onto a helicopter about to take off. "Mr. President," said the Marine guard, "your helicopter is over there." "Son," said Johnson, "They're *all* my helicopters."

A practical consequence of the Eight's territoriality is that Eight bosses feel free to barge in on their subordinates, who, after all, are only extensions of themselves. When I worked in government I once had an Eight boss—Bob, the general counsel—who cut internal windows into the offices of all his professional staff so he could see from the hallway what was going on. "The quickest way to see Bob," we used to say, "is to shut your door."

As part of their sense of being masters of their domain, Eights (like their neighbor Nines) feel free to get involved in and distracted by minor details or irritations. So Robert Maxwell, the British publishing magnate, insisted on approving and sometimes then disapproving ridiculously minor expenses, thus disempowering and humiliating his most senior managers.

Working with an Eight
Influencing an Eight

Eights will naturally respond to your requests if you show how what you want will consolidate their power and influence. (Compare with Fours, who open to the world of feelings and impressions, or Sixes, with whom you can appeal to your private agendas or differences.) In addition, Eights are centrally concerned with justice for themselves and for others. Appeal to their desire to settle scores and to their sense that wrongs will be righted, that the unjust will be punished and the just rewarded, that the powerless will be empowered, and that it all will be exciting or explosive or fun. "Why should you do this film about enterprise zones? Because that's where the juice is. Because people are pulling themselves up by their bootstraps against all odds. You can change the world." Eights like to feel their efforts make an impact.

How to motivate an Eight? Tell her she can't do it. Says Diane, an Eight production manager, "I love it when people tell me I can't do something. It's like mother's milk. I always go on pushing ahead, whether I know how to do something or not."

An Eight wants to be the hero with the black hat: the bad-guy drill sergeant who will save your life, the tough-love school principal who carries a baseball bat and brings the school back to discipline and respectability. So throw down the gauntlet: Say, "Here are our options. If you go this route, it will be more difficult. It is unconventional. We'll have to power our way through. We may be ridiculed. We'll have to be tough. But the difficult route gives us these advantages. It can work. It is your decision." This is very seductive for an Eight. Eights love to test themselves in an environment without a safety net.

At their worst, Eights brook no opposition or open discussion. Like Saddam Hussein or Lyndon Johnson, they demand that information and discussion support preconceived notions. But at their best, they bring effective skills to an open argument. They are not afraid to test people's integrity and commitment or level of skill or to expose any self-delusions that the combatants may be selling. They are not afraid to let it all hang out. The battle over, high-side Eights are realists who can reevalute their own position.

Eights don't react well to being squeezed on the wrong end of a power play. Many will find it laughable that you are trying to force them to do something a certain way. Says Penny, the high-tech department head, "My back goes up and I get very stubborn when somebody says, 'You'll do it my way!' Ha! I'm not someone you can just roll over."

But acting weak with an Eight is a mistake, as well. While Eights protect the *noble* weak, who can't protect themselves, most Eights have utter contempt for wimps, whiners, and bluffers. Eights pay respectful attention when you have views and stand up for them. You don't have to do obeisance.

Eights like colleagues who will tolerate their explosiveness at a meeting. But if you make it a question of your power versus your Eight boss, he will have no choice but to fire the big guns.

Most Eights *prefer that you move toward them.* Respond to the rage, not in kind, but directly, firmly, intentionally. Stand your ground. Feel your own power. "I don't agree with you," you can say. "The Frumholtz contract is completely in hand. Here are the figures. I am in direct contact with each of the project managers. I *am* in control here." (Al Haig said it best for power-fixated Eights.)

When an Eight is out of control, you may choose to move away, if you retain your power. You can even say words to this effect: "I need to talk to you about something important. I'll be back after the fireworks are over."

Another excellent rejoinder to an exploding Eight, if your relationship will accommodate it and if it is true, is, "You're believing your own bullshit!" This may stop your Eight in his tracks. The notion of *exposing* bullshit, even if it's their own, is highly attractive to Eights. *All* Eights think they are on a special mission from God to expose bullshit wherever it may be found.

A now-senior Eight manager, chief of a division in a multinational firm, told me of a small dinner that he had thirty years ago with the then CEO. "I was the youngest one there. It was my first real meeting with the old man. I had been blustering away, offering advice about the business and life—*bullshitting*—when the old man turned to me and said, 'I am not a fool, sir.' Of course, I wanted to crawl into a hole. I realized I was holding forth just to hear myself talk. The old man busted me, and it was the central event of my career. I can still feel the pain of that moment thirty years later. I learned to check myself for bullshit, and that has saved me many times."

Eights hate to be blindsided. They'd much rather be told that they are over the top. The best Eights have learned from experience that in many situations important nuances escape them, and they may appreciate the report from someone they trust.

How an Eight Makes Decisions

Eights are impulsive and hot. They make decisions in the heat of the moment. They hate to chew things over. The tension of ambiguity is too much for them. (Eights are at core as obsessive as Nines, but their impulsiveness is a reaction to their inability to hold on to more than one position, as do Nines.) If you know what you want, present it directly and forcefully. You may want to offer several alternatives or just one, but either way the Eight wants to hear, "It's your decision."

Eights don't have the patience to explore the dark underbelly of each alternative, like Sixes. Information processing is not Eights' strong suit. They like to go by their gut. "If I don't have a gut reaction, I'm not where I need to be," says Don, an Eight trial lawyer. "I know what result I want and then I go get it. When I know what needs to be done, there is a sense of rightness about it."

Of course, haste sometimes makes waste. But Eights would rather pick up the pieces than exercise restraint. I am reminded of Yankee owner George Steinbrenner's repeated firings of manager Billy Martin and the repeated reconciliations that followed.

Some Eights are dictators and simply won't take your opinion into account. As Charles de Gaulle (a Huit) put it, "I have heard your views. They do not harmonize with mine. The decision is taken unanimously." Others will give lip service to participatory decision making and then continue to make decisions on their own behind closed doors. The chief executive of one of America's largest companies once said in my presence, "We will implement this participatory mode of decision making. If any of you can't make it work, step into my office and we'll have it working in ten minutes."

For many Eights, the opinions of other people seem pale and distant and small, as if seen through the wrong end of a telescope. Consulting with others seems superfluous. And Eights are unlikely to be swayed simply because the preponderance of opinion is against them. Says my colleague Stanley, an Eight management consultant, "I don't think too many Eights would fall for that experiment where eleven people say something's black and the twelfth one goes along, even though she knows it's white. The Eight would stand up and say, 'You're all nuts!'"

The Eight Leadership Style

Eights are natural tyrants. In ancient Greece, tyrants were self-made men who seized power without having inherited it, as had a king. Many tyrants were very popular; others were overbearing.

Some Eights manage by tantrum and fear of reprisal. Others are benevolent dictators. Either way, Eights like to *manage by decree* rather than by relying on stultifying ongoing procedures. Boris Yeltsin insisted on such authority when he became president of Russia and has issued many decrees in an attempt to circumvent the legislature or the political process. De Gaulle wrote similar powers for himself when he became president of France. Of course, Saddam Hussein retains such authority as well.

Managing by decree is not about maintaining efficiency or cajoling sales or fine-tuning, which are Three concerns. Managing by decree is useful, even desirable, when things are falling apart and you need a strong leader, not warm fuzzies. And if you need to change your decree, you are not bound by any participatory democracy. You just issue another decree.

Eights can be magnificent, bold wheeler-dealers and behind-the-scenes consensus builders. Nines create consensus by finding the overlap in people's positions and progressively fuzzying the boundaries. Eights hammer out agreement, like the physically intimidating, in-your-face Lyndon Johnson did when he was Senate majority leader. Compare Johnson's forceful, gut-based Eight energy with the sharp-edged cerebral energy of House Speaker Newt Gingrich, a Seven, who aligns his troops around enthusiasm for "new ideas" and mental gymnastics. Or compare Johnson to the previous Republican House leaders Gerald Ford and Bob Michel, both round-edged Nines, who settled into comfortable collaboration with the opposition without causing much of a ruckus.

The Eight approach is effective in taming unstable, uncharted environments where strong force of will, even brashness, is needed. Eights don't get distracted by the needs of others for structure or clear agreements (like Ones) or excessive consideration for the rights of others (like Nines). Certain rough markets are the Eight milieu: real estate development, heavy industries, big oil—all of which have histories of riding over people, competitors, government agencies, and Mother Earth. Eights can also be useful in the rough-and-tumble environments of telecommunications, media, and high technology.

Frequently Eights don't realize how intimidating they can be. Oscar, an Eight who is the new chief operating officer of one of the East Coast's largest medical centers, introduces himself to people around the building by approaching them without so much as a hello. He examines their name badge and demands, "Tell me who you are, what you do, and why you're qualified to do it." He thinks he's getting to know the troops. People run the other way when they see him.

Most Eights enjoy crushing challenges to their authority. They don't have much respect for lines of authority that don't go through them. I once asked Oscar if he felt that he was a team player. "Damn right," he said. "Team captain." Says Hugo, an Eight professor, "I like tough intellectual challenges to my ideas—and I despise intellectual wimps—but my students damn well better remember whose class they're in. Fight as hard as you want, just so you remember it's my gym."

The Eight Work Style

Eights generally prefer jobs that allow them a high degree of autonomy and working environments where relationships are fluid. The less an Eight employee has to deal with complicated office procedures, the better. Sue, a former flight attendant and an Eight, liked her job for that reason: "We rarely followed the manual when we were doing the service because we had all figured out a much better way. Fortunately, we had very little direct supervision. And working with other flight attendants was no problem because you knew it was never going to last. You'd have somebody else to work with the next week."

Eights easily come into their own when empire building and entrepreneurship are required for success, and where a strong will and a thick skin count as advantages. They excel and are happiest as managers of their fiefdom, whether in sales or marketing or logistics or running institutions or factories or franchises. They can be magnanimous and terrific when they feel they have the power they need but aggressive and unpleasant when they feel oppressed, impotent, or under somebody else's thumb.

Eight employees can work especially well with, or against, Eight bosses. "I don't have a problem working for a boss if I can respect him," says Tom, who works for a real estate developer, another Eight. "If he's not worthy of respect, he shouldn't be king of the mountain and he won't be for long." Both Eights understand the rules of a power game. "I don't have a problem working with anybody," says Don, another Eight. "Sometimes people have a problem working with me."

Some Eights are not cut out to be employees, ever. In her one-woman off-Broadway show, *Blown Sideways Through Life*, Claudia Shear, an Eight, describes the sixty-five jobs she's held in her short life. The slightest whiff of humiliation caused her to quit and move on. "To smile and say yes makes me feel like my mouth is packed full of sand and shit," she declaims. "I'm not letting the world of bosses and money define my day." Shear sees herself as a gladiator, not as a go-getter employee, like a Three. To her, holding down a job involves "suffering and striving in great feats of strength and tests of character."

The Eight Learning Style

Eights, like Threes, favor hands-on experience. They want to test things out in the real world. In a workshop or training session, they want contact. But unlike Threes, who want to get with and star in the program, Eights are provocateurs who ask bold questions. They won't be tied to their chairs. They like to move around, to engage their bodies. Mind games bore them. Give them the stimulation they crave. Don't be surprised if they're contentious or take up a lot of space; they enjoy people's reactions to their outrageousness. Let them have their fun if you can. But Eights like to test the boundaries; make sure you are clear where they are.

The Eight Organization

The Eight system is a response to a rough-and-tumble marketplace where there's not a lot of time or space for ruminating, for give and take, or for creating consensus. A flood rescue team, for example, can't worry a lot about ruffling feathers in the middle of a crisis. Success in such a setting requires a strong, directed will and the ability to act on it—both Eight attributes.

In such an organization, complex human issues take a backseat to will and power. Problems tend to get resolved by the contestants knocking heads; toe-to-toe hashing it out is standard fare in this culture. Shrinking violets don't do well here.

Such environments as the worldwide media conglomerates, real estate development, shipping, heavy industries, and, in the last century, steel and railroads, would have invented Eights if they had not already existed. Such industries value the Eight ability to stand tough against the ruthless competition, against government regulators, against competing stakeholders (like landowners or, more lately, environmentalists), and most especially against the chaos of their market sector. (Interestingly, once they have accomplished their powerhouse mission, many Eight organizations, such as railroads and steel, seem to turn into Nines.)

Eight organizations are the best when you need to move swiftly and decisively—perhaps brutally—to eliminate the competition and to firm up market share. They're generally organized around the imperatives of the Great Leader or the Grand Plan, either of which aims to "rule the world" by gobbling up or pulverizing the competition and other obstacles in the way. Anheuser-Busch, the brewer, is an Eight company—there is no one more belligerent in the beer business—who crushes the competition with inundatory advertising and overpowering distribution.

Microsoft is another case in point. Its cravings for power seem endless. *Fortune* magazine asks, "Is there anything Bill Gates doesn't want?" In its current incarnation, Microsoft's reputation is not for efficiency or for developing the most ingenious or highest quality of products or even for getting to the marketplace first. Indeed, says *Fortune*, "Microsoft has been notorious for producing inelegant products that are frequently inferior to the competition and for bringing them to the market way behind schedule."[7] Rather, Microsoft is famous for crushing negotiations with those with whom it deals and for unfettered use of its marketing muscle. (Compare with the Three operation McDonald's, which intentionally made its suppliers—the bakers, potato farmers, and paper goods manufacturers—part of the team and fabulously wealthy. McDonald's tightly held its suppliers to strict specifications but as part of a collaboration.)

At its best, the Eight organization's power and strength really do get the job done. Eight organizations create action and excitement and set the rules of the game, the standards by which others play. They take bold risks. When these pay off, as with Microsoft, Eight organizations leave their mark on a grand scale.

Getting the Best from an Eight

When Eights are stressed, they feel their isolation and impotence at Stress Point Five. The big bear retreats into the cave to lick his wounds, mend his boundary fence, and get some perspective on events.

Instead of being bulls in the china shop of life, using their power to take what they imagine they want, Eights evolve when they use their power in the service of others, the perspective of Eight's High Performance Point Two.

Eights, tough pragmatists, leave their illusions—and their idealism—at Shadow Point Seven. When Eights balance Seven's idealism about *the way things should be* with Nine's acceptance of *the way things are*, they act with natural power. Innocence is the virtue of Eight. Ally Point Nine is Eight's peaceable kingdom—what every lion king or queen wants.

Stress Point: Five

Eights express anger easily, both in the normal course of business and when they are upset. You may say about your Eight boss, "The old man is yelling and screaming and barking orders. He must be under stress." But Eights naturally operate at full blast. Knocking heads, even in a pretty boisterous way, is generally agreeable for an Eight. They thrive on big feelings.

When Eights *really* experience stress, the famous Eight power plant goes into meltdown. Eights at Stress Point Five feel their power source dry up. That is truly stressful, even terrifying, for an Eight. Under stress, an Eight may feel like she's losing it or falling apart. You'll know the Eight you work with is under stress when you see her being a voyeur instead of an actor, being introspective and trying to figure out what's going on, feeling that she doesn't have enough facts to decide what to do next (which normally won't give an Eight pause).

But Stress Point Five isn't all bad for Eights. At Five, Eights pull back. They regroup and are thoughtful instead of active. They look dispassionately at events, amass information, gain perspective, and renew their energies. Said Tom, an Eight manager who was afraid he might be fired in a round of downsizings at his plant, "I got very quiet and very prepared every day. I just concentrated on my own work. I broke all the assignments down and parceled them out. I got all the information I needed so that I could think clearly.

When they brought me in for a long talk, I think I saved myself because I was low-key and I had my ducks in a row."

The Eight-Five line is about knowledge at one end and power at the other, two sides of the same coin. Fives know that knowledge is power. Eights know that power is knowledge: that acting with power in the world is the only pathway to real knowledge of it.

High Performance Point: Two

When Eights move to Two they use their mighty powers and charisma to champion the individuals in their care. They become protective and nurturing *servant leaders*. Their goals become aligned with the goals of those for whom they are responsible. They make it happen because they honor and are affected by the sensibilities of others.

Viola, an Eight entertainment attorney known for her gruff, combative approach, told me how much easier and enjoyable it was for her to negotiate an agreement when all the principals and lawyers involved were women, because, she said, "Regardless of where any of us are coming from, we all meet at Two. My whole approach just changes. Everyone's focused on making the deal reflect the best interests of all the others. Nobody's trying to walk over anybody because our feelings are right on the table with everything else for all to see. There is a mutuality that just doesn't happen in the rest of the business. Everyone is looking out for everyone else, and everyone trusts that nobody's trying to do anybody else any harm; if they did it would come back to them in spades."

Wings

Shadow Point: Seven

Eights are as idealistic as Sevens. That's why they get so angry. Eights believe in a just world (as they see it) and explode when they see an injustice—to themselves or others. Their anger boils over when their vision is frustrated.

Eights are brutal realists on the surface, but underneath they are playful idealists, sentimental about the possibility of a positive future (just like Sevens). Eights spend a lot of their time puncturing the inflation of others, but owning their own shadow can carry these generally earthbound folk like a balloon. They increase their effectiveness with a lighter touch and a more expansive outlook, the view from above. Instead of hacking out a path straight in front of them, they see a plethora of alternatives, choosing the appropriate one with agility and grace instead of trying to power the square peg into the round hole.

Ally Point: Nine

Eights have the same problem with bold, direct action that Fours have with feelings: they are so inside any activity they undertake that they lack a context or frame of reference by which to appreciate or understand it. When Eights move to Nine they are still profoundly powerful actors, but they are aware of the frame of reference (the other people, the team, the company) in which they operate.

Nine is the homey, peaceable kingdom where the Eight lion king can lie down with the lamb. When they move to Nine, Eights go with the flow instead of making their own. Nine, the Enneagram home of balance, is *the* natural moderator of the Eight's habitual excess. Nine's power comes from merging and yielding, which practitioners of the martial arts know is the most powerful stance of all.

"Eight's energy is as an igniter and an empowerer," Bob, an Eight union activist, told me. "Once you've empowered people, then you need to shut up and get out of the way. That's the hardest thing for an Eight to do." Eight instigates events. Nine allows them to happen. The best advice for an Eight is: allow, allow, allow.

Cardinal Rules

If You Work with an Eight

- Show up. Eights hate it when you flake out on them.
- Spit it out. Eights like the news quick and straight. Don't waffle. Don't embellish.
- Don't whine, either. The Eight doesn't want to hear your excuses; she wants results.
- Eights want respect. Much like Twos, who need to be respected for their indispensable contributions, Eights need to be respected as substantial figures, not petty functionaries.
- When you're blasted by an Eight, don't simply blast back. Standing up to an Eight is different from raising the stakes, which gives them no choice but to annihilate you in return. Acknowledge their power but acknowledge your own, too.
- Don't ever tell an Eight what he can't do. You will bring down molten lava on your head as he proceeds to do it.
- Explain problems in black-and-white terms. Eights have little tolerance for subtlety or philosophical context.

- Do you need this fight? If not, close the deal without it. Is this clause essential to the deal? If it is, explain to the Eight that it is a deal breaker, and be prepared to back it up.
- Tough as it may be, Eights invariably prefer that you tell them directly and bluntly when they are screwing up or making you mad instead of holding on to your anger and resentment. Iciness drives them nuts. Silence is their stress point. Much better to have it out and get it over with; the Eight's not likely to hold a grudge in this type of situation.
- Eights like to be in charge of their bailiwick, which they naturally try to expand. If you don't want your Eight employee constantly nipping at your heels, set clear limits and be prepared to for him to test them repeatedly. (He can't help it if he's an Eight.)

If You Are an Eight

- Feeling screwed is not the same thing as being screwed. Check your automatic impulse to retaliate until you've checked out the situation.
- Become an even more powerful Eight by expanding your arsenal to include listening and negotiation (see Ally Point Nine). Let other people finish thinking and speaking before you jump in. Give their views the merit they deserve.
- Choose your battles. Ask yourself, Is it worth it? Before you bulldoze someone, ask yourself whether you're willing to deal with the consequences (such having to apologize—or being fired).
- Don't burn your bridges so quickly. What goes around comes around. People who annoy you don't need to die a painful death for every mistake they make. Maybe you can still get some good things out of them.
- For many people, your threats, tirades, and tantrums are just not effective, no matter how enjoyable they may be for you. Be specific about what action on the part of the person you are threatening will actually satisfy you.
- Don't assume it's okay for you to intrude. Instead, ask permission. Be diplomatic: "Can I come in?" "May I offer a suggestion?" Listen for the response. Learn what rules you are violating before you violate them.
- Find ways of drawing on the talents of others so they can join your team with a sense of ownership and empowerment rather than as hired hands. This comes from learning their aspirations (the perspective of High Performance Point Two). Instead of habitually testing for their weaknesses, use your Eight powers to power up their positive potential (see Shadow Point Five).

- Be aware that your impulse to excoriate someone may be a sign of your insecurity about keeping control or your fear of your own exposure or your own vulnerabilities.
- Consider whether your preoccupation with fairness and protecting the underdog puts others on the defensive unnecessarily.
- Be aware that exhausting yourself through rage or sensual indulgences may be a way of avoiding uncomfortable feelings.

1. Leo Rosten, *People I Have Known, Loved or Admired* (New York: McGraw-Hill, 1970), 66.
2. Charles Barkley and Roy S. Johnson, *Outrageous!* (New York: Simon & Schuster, 1992), 47–48.
3. Barkley and Johnson, *Outrageous!*, 27–28.
4. Barry Diller, quoted by Robert Sam Anson, "Heave-ho, Heave-ho! Mike Eisner Drives TV Head Out of His Grumpy Kingdom," *New York Observer*, March 27, 1995, 20.
5. Anson, "Heave-ho," 20.
6. Roy Greenslade, *The Rise and Fall of Robert Maxwell and His Empire* (New York: Carol Publishing, 1992), 102.
7. *Fortune* (January 16, 1995), 35.

NINE

The Mediator

AKA	The Natural, the Peacemaker, the Negotiator
Worldview	Everything will work out if we stay calm, amiable, and connected.
High Side	Empathic, available, unaffected, steady, reliable, humble, warm, salt of the earth
Low Side	Apathetic, lazy, resistant to change, indecisive, boring, wedded to habit, lost in space
Leadership Style	Collegial, participatory, inclusive, reactive, sharing credit; and—sometimes—passive-aggressive and stubborn
Credo	Let it be. Don't push the river.
Appeal to	Peace, harmony, unity, team spirit, fairness, selflessness, inevitability, least disruptive alternative
Don't Appeal to	Competition, one right way, your authority, their authority, deadlines
Talk/Communication Style	Sagas, epics (lengthy, rambling, repetitive narratives), maundering
Makes You Feel	Accepted, understood, calmed, warmly held; and—sometimes—uncertain as to what is wanted, cotton headed, lost, overwhelmed, and furious at their sweet stagnation
Appearance	Calm, simple, lived-in, comfy, homey, sometimes disheveled and unkempt
Good Work Setting	Stable and predictable, with clear delineation of responsibilities, collegial, mutually supportive, low conflict

Difficult Work Setting	Authoritarian, high pressure, low human relations component
Books	*On Becoming a Person* by Carl Rogers *The Functions of the Executive* by Chester Barnard *Confessions* by Saint Augustine
Sayings	"I have spent most of my life studying the lives of other peoples." —Margaret Mead "Let me chew it over." "Learn to live with it." "We shall not be moved." "Don't rock the boat." "Don't argue. Just don't do it." "We are the world." "Live and let live."
Of the Nine Persuasion	Dwight Eisenhower, Ronald Reagan, Gerald Ford, Lance Ito, Julia Child, Ringo Starr, John Major, Bruce Babbitt, Chester Barnard, Carl Rogers, John Goodman, Gabby Hayes, Dan Quayle, Edith Bunker, Margaret Mead, Queen Elizabeth II, Nancy Kerrigan, Jerry Seinfeld, the U.S. Postal Service, Bali, Polynesia
High Performance	3 Direct, focused action toward a clear goal
Stress	6 Driven to action by paranoia, doubt, fear of catastrophe, or the intentions of others
Ally	1 *Energized* by order, by getting priorities straight, by knowing there is a clear right and a clear wrong
Shadow	8 *Grounded* by the direct exercise of power, by feeling, expressing, and acting on will, anger, and dominion, by being willing to engage
Virtue	Right Action
Vice	Laziness

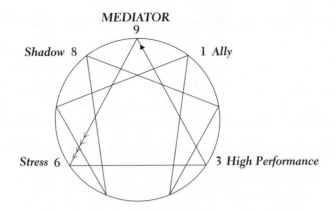

Getting to Know a Nine

Tom's Story

Tom, director of social services for a Midwestern state, has worked happily in state government all his life. Before being promoted to the top spot, he was deputy director of his agency for many years under three different directors. Tom was never sure he wanted the head job, but eventually it fell open, the governor was in a hurry, and Tom had so much experience and so few enemies that he became the consensus choice. He's been a huge success.

"If you don't know him really well he seems to have the soul of a vice president," says one member of the agency's board of advisers. "He always seems concerned with how everyone else is doing. Do they have what they need to get their jobs done? Do they feel their careers are on track? The joke about Tom is that when he dies, someone else's life will flash before his eyes."

Tom's employees describe him as "extremely likable," "unassuming," and "not the kind of guy to get upset." "His most prominent trait is a spirit of collaboration. He's a partnership guy," says Aaron, a key deputy. "This makes him very well regarded, even by factions who don't get along themselves." Not one to micromanage, Tom gives very broad directions and plenty of latitude to carry them out.

"I've never heard him raise his voice or lose his cool," says Nancy, one of his managers. "He's very good at seeing his own weaknesses and the truth in what other people say," she continues. "You go into to argue with him, and he encourages you and agrees with you!"

While Tom is calm, the people who report to him always seem to be arguing about something. (I pointed out to him that they're graciously doing his arguing for him.) In particular, they argue about what direction to take in the absence of clear direction from him. "He's a great guy," says one employee. "I just wish he'd make clearer what he wants us to do on these tough questions. But he hates being pressured. The worst thing you can do is go in there with a sense of urgency and try to force a decision out of him. He'll listen and nod pleasantly, but he won't do anything. But when we go in there with a clear dis-agreement among ourselves, he's brilliant. He seems to come alive. That's how he likes to decide. He lets us argue, and he mediates a solution."

Every year for the last twenty Tom has ridden in a seven-day bicycle rally — not a race — that goes from one end of his state to the other. Thousands of people participate. Tom rides with his friends from college, with whom he shares a support van; hats from each year of the ride are arrayed on his office wall. "Why do you continue that, after all this time?" I kid him. "I like keepin' on keepin' on," he says. "I do the same thing in my work. I stick around, and the results that are supposed to happen do happen."

The agency's nationally acclaimed mediation program is a case in point. Tom's baby, the program is staffed by volunteers who offer mediation as an al-ternative to state-mandated "due process hearings" for welfare recipients who want to contest rulings of the department. Tom was extremely committed to the program for many years. But he never forced it on people. "The legal people, the financial people, and the bureaucrats all had objections," Tom says, "but that mediation program had a life of its own. We just kept proposing and reproposing until we had some consensus, or maybe everybody else just ran out of steam. I just stayed with it."

"This is a service organization," says Tom. "It's not about us. It's about the clients. The mediation program makes sure everyone gets a chance to be heard. *Then the solutions find themselves.*"

"Nobody is more connected to the clientele than Tom," said one em-ployee.

He points over his shoulder. "Now you know why I have that F. Scott Fitzgerald quote on my bulletin board." It reads: "The test of a first-rate intelli-gence is the ability to hold two opposed ideas in the mind at the same time and still retain the ability to function."

Do you recognize Tom? Tom is a Nine.

The Basic Premise

Nines are the most easygoing of all the Enneagram types. Able to compromise easily, they're so in tune with the intentions of their fellows that they lose sight of their own intentions, desires, purposes, and needs. Their *selflessness* and their sensitivity to other people's often-irreconcilable views makes them naturals for mediating, counseling, consensus building, and calming things down.

Deliberate and *slow moving*, Nines resist succumbing to pressure, especially pressure for closure. "It'll happen when it happens," says a Nine. They take the time to listen to your story, to discuss your project's pros and cons, and to allow the proper direction to emerge naturally. ("Never run for a bus," advised Mel Brooks as the two-thousand-year-old man, a Nine. "There will always be another.") At the same time, this laid-back attitude sometimes means Nines lack a sense of purposefulness. Co-workers may see them as spacey and neglectful, slow-talking and slow-walking bureaucrats who are easily overwhelmed and don't do what they say they are going to do.

If the go-getter Three is a typically American style on both coasts, Nine is a characteristic social style of the country's middle. Many modern presidents who were Nines came from such middle American stock: Eisenhower, Ford, and Reagan were all beloved, with sunny dispositions and a healthy respect for tradition, quintessentially *folksy* men, amiable fence-sitters who were tranquil and warm amid the tumult that swirled about them. Nines tend to be decent, persistent, "the salt of the earth." They can be beguilingly self-effacing, as was Gerald Ford in his first speech to Congress as president. To the many doubting his ability to perform magic in tough post-Watergate times, he emphasized reliability over flash. "I'm a Ford, not a Lincoln," he said unassumingly, like a true Nine.

At their best, Nines are the philosopher's stones of the Enneagram. The magical philosopher's stone had the power to change base substances into pure gold, without itself changing. Nines can see your gifts, your real needs, and your calling, and they naturally have the empathic skills to bring these forth, often without your realizing it.

What Nines sometimes give up for the ability to bring out the best in others is the ability to do the same for themselves. Nines lose their own way when they get swept up in other people's agendas and projects. They may wake up hours or days or years later and feel betrayed, frustrated, and furiously angry for having lost themselves.

Nines can see the Promised Land, they can direct others to it, but all too often they fail to claim it for themselves. The biblical Moses, a reluctant leader and a quintessential Nine, resisted claiming his own destiny as long as he could, telling God that God had picked the wrong man. Like a typical Nine manager sandwiched between his boss and his employees, Moses was torn between a jealous God whom he had to appease and a whining, disobedient people he had to chastise. But he rarely lost his patience—until he descended from Sinai and discovered the Israelites worshiping a golden calf, at which point he hurled to the ground the tablets on which God had written the Ten Commandments, breaking them. This rare display of anger, according to some accounts, cost him his right to enter the Promised Land, the worst possible punishment for a Nine who just wants to be part of the group. It is no wonder Nines have learned to be cautious about directly expressing their anger. Like Moses, every Nine can tell you a story of how he angrily went to bat for himself and got whacked.

Psychology

As children, Nines learned to repress their own longings for the sake of avoiding conflict and staying connected to those they cared about. Likes Eights and Ones (their fellows in the power triad), they adjusted their own will in order to survive. Eights responded to this dilemma by insisting on their own way in all things, and Ones by identifying with the oppressor and insisting on the *oppressor's* will in all things. Nines, in contrast, took the middle route between adherence at One and defiance at Eight. They learned to expertly maintain the peace and stay connected to others by appearing to acquiesce, by empathizing with all sides of a question and all parties to an argument, and by squelching their own needs, views, desires, and will. Secretly (usually unconsciously), Nines resented that they had to give themselves up.

Some Nines had warring parents, and the Nine was torn between them. Other Nines came from big families, where expressing strong individual desires was impossible or disruptive. Some Nines had an intrusive or willful authority who did not consider the Nine's position. This is reflected in what Freud called "the battle of the chamber pot." Nines gave in, or appeared to have given in.

Nines' strategy was to go along to get along. They learned to deaden any extremes of feeling, most especially the feeling of *desire*. Having desire means wanting and choosing—dangerous enterprises if you want to stay merged with others and free of conflict. (Compare with Four, who is addicted to desire *and* the feeling of being a solitary exile.) This deadening of feeling makes adult Nines appear comfortable, at ease with themselves, even spiritually advanced. Everything seems to be copacetic with them. But in fact, many adult Nines have forfeited their highs and lows as a result of this false compromise with the world. "Accept me," the Nine says, "and I'll give up my anger, my strong feelings, my own agenda, my self." But these feelings can be suppressed for only so long.

The Good News

Nines are people of enormous *goodwill*. Slow and steady, they can labor away in the pack, supporting and encouraging the needs, ideas, and agendas of others. Unlike Threes or Eights, they don't seek the limelight; but if it should come toward them, that's fine, too.

Natural Mediators

Nines intuitively sense what the ancient Eastern sages knew: that what appear to be opposites are really just differences in perspective. They have an uncanny ability to create balance. More than anyone else on the Enneagram, they know how to *tolerate paradoxes* and contradictions. They can see the truth in contrary opinions (and Enneagram styles) simultaneously and move from position to position with integrity. At their best, Nines are the true masters of the Enneagram.

Rarely drawn to extremes, Nines expertly work the middle. A Three who hears complaints in the customer service department of a large store is likely to see himself as representing the store to the public. An antiauthoritarian Six might see herself as a consumer advocate in opposition to management. A Nine is likely to see herself as occupying some kind of middle ground, a mediator between the company and the customer.

"Being in the middle means appreciating both sides," says Donna, a director of human resources. "I usually see a lot more wiggle room than the people I work with."

Nines are terrific team builders precisely because they are able to see so many different perspectives simultaneously. "I'm always very conscious of what contribution people are making to the group, even if they're unaware of it," says Steve, a Nine product manager. No one who works with an evolved Nine feels left out.

A similar process is at work in mediation. Because they have the special talent of identifying with whomever is speaking at the moment, Nines give all of the parties in conflict a sense of being heard and understood. This is precisely what makes mediation work. The best mediation involves a reciprocal disclosure that leads to mutual understanding. The parties come to an agreement because they understand and empathize with each other's positions. Many of the other Enneagram points think they are good at this, but Nines are the real naturals.

Expert at Empowering Others

Nines at their best know how to get the best out of the people who work with them. While unevolved Nines who don't know how to say no take on other people's problems and get stuck in them, evolved Nines know that each individual has his or her own best answers. "I used to think that when my employees came to me with a problem I either had to tell them how to solve it or do the work myself," said Linda, the director of a philanthropic foundation. "Now I figure out how to help them do it, without getting sucked in." Nines empower others by respecting their ability to be independently competent and capable; the odd paradox is that Nines don't always do the same for themselves.

Kerm Campbell, the CEO of the leading-edge furniture manufacturer Herman Miller, tells of an encounter with a longtime employee. "He was working on a program, and I asked how it was coming along. He replied he hadn't done much about it and wanted to know what my position was. I told him simply that my position was his position. He seemed quite surprised, but he got the point."[1]

The great Nine psychologist, Carl Rogers, based a whole psychotherapy on this principle. Declining to suggest or impose solutions on his clients, he offered them instead what he called "unconditional positive regard," acknowledging their worth and significance without evaluating or judging them. According to Rogers, such emotional acceptance freed up answers the client already knew but were hidden from view. This is something that Nines tend to do for others quite naturally. It is also the best way to help a Nine thrive at work, since Nines prefer not to push themselves or their ideas forward, and they tend to wilt under criticism or in overtly competitive situations.

Sometimes people confuse Nines and Twos because both types seem to focus on serving others. But Twos expertly track your feelings as they keep their own goals in view, adjusting their persona but not their agenda. Nines, on the other hand, keep their persona the same, but their agenda is as malleable as silly putty. Twos actively seek out the specific needs and desires of others and pointedly respond to them; Nines create the opportunity for you to be comfortably yourself rather than hopping to meet your specific needs. Lisa, a Nine who is the head of public relations for a large university, says, "I work very hard to get senior management to spend time with me. Every one of them is different. Some like a formal agenda with scheduled time. The president likes me to be available for Sunday afternoon phone calls. A lot of the deans like to catch me on the fly. The best way for me to do my job is to make it easy for those I work for to take the time to share their priorities with me. In order to do that I am extremely flexible and responsive. Please don't think I'm not aggressive. I aggressively harmonize with their schedules and their styles. Creating time and space for others is not an easy job."

Easygoing

Nines are the best on the Enneagram at "going with the flow." Unlike Ones, they rarely impose a rigid agenda or, as Fives do, a problem-solving framework. Responsive to the other players, they have a sense of the larger picture and are happiest operating by feel. For Nines, life and work are complex *organic* processes that you mess with at your peril. Here is the most influential management theorist of the 1930s and '40s, Chester Barnard, a Nine who was an executive with the telephone company: "There are an enormous number of things that people have to do on this earth that have to operate just as the physiological system operates, without conscious control. The minute you get conscious about it you lose the control." Such an organic Nine organizational approach is being revisited as systems theory, chaos theory, and group-as-a-whole approaches.

Consistent and Committed

Nines are consistent. Sevens are great planners; they have great ideas and enthusiasms, but you can't rely on them day in and day out. Nines, creatures of habit, make planning possible. "I like to get in at my regular time, get my coffee, read the paper, then get into my routine," says Donna, the human resources manager. "My employees know how I like things. My bosses know what to expect. I get a lot done. I've always found that you get a lot of credit just for being consistent."

Although they may prefer not to act or may wait until they are forced to act, once they get going Nines, like their colleagues Eight and One in the power triad, are hard workers who are quite methodical and deliberate.

The Bad News

Well, he's a good listener, but he really doesn't seem to hear.
—Said of Ronald Reagan

The core problem for Nines is that they substitute others' values and agendas for their own. This can lead to a warm and fuzzy sense of belonging bought at the price of their own aspirations.

With their urge to merge, Nine employees often fade into the background. Nine bosses generally can't afford to be invisible, but they will tend to diffuse even functional boundaries and goals. This can make cottonheads of those they work with. When Odysseus's men stopped in the Land of the Lotus Eaters they lost any desire to do anything, forgot their way home, and nearly sucked Odysseus in with them.

Lotus-eating Nines can do that to you. Friendly and accepting on the surface, they seem to say, "Come in from the cold, hard world and work with us. Our department/division/company is cozy and warm." Who could argue? But the dark side of Nine harbors lethal intent. "To work with us, you'll have to give up the parts of you that don't fit. You'll have to give up the rough edges of your personality, which do not contribute to harmony. We are completely accepting of you so long as you merge with us." Nines at their most invidious give lip service to diversity but force everyone to conform on matters of the will.

"I once switched divisions at an electronics manufacturer from a large, cutthroat, production-driven division run by a Three to a small, offbeat research division run by a Nine," recalls Leslie, a One. "At first I was ecstatic because everyone seemed like one big happy family. But it didn't take long to see the price my colleagues were paying. The job was sold to me as 'not driven by the bottom line,' which was true, but that also meant there was no individual feedback. Our Nine boss wanted everyone to feel part of the team, not competitive with others. But he made it hard to get excited about your job or to be imaginative. I thrive on feedback, but we never had any performance reviews, and he hated it when I would try to schedule a meeting with him each year to talk about my compensation. The year I gave up and didn't ask for a raise was the year I got the most substantial raise of all. I think I was rewarded for finally getting with the program and not causing him aggravation."

Conflict Avoiders

Nines avoid confrontation and conflict, not because they're political or strategic like Sixes, but because they prefer, as we've seen, to "go with the flow." This can be a wonderfully high-minded approach or the ultimate in selling out. Nines are the grand appeasers of the Enneagram.

Judge Lance Ito is a case in point. The qualities of judicial temperament that led to Ito's assignment to the O. J. Simpson trial in the first place—his calm, even, slow-to-anger style, his obsessive balancing of both sides—also served to undermine his control of the proceedings. Ito's informality and self-effacing humor diffused a good amount of tension and conflict during the early stages of the case, but while striving to be a "nice Nine" he forfeited his power and authority. He let the trial meander without a definite schedule. He allowed himself to be pressured by angry lawyers on both sides who argued that the other side was getting preferential treatment, a pitch brilliantly calculated to put a terminally evenhanded Nine on tilt. When he did get upset, he would quickly apologize, somewhat embarrassed, rather than letting his justifiable anger have real impact.

Unwilling to take strong positions and stick by them, Ito regularly waffled. Very quickly the attorneys discovered that the firmest of his stern threats, rules, and rulings were open to negotiation. When late in the proceedings he tried to stick to his guns on several rulings, he seemed tinny and overbearing.

Nine managers regularly find themselves pulled in different directions. Bob, who runs a career counseling franchise with twenty full- and part-time consultants, is forever trying to figure out how to divide up resources. "Bob pretty much goes along with whoever spoke to him last," says Maryellen, who works for him. "He just doesn't want to disappoint the person he's looking at."

For Nines, the desire to avoid conflict often results in a certain resignation. Because they feel ineffective to begin with, and because the entrenched forces seem immutable, making a change or taking a stand seems to require so much energy and focus. Instead, Nines tend to accept what's presented. "And that's the way it is," sighed the Nine Walter Cronkite every night. Cronkite also remarked, "The very constraint against taking positions is a mark of the professional in journalism. I've spent a lifetime suppressing them."

Slow to Take Action

Either this man is dead or my watch has stopped.

—*Groucho Marx*

For many Nines, the evil twin of "going with the flow" is a determined resistance to conscious, planned change. Nines are the best stonewallers on the Enneagram. They have a special talent for stubbornness, for digging in their heels, for feeling eminently justified in refusing to act, all the while appearing to agree to go along.

Many Nines come off as sluggish and inert. Like a big oil tanker sitting deep in the water, they can find it hard to get started, and then once they do, it is hard for them to change direction. Why is this? Because so much must be taken into account when Nines make a change: their own views, those of their fellows and the company, the views of their customers and competitors, politics and technology, even ethical and philosophical considerations. Obsessive Nines naturally ruminate on such things as part of an ongoing stream of consciousness that may be barely noticeable to outsiders. For them, there is no small change, there is only the prospect of exhaustion.

June, for example, is very bright, but she has settled into a cataloguer's job at a large direct-marketing firm, despite the fact that she is trained as a computer programmer. When programming jobs come up in-house, as they do with some regularity, she makes herself dizzy with "considerations": "Oh, so-and-so is also qualified, and he wants it more than I do," or "I'm okay where I am. Why stir things up?" Just recently, she became friendly with the manager of another department, who offered her just the type of programming job she's said for months she wants. June is pleased that the manager came to her (many Nines prefer to be discovered than to audition). Has she leaped at the chance? Not yet. "I have to stay unemotional," she told me, "because getting too excited can throw you off. The problem is that if I really wanted a programming job I could probably do a little better at another company.

"I hate to be disappointed. If I don't want it too much, then I won't be. I never go whole hog for anything, so there's some consolation when I don't get it."

Can't See the Trees for the Forest

Nines invariably see events in a larger context. Nines are remarkable for understanding the dynamics of larger systems, but when it comes to the Nine's own work life, taking a global view can lead to stagnation. "What does it really matter?" asks this type of Nine, for whom no events are of consequence. Other Nines, overreacting against getting subsumed by the global view, hold on for dear life to habit and rigidly overfocus on small but manageable details. "If you want red file folders, you have to buy them yourself and keep them in your office," said Emily, a Nine office manager. "The only ones we order for the supply cabinet are manila."

An industrialist and investor from South America, a Nine, called me about a conflict he was having with some partners in a mining business. I asked him to describe his role in the venture. I expected a two-minute disquisition. Instead he said, "To understand me you have to understand the Spanish colonization of South America." And he began a fascinating hour-and-a-half discussion of the history of the Spanish and their wars with and domination of the Indians. He told me with outrage how the Spanish raped the mines. They didn't understand consequences. Neither did his current partners, which was the basis of his struggle with them. They wanted to get in and get out quickly. He saw the advantages of the business deal, but he also wanted to respect the physical environment and the workers. He saw that the government would be involved. And he did not want to repeat the mistakes of history.

At first I found the industrialist's point of view admirable. A true Nine, he understood the ripple effect of his actions. Then I began to feel sorry for his partners, who wanted a simple business plan.

The solution was an easy bit of magic for a Nine: Why not both? Sometimes Nines become rigid because, from experience, they are so afraid of giving themselves away. Masters of compromise on behalf of others, they fear that any compromise they make on their own behalf means someone will run roughshod over their aspirations, as happened when they were children. They forget to negotiate on their own behalf, even though no one is more equipped on the Enneagram to accommodate multiple realities. "Grind out the business plan, like a Three," I said. "But that needn't limit you. In addition, explain to your partners where you are coming from, or you won't be able to work with them in a serious way."

He was completely delighted. He hadn't thought he could have his way and also have the deal. He was afraid he would have to choose his partners' way or lose his connection to the venture. Nines can be hopeless and resigned; the notion that they can get their own needs met *and* stay connected to their group is life changing.

Easily Distracted

Nines' reluctance to narrow their focus sometimes means they're attracted to the irrelevant and inconsequential like moths to a flame. They pursue distractions the way Sixes pursue plots against them. (They'll find them, whether they are there or not.) Masters of trivial pursuits, they can be easily sidetracked by interruptions and by other people when they're trying to do their own work.

At their worst, Nines pay attention to the circumference rather than the central point. They may talk a lot, but their circumlocutions serve to obscure rather than clarify. At the same time that they're telling you more than you want to know, they're also telling you less. Jan, a Three who works in marketing at an international manufacturer, says, "The reference librarian here is a Nine. Sometimes I need a quick answer to a question, but I dread calling her. She keeps you on the phone forever turning the problem every which way. Then she sends you reference books, magazine articles, printouts off the Internet, more than you could ever need. By the time the stuff arrives, you've forgotten your question." At some level Nines don't believe that you have heard them or that they have made an impact, so they bombard you with words and material to make sure they have connected. (Compare with Fives, antipodes across the Enneagram, who are so sensitive to contact that they are stingy with their goodies. A little seems like a lot.)

When work requires intense commitment and focus, Nine's tendency to keep too many questions open can get in the way. Scratch a Nine who's spending an inordinate amount of time and energy selecting new stationery or office plants, perhaps even wondering if he is in the right career altogether, and you may well find someone who feels unable to fight for a desired career track within a company or claim important turf after a reorganization.

Disengaged

Nines may appear mellow and without a care in the world, but in worldly matters, at least, their very unflappability can make them careless about details and follow-up.

When my uncle died some years ago, I was responsible for transferring his stock portfolio from his estate to an account at a brokerage firm and then distributing it to the rest of the family. The firm completely screwed things up. I was upset. "Don't worry," said the manager of the firm's District of Columbia office, a Nine who was not even slightly exercised. "In a hundred years no one will care." He meant to soothe me, but instead he made me furious, a common reaction to Nine's lack of engagement. In the end, everything came out as it should, except that it happened on "Nine time." You can't hurry Nine; you'll just have to wait. Try to hurry them, and they'll dig in their heels.

Shelly, a therapist who runs a county counseling agency, almost never returns a phone call on the same day she receives the message, even from colleagues. "There is nothing so urgent," she says, "that won't benefit by a little cooling off. Often the problems take care of themselves." Some problems do; others, however, don't. Either way, Nines invariably choose the slow cooker over the pressure cooker.

Camouflage Artists

Nines camouflage their own power out of a desire for harmony. Unlike chameleonlike Threes, who blend in just to stand out, Nines shroud their impact and consequence behind an easy smile and by obliging and going along. Often they pretend to be—or feel they are—the victims of events outside their control. "A raise is definitely possible," a Nine boss might say. "But right now, the economy's too uncertain. We don't know what the competition will do. Let's definitely keep talking about it."

Some Nines overcompensate for their reactivity to others and their inability or unwillingness to set clear boundaries by being overly rigid or fussy or directive or cranky. But beneath this protective camouflage, they are still organized around their attention to the agendas of others and not their own.

As part of the power triad, Nines are as willful as Eights and Ones, but given their reservations about direct aggression (which is well hidden at Nine's shadow, Eight) Nines assert themselves, their authority, and their views indirectly, albeit quite strongly. More passive-aggressive than any other Enneagram type, Nines may say yes, they will gladly read your grant proposal or write you a letter of recommendation, but the proposal sits on the desk or the letter never arrives at its destination, despite repeated requests from you and ready agreement from the Nine. Still fighting the unsatisfactory parent who did not consider the Nine's wishes, Nine says, "You can make me say yes, but you can't make me do it." To read Nine's mighty will, remember John Mitchell's admonition when he was attorney general, "Watch what we do, not what we say."

Easygoing Rob is an agency director at a midsized Northeastern city. Considered knowledgeable and experienced, he rarely gets angry, at least outwardly. From his point of view, he keeps a tight rein on the office without needing to be unpleasant. When Rob heard that one of the five department chiefs reporting to him was bad-mouthing him on the sly, he said nothing directly, but when the opportunity arose, Rob transferred him to head a far less desirable department. "I sold it as cross-training," he told me, "but everyone knew it was punitive. I didn't have to say so.

"Now this fellow is very good at what he does," continued Rob. "I never wanted to get rid of him. He reorganized the new section and improved it considerably. He inherited a bad disciplinary problem himself, which is really a problem in the public sector. He took the guy right on. He needed my support and he got it. He saw that I wasn't just a wimp and that I would go out on a limb to support him.

"He figured out on his own who the boss was. That was the point of the exercise. Then I put him back in his old slot, as easy as pie. He's been there two and a half years, and he's very happy and a lot wiser. And a big supporter of mine. And I of him."

Working with a Nine

Influencing a Nine

When working with a Nine, don't be afraid to state your own position, priorities, and goals. Nines enjoy and are skilled at seeing things from your point of view, and they will not ignore what you say. They like you to go first so that they can bounce off your ideas. Be collaborative, not confrontational, disruptive, or willful; Nines are as willful as anyone on the Enneagram. Their will is that things go smoothly.

The best way to influence a Nine is to emphasize what you can create together through your collaboration. Nines generally don't like overt competition within a team. "I don't like it when people beat their own drums," said Brad, the Nine manager of a division in an educational software firm. "I resent it when people are aggressive or self-promoting. We're supposed to be on the same side around here."

Working with a Nine can be frustrating, like pushing on a rope. Pull the rope instead. Most Nines are happy for you to take responsibility within the areas of your concern (and even beyond if you're not bossy or intrusive). If you're on a work team with a Nine, take responsibility for designing the work and ask for your colleague's collaboration. If you work for a Nine and want to advance, make a prospective career plan and check it frequently with your boss, making sure that he understands it's part of an ongoing discussion. If you still need a decision at deadline, be prepared to make it yourself, and ask for the boss's concurrence. Don't be pushy or arrogant; Nine is very sensitive to both and you will lose. Be collaborative instead.

How a Nine Makes Decisions

Not to decide is also to decide.

—*Chester Barnard*

The problem with decisions is that they almost always necessitate more decisions.

—*Ian McNett*

Saint Augustine, a Nine, said, "To act is to sin." Nines like to ruminate. They go back and forth, content to chew their cud. Forcing a decision may seem like an intrusion on the processes of nature. That's why Nines may be hard to pin down. They would rather wait for things to work themselves out.

Nines commonly avoid decisions by asking for more information, by counseling prudence or restraint ("It's not the right time"), or by pointing to the decision's likely impact on other people's feelings. A favorite Nine avoidance tactic is to insist that the views of more people need to be heard. "If we wait long enough," says Nine without coming out and saying it, "the proper course of action will emerge."

When Nines do take on decision making directly, they can get especially good results because they take so many positions into account. Nines like their decisions corroborated. Like many Nines, Ronald Reagan had a "kitchen cabinet"—easygoing collegial types who went back and forth on the issues and made recommendations without letting their own individual ambitions or egos get in the way. (If they did they were booted out.) "What [Reagan] most often asked his advisers to do," according to his biographer Lou Cannon, "was 'work things out' by finding a middle ground where none existed between incompatible options."[2]

Nines prefer collaborative decisions, which at their best enfranchise everyone but at their worst degenerate into "groupthink," a term devised by the psychologist Irving Janis to describe situations where everyone relies on everyone else to be thoughtful and responsible. Many times decisions are hard for Nines because they have trouble laying their claim on matters that are central, while they can spend a great deal of time being persnickety about minor details (and thereby giving the illusion of being decisive).

The most stressful setting for a Nine is one where they are bombarded by a constant stream of situations requiring on-the-spot decisions that cannot be made by referring to how such decisions were made in the past, and where there is no time to ruminate or develop a consensus. Fast, nonroutine buying and selling or interpersonally contentious negotiating tends to put a Nine on tilt. Creatures of precedent, Nines assume that tomorrow will be and should be like yesterday and the day before. How should we plan? "Let's look at the past and project it into the future," says the Nine. This is a good way of not having to reinvent the wheel and be responsible for the consequences.

Since they like to go by their gut, Nines can get constipated. When Nines are stuck, here is how you can help them digest all the choices: It's hard for Nines to say, "I want that." But most Nines can decide what they want least. Present them with all the alternatives and help them eliminate the least desirable ones until a decision is made. Ask, "What would make you most uncomfortable?" until the options are narrowed. Nines, so accommodating, are happy to adjust to what's left.

The Nine decision style is useful:

- when there is lots of input or many stakeholders whose opinions need to be taken into account
- when the potential for conflict is a problem
- when issues need to be thoroughly considered and there is time to do it
- when the best outcome will be a result of having included as many people and points of view as possible.

I have consulted with community planning agencies who are charged with creating development plans. When overheated merchants, homeowners, and various interest groups and activists need to collaborate, the mediative Nine approach is the best. Even though it may be tedious, structuring a meeting process based on the Nine—where everyone is heard, where judgment and censorship are kept to a minimum, and where issues are thoroughly discussed—not only mellows everyone out; the best kind of decisions in this situation come when the most diverse views are heard and understood by the competing stakeholders and everyone feels included—the high side of Nine.

The Nine Leadership Style

Of a good leader, who talks little,
When his work is done, his aim fulfilled
They will all say "We did this ourselves."

—*Lao Tzu,* Tao Te Ching

The best Nine managers are genial and nondirective, nonactivist coaches who inspire and operate by consensus. They lay out a global, unifying vision for the enterprise, establish warm relationships with people, and then get out of the way. Aaron, a Three who works for Tom, the social services administrator, says, "Tom gives very broad directives and lots of latitude to carry them out. He wants to stay part of the loop, but on most things he doesn't need to hear from you in advance, and he rarely second-guesses you." Sometimes the vision is so general that it amounts to little more than collegiality and mutual respect.

Ronald Reagan was the prototypical Nine manager. According to Lou Cannon, Reagan

> delegate[d] far more to cabinet officers than most of his predecessors had, granting them broad authority and a long leash. Seen on one level, this delegated presidency was a useful mask for Reagan's ignorance of many issues. However, it was just as legitimately a reflection of his belief in the virtues of cabinet government and of his confidence that he could select able managers to carry out his policies. By temperament and training, Reagan simply was not a detail man. Even on issues where he was well-informed, Reagan chose consciously to focus on the broad goals of what he intended to accomplish and leave the details to others. He was appalled at the stories that President Carter had become so involved in detail that he took time to determine who used the White House tennis courts. [Jimmy Carter is a One.] Reagan . . . saw himself as a leader, a communicator, an executive decision-maker, a chairman of the board.[3]

For Chester Barnard, the Nine management theorist, the manager's job was not to micromanage but to delegate: "You cannot direct from the top the multifarious activities of the groups down below," he instructed, arguing for the empowerment of middle managers a half century before it became chic. "There has to be a reaction and a response to local conditions that can't be conveyed to anybody at a distance. . . . You put a man in charge of an organization and your worst difficulty is that he thinks he has to tell everybody what to do, and that's almost fatal if it's carried far enough."

The best Nine managers manage by carrying on an ongoing conversation with their employees in which they elicit the employees' own ideas of how to proceed. The worst Nine managers try to prevent their employees from proceeding at all, so fearful are they of being forced to act.

Nine bosses have a great many techniques for avoiding confrontation with problem employees. Typically, a Nine manager will write a memo to the entire staff instead of taking a particular employee to task. "If someone comes in late, I'll send a memo to everybody reminding them what time they're supposed to be in," says Rob, the agency director. "That way I don't have to embarrass anybody." Keith, a Nine who is a high school principal in rural Virginia, used the same indirect approach to influence a new teacher who wore sweatpants and T-shirts to school. Instead of telling Jeff that his attire was inappropriate, Keith waited to take any action until the other teachers began to complain to him that Jeff was unprofessional and the students began to gossip about Jeff's clothes. Finally, Keith adopted a formal dress code for the entire faculty, and Jeff took the hint to leave his casual clothes at home.

Generally, Nine managers are process oriented rather than problem oriented. Most people try to solve problems by isolating them and figuring them out, perhaps assessing blame for failure, and moving toward a logical solution. Nines are not generally interested in assessing blame because blaming excludes people. They're much more interested in coming up with systemic solutions that allow employees, even problem employees, to continue contributing and participating.

The Nine Work Style

Nine employees value cooperation, teamwork, and goodwill. They favor a low-stress, low-conflict, low-deadline, low-reporting environment. But, terminally concerned that they're invisible and may be overlooked, they need to be seen and appreciated. To feel secure, they like to have a sense of their place in things. Clear job descriptions and lines of authority are made for Nines, who are happiest when they know what the game is. So are routines. Whereas Sevens and Fours are frustrated by office procedures because they stifle initiative and creativity, routines for Nines can be liberating. Many Nines, as we've seen, know that relying on a well-functioning routine is the best way to respond equitably to a large clientele, such as the clientele one encounters in government bureaucracies or utilities.

You may notice a certain passivity about Nines at work, which parallels the understanding that if you take a long enough view everything will work out in the end. A Nine is comfortable making a deal with significant portions unsettled because he knows or believes there's goodwill on both sides. Substantial details can be worked out later. The prospect of a mistake or two is not particularly alarming; errors don't carry the same valence as they do for a One or a Six because Nine believes there's generally ample time to correct them.

Nines rarely set specific performance goals for themselves; instead, they rely on passive prioritizing. They believe that what needs to get done will get done, and what doesn't get done didn't need doing. Often they're more comfortable being reactive than proactive. Linda, a Nine whom I sometimes have as my consulting partner, says, "I don't like to start with a blank slate. That doesn't mean I don't have my own opinions; it means that I work best when someone else primes the pump. Then I have a lot to say."

Make an active effort to collaborate with your Nine colleague or employee. Ask what she thinks. Then ask what *else* she thinks. Many Nines swoon with pleasure when you solicit their opinion and tolerate their on-the-one-hand, on-the-other-hand approach. They've learned from experience to give short answers, lest they appear to run on. They sit on what they know. Nines may expose their thinking tentatively at first, then the floodgates open. (As Lord Chesterfield said, "Many a man would rather you heard his story than granted his request.") Nines are magically sensitive to a range of opinions that you may have overlooked, but you need to give them just what they give you—time and space to flesh them out. Be sure you ask Nines for their range of experience and opinions.

The Nine Learning Style

Nines learn by *osmosis*. Osmosis is an organic process (Nine's favorite) in which solutions of different concentrations on either side of a membrane reach a balance. Simply put, Nines readily absorb both what workshop leaders and fellow workshop participants have to offer. They learn well in immersion courses or at extended workshops and retreats where they can relate to the rhythm and intimacy of the group as a whole. Indeed, Nines do especially well in groups, where they merge with what is expected and where they can test their learning and sense the progress of others as part of a safe, ongoing conversation. Nines do less well in a high-pressure, competitive, fast-moving, highly evaluative format.

The Nine Organization

This place needs a laxative.
—*Bob Geldof, rock promoter, on the European Economic
Community bureaucracy*

Nine organizations create order out of chaos. They standardize production or decision-making procedures in order to be able to handle numbingly high volumes of routine input in a dependable, predictable, and orderly manner. Nine is the overriding culture in such organizations as the U.S. Postal Service, insurance companies, public utilities, railroads, large school districts, bureaucracies, and, of course, motor vehicle bureaus everywhere.

Bureaucracy, as described by sociologist Max Weber, developed in Europe in response to unreliable Eight environments in which kings or strong leaders operated government services impulsively and arbitrarily, putting their friends, relatives, and sycophants in office. Weber argued that government decisions should not be dependent on nepotism or the whims of individuals. Bureaucracy was conceived to create an *honorable,* constant framework for exercising authority and making decisions. Nine organizations at their best strive to diffuse conflict by relying on procedures that emphasize fairness and require that everyone be heard.

When decisions are arrived at in such an organization, the meaning or import may be fuzzy or open to interpretation. Such policy agreements are common in diplomacy, where the fact of a treaty may be more important than what it says. Nine systems value communication and cooperation and teamwork—the process of goodwill—over the actual substance of the decisions. This helps the parties get on with it, without having to hammer out every bit of minutiae. Muddling through is the special gift of Nine.

The low side of bureaucracies, like the low side of Nine, is the failure of substance: Nine organizations hold too tightly to routine and procedures— how things are done—and avoid focusing on goals that may rock the boat, such as clarifying the mission, cutting costs, or being more aggressive in the marketplace. In such an organization, it's sometimes hard to measure the results of one's work. All results tend to be of equal value, and second in importance to following customs and procedures that keep interpersonal relations free of conflict. The process runs amok.

Nine organizations value the organization over individual entrepreneurship, the tribe over the individual. Employees in a Nine system—such as the middle and lower grades of the civil service of the United States—generally have job security and are promoted without much attention to their level of competence or productivity. In a flawed Nine system, sticking it out (seniority and endurance) is valued over quality or excellence or personal ownership of the work.

Getting the Best from a Nine

Instead of playing both ends against the middle with disorganized, distracted aplomb, Nines evolve when they claim their power and their will (at Shadow

Eight) and make strong, value-based preferences (at Ally One). This frees the Nine to act efficiently, effectively, and single-mindedly, with clear goals—the perspective of Nine's High Performance Point Three. The virtue of Nine is Right Action. When Nines are stressed, they move to Stress Point Six, where they feel isolated, untrusting, and the victim of paranoid, critical people. But Six's worry is also a wake-up call that gets Nines off their duffs and into action.

Mike's Story

Mike, a Nine, is the head of employee assistance programs at an Iowa manufacturing plant. "He's genuinely terrific," says Dave, a Six and the plant manager. "Everyone loves him. He counsels individuals who are in crisis. He gets them into programs to deal with alcohol or drug abuse or financial problems. He's the world's greatest facilitator. He's basically an okay manager, even though he doesn't read his mail or do his statistics or always come to the meetings he's supposed to. He's not a good enforcer of the company rules, which bothers me and which we would not ignore in a line manager, but we rely on Mike in other ways.

"We've got a big problem right now, though," Dave went on. "Like most other companies, we've had to look at downsizing our work force. I need only one slot from Mike—he has five people and we want to leave him with four. I left it up to him which one of his five people to lay off. Mike said, 'Okay, I hear you.' This was nearly a month ago. Nothing's happened."

Mike told me he wanted to wait and see if things would change. "Maybe it'll work itself out," Mike told me. "Maybe we'll get a big contract or something."

But Dave didn't have any more time. He told Mike, "Look, either you do it, or I'll do it."

"I'm really torn," said Mike. "I completely understand Dave's position."

Stress Point: Six

Nines go to Six when they are frustrated and overwhelmed. In this stressful state, they feel themselves to be the victims of small-minded, untrustworthy, or argumentative people who have a secret agenda. No longer easygoing, they suspect bad intentions on the part of others.

"I really wonder whether Dave and the bean counters know what they're doing," Mike said to me. "He's being so shortsighted. I'm not sure he knows the impact these layoffs are going to have on company morale. It will come back to haunt him."

When Nines go to Six, they worry. They look for how they are going to be done in. Comfort-loving Nines can get uncomfortable at Six. But Six is also a good wake-up call for Nine. "When I go to Six," says Nancy, a self-employed Nine consultant, "I worry I'm going to be a bag lady. It's so uncomfortable, I go out and drum up some business right away."

High Performance Point: Three

Nine in Three sees what needs to be done and does it; the focus is neither too broad, like a stuck Nine, or too narrow, like a Six. Nine, who may normally seem to be laid-back or lazy, frees up the enormous energy lost in constant ruminating. At Three, the emphasis is on flexibility, pace, and forward movement.

Mike and his department wrote job descriptions for part-time workers, clearly outlining lists of tasks. They developed a plan that showed how they proposed to manage the paperwork, keep everybody on health insurance, *and* keep the department running.

Mike's solution, which became known at the plant as the Eighty Percent Solution, required him and the team to be a tight ship, since not everybody on the team was around all the time. Mike's influence, already considerable, increased. He was asked to speak to teams and do more in-house consulting. Editors at a training and development newsletter wrote up the situation, and Mike spoke at a conference. "Doing this made us far more committed and conscious. Just making out the detailed lists of tasks that each of us does was empowering. We had been operating on good vibes and goodwill. We get lot more done and we're more efficient now because we're more conscious about what we have to do—we're forced to make choices—and more committed to proving we can make the solution work. We're all Threes now!"

"Well," Mike said, "Why not see whether I can keep all five of my employees on part-time?"

Wings
Shadow Point: Eight

Beware the anger of a patient man.

—Dryden

Mike tended to reject his Eight shadow, the direct expression of anger and the willingness to engage in conflict. *Eight creates justice through power.* When Nine owns Eight, the power of anger is grounding: everything else can be built upon it. Anger is not something for a Nine to "work through." It's more like a touchstone that makes taking a clear position the most natural thing in the world.

Because Nines run from their anger, it is delayed. As Nines develop a relationship with their anger, the lag time between the event that makes them angry and the expression of the anger is diminished. That's the path of growth for Nine.

"I'm going to the mat for my people," Mike told Dave flatly. "That's how its going to be. I will keep all of them on. I've talked it over with them, and we agree that if each of them has to work only 80 percent of the time, that's fine."

Ally Point: One

Nines get stuck trying to satisfy everybody's positions. They get freed up when they satisfy guiding principles (Ally One). Standing on principle is the key to decisive action for a Nine. Nines need to find out what it is they stand for; all else flows from that. Unlike Nines, Ones are clear that some things are more important than others; it's easy for them to prioritize. "I valued team unity. Once I realized there was no honorable way to let one of my people go, that was the decisive moment," Mike says.

Cardinal Rules

If You Work with a Nine

- The Nine boss's commitments are soft and filled with contingency. Confirm them and your actions in a memo and with follow-up action.
- Don't mistake a Nine's silence for agreement. And don't necessarily take yes for an answer; the Nine may not even know she doesn't mean it. If you're unsure about where your Nine boss stands in relation to something you need, ask her. Find out what's really possible and what she has agreed to.
- Nines hate pomposity and pretension as much as Eights. Naturally humble, Nines want you to be that way, too. Don't pretend with a Nine that you know more or have more power than you do; and if you do have it, don't flaunt it.
- Establish very clear performance goals. Nines get fuzzy and forgetful when it comes to agreements, so it's good to have them in writing, even better if Nine creates the writing. If you're concerned about a Nine employee's ability to complete a specific project, ask him to repeat and summarize the commitment, focusing especially on agreed-upon stopping points and deadlines. If your boss is a Nine, you should take the responsibility for writing job description for yourself and standards for review.
- Nines talk themselves out of their own importance. That's one reason they don't follow up well. They need to be reminded that their assignments are

important, that they are important, and that people are depending on them to get their work done.

- One of the best ways to encourage a Nine to get with the program is to ask her what she thinks. Nines are so agreeable that they are often overlooked. Asking for their input helps them focus—and makes them feel valued. And when Nines feel understood and valued, something magical can happen.
- Nines get overwhelmed by considering the whole of a project and how it's connected to other things. They need to know their part. Make it explicit. "Your ideas about hazardous material management are more than welcome, but let's catalog these chemicals first." Some Nines out of habit and experience learn to do just their job, but Nines do best when they have a sense of the larger responsibility.
- Don't be controlling or domineering. Nines resent it. Work toward collaboration and cooperation.
- Give your Nine employee a regular meeting if possible. Nines won't assert themselves to claim the time they need, but they do extremely well when they have your undivided attention. Make sure it's really their time: Nines will be deflated if you are distracted by phone calls, interruptions, or other work.

If You Are a Nine

- Never again ask what you need to *do* next. Better to ask what you need to *finish* next. Then finish it. Even though distractions will tempt you, learn to finish whatever you're doing, if only to practice discipline.
- Write a One-ish mission statement for each of your projects to clarify where you are going and why. Do the same for your life. State your intentions clearly. The romantic notion of living life without goals is a false promise for a Nine.
- "Follow your bliss," said Joseph Campbell. Learn from Fours. Be willing to tolerate the discomfort of desire. Don't settle! Take some time to find your own position. Then let it be known to others early, or even first, as a way of committing yourself to act.
- Don't leave less desirable options in play. Play them or eliminate them. Don't let decisions that *can* be made drag on. It's neater and less confusing to make the decision and move on.
- Ask yourself in each issue you confront: Is this *your* issue? Or have you unnecessarily taken on someone else's problem as your own? Be clear about how your goals and responsibilities are separate from those of others. Why not empower them instead to solve their own problems?

- Narrow your focus. Though you want to relate everything to the global picture, this may not be appropriate all the time. Narrowing your focus will make many issues easier to resolve.
- State what you have to say without qualifying it or undermining it. When you hear yourself equivocating, stop. Learn to be specific and direct. And don't feel obliged to repeat yourself—you're not invisible. Trust that people will hear you the first time. When Elizabeth, a Nine training consultant, was starting out she used to get criticized for being repetitive. "I couldn't make a point without making it again," she remembers. "When I realized that people actually heard me the first time, I was deeply affected."
- Don't blow off your subordinates' requests for decisions. Sometimes employees need real guidance, and customers need an answer—not just pleasantries and acceptance and trust that "everything will work out in the end."
- As "big picture" folks, you have permission to hire people to take care of details and follow-through. Get a One to help you get organized.
- Don't give it all away: the credit, the authority, the responsibility.
- In particular, don't give away the rewards that say you are a substantial and important person of authority and influence.
- Harmony and rapport are your birthright, but you don't need them all the time in every situation. There are many other criteria for judging effectiveness of the work team.

1. Charles R. Day, Jr., "Kerm Campbell," *Industry Week* (November 7, 1994), 36.
2. Lou Cannon, *Reagan* (New York: Putnam, 1982).
3. Cannon, *Reagan*, 341.

One on One

One Working with One

Jimmy Carter and Rosalyn Carter, both moralists who are sometimes moralistic, are a partnership of Perfectionists.

If both Ones agree on what is right and wrong, then you can have an effective, highly productive, high-minded collaboration, a team that is a voice of conscience like the Carters frequently are. Otherwise you may find you've got a snooty, holier-than-thou collusion against those who are "incorrect." The collaboration may turn into a battle over whose vision is more perfect. But no matter how critical Ones may seem of each other, the real battle is between each One and his or her own standards, superego, and sense of what is right.

When One is boss. If you're a One boss of a One, your worker may share your energy and commitment but not your understanding of what is appropriate. Or your particular standards. A One administrative assistant thought that her One boss would see and surely appreciate her late hours and extra work, but her boss felt that the extra effort was the minimum required, so no special kudos or bonuses were forthcoming.

A One typically runs into problems with a One boss because both think they hold the high moral ground or the better understanding. Neither compromises easily because compromise feels like admitting a mistake. Don't "should" your employee. Ones are already "shoulding" themselves to the max. Ones do better when they consciously have an opportunity to apply their values, along with their enthusiasm and high energy, to making a beneficial difference. Ones will always be committed to doing things right as they see it. The key for Ones is always to make an effort to understand the value systems of others rather than just being certain they hold the franchise on correctness.

One Working with Two

This is the relationship between the Perfectionist and the Helper. The Perfectionist One is committed to eternal verities—the law as written—while the Helper Two is committed to equity—bending the rules for specific people under special circumstances. Ones are principled, while Twos are relational, customizing flexible solutions to the people and the problem.

Debbie, a One, and Marianne, a Two, work together at a county welfare office in New York state. Says their boss, Mandy, a Three, "Debbie's always tattling on Marianne. Marianne is always breaking the rules, and Debbie is in here four times a day pointing that out. We're a government agency, so we have to follow the rules, so I always agree with Debbie, but I never do anything about it, because almost everything that Marianne does is so damn helpful to the clients."

Sometimes Ones think they *are* Twos because, after all, they are just trying to help. Indeed, both Ones and Twos compulsively try to help each other; at their best it's mutual. "Don't worry," they say to each other in their different ways, "I know what's right for you."

When One is boss and Two is employee. Ones go by the book, and Twos, who are super-focused on pleasing their boss, can usually jump through those hoops with ease. The Two will often soften the impact of a harsh or brusque One boss on employees and clients. Maybe the One has pissed off a colleague but the Two is on good terms with his secretary, so that the One still gets what she needs, often without even knowing that something is wrong. But make no mistake: Two's main focus is in aligning with the boss. If there's a workplace battle, the Two is in the fort with the boss and the other managers—maybe the only employee in there (he'll know about the upcoming layoffs or bonuses)—while all the others are attacking from the outside.

If you're the One boss, remember that Twos of all stripes work for more than money: they want you to genuinely appreciate them for all they do and for their uncompensated devotion to you, which you take for granted. Satisfaction that they've adhered to your principles and procedures is not enough. Remember, too, that your tirades are guaranteed not to be the corrective you mean them to be: the Two is likely to go home in tears, and the wound can last a long time. Twos will take their revenge.

If you're a Two employee with a One boss, you'll be far more aware of your boss's personal and emotional needs than she is. When she's doing her One thing, though, you'll want to stay out of the line of fire or stand alongside her on the firing range. When you are criticized, admit your mistake and be able to express clearly to the One what you have learned from it ("You've made me a better person by showing me . . . ").

When One is employee and Two is boss. Ones try to apply the same rules to everybody. Twos play favorites. This may freak out a One employee who wants to be clear what it takes to get ahead and who prefers the standards to be impersonal. If it takes schmoozing or, worse, being gushy, many Ones will fall by the wayside. Even Ones who feel valued will still have to live with Two's impulsiveness, plasticity, and tendency to be fickle.

If you're a One employee with a Two boss, consider adjusting to your boss's flowing personal process instead of rigidly insisting on your own brand of etiquette. This relationship hums when the One remembers that warm rapport and interdependent mutuality are not a compromise but actually can help the One get where he wants to go. It's especially salutary for One to become a student of Two's gracious techniques. "I used to say, 'I don't understand you,' cross my arms, and wait for the other person to explain himself," says Jim, a One. "My Two boss, Jennie, taught me to say, 'Let me see if I understand you.' It's much less confrontational and makes everybody feel that we're not just placing blame but collaborating on a solution."

If you're the Two boss you need to remember that your One employee is looking not for strokes but for specs: what it takes to get the job done. But watch out: if the job you've given her raises sensitive issues for others, your One may not know what to do. "When I give Diane an assignment, she reads everything, talks to everybody, and then comes back with the perfect report," says her boss, Louise, a Two. "But if I tell her to implement a change, she has a mutiny on her hands. In her zeal to do everything right, she makes everyone else feel they're doing it wrong." Be prepared, if necessary, to cover for her.

One Working with Three

This is the relationship between "quality control" and "sales." At best they support each other, Perfectionist One keeping the quality high and Producer Three bringing the product to market. At worst they undermine each other, One keeping standards unrealistic or irrelevant to the customer and Three overselling or making promises that can't be kept.

Perfectionist Ones and Producer Threes span the difference, as Peter Drucker described it, between being efficient and being effective. Being efficient means doing things right, like a One. Being effective means focusing on results, like a Three. "She wants to do it right," says the Three boss of her One employee. "I want to do it right, too; around here that means turning things around quickly so we can move on. I don't like to get bogged down in details that won't show and won't matter."

Both Ones and Threes are compulsive and committed about work. Both have lots of energy, which can mean the relationship has a lot of "charge," and One and Three are often engaged, entertaining, and mutually supportive as both approach the task from their different perspectives.

But these high-energy, responsible styles can chafe each other. Threes, who stand out by fitting in, can think sharp-elbowed Ones are uppity on their moralistic perch or hung up on the irrelevant; Ones can think Threes are reckless, superficial, and deceptive.

When One is boss and Three is employee. If you're a Three who works for a One, your boss will be impressed with your bright eyes and bushy tail, but if you take these to extremes, you may seem more like flash and dash. Slow down. Your boss appreciates it when your work is meticulous and your decisions well considered.

If you are a One boss with a Three employee, make the high standards that you seek a goal to be won, with appropriate rewards. Threes can operate in a One universe if there is a Three payoff. And don't expect your Three employee to be as self-punishing about mistakes as you are. Threes recast mistakes as a kind of success: they learned something, got redirected onto a more productive path, or made some important contacts. You might learn from their example!

When One is employee and Three is boss. If you are a One employee, your Three boss is likely to find your reporting too detailed. The "perfect" way to present the material is so that it is useful to the Three boss. Always try to keep the market in mind (that's the Three specialty). Most Ones can readjust and create a streamlined executive summary for the Three boss, even though they wouldn't be comfortable with same thing themselves.

Three bosses like a sense of easy teamwork, a commitment to the task rather than a private agenda. Ones usually buy into the official rules but execute them stiffly or formally. If you're the One employee, a little interpersonal schmoozing goes a long way. Let the Three know you are on the team.

One Working with Four

Both Ones and Fours are perfectionists. One's ideals are moral, with "objective" standards; the Connoisseur Four's ideals are emotional and aesthetic, with subjective standards.

At work, both like to see things done impeccably and exquisitely. Fours are as critical and contemptuous as Ones when people don't measure up. They know what's right, others don't. Both are relentless and energetic when it comes to getting things up to snuff.

But holding to standards is not done out of mean-spiritedness or lack of heart. One and Four are both concerned with the gap between the way things are and the way they should be. Their intensity bespeaks passion, commitment, and engagement. Both can have trouble seeing alternatives to their way. But when they do get their way, something a cut above is in the offing.

When One is boss and Four is employee. For your One boss, the rules have an aesthetic all their own: form follows function. Beauty comes from unpretentious, unadorned alignment with purpose. This is the spare but profound Shaker gracefulness ("'tis a gift to be simple").

Ones run a strict shop. Neatness counts. The rules count. Principled action counts. Volatile Fours find that the One realm can be a terrific home base for them. One is the master editor of the creative Four's endeavors, regardless of what kind of work we are talking about. Fours who trust their One bosses have enormous freedom to push the envelope, knowing that they can experiment with and rework their creativity under the sober eye of a One who will tell them the truth without patronizing them. But don't expect a special dispensation if you're running late or "having feelings." Ones typically have little sympathy for Four's insistence on a special set of rules. Excrutiatingly fair, Ones like to treat everyone the same at the boundaries.

On the low side, some One bosses will stress out their Four employee with attention to details that the Four considers distracting, tedious, uncreative, or trivial (like finances or formal reporting procedures). "This project is special," says the Four. "Why limit it by doing it the way things are usually done?"

Ones are blamers and Fours blame themselves. Said a Four remembering her One boss, "Whenever anything went wrong, he thought it was my fault and so did I."

If you're a One boss with a Four employee, you may be put off by his histrionics and his moods. Use your One's highly effective habits as a rudder, not a club.

When One is employee and Four is boss. Creative or artistic Four bosses often have a One administrator or financial officer working for them. This arrangement can work extremely well. The Four supplies the vision; the One organizes, develops policies, codifies systems, follows through on deals, keeps records, and prevents the Four from going over the edge. One also hones Four's ability to stay calm in a crisis.

But if you're the Four boss, you may find that you feel criticized or restrained by your One employee. If you're the employee, you may feel resentful that your boss is such a character, so impulsively driven by bursts of mood.

Fours need to remember that with Ones it's not personal. Ones need to re-member that with Fours it is personal. When One and Four direct their fussi-ness toward the task, the sense of personal wounding gives way (although bickering may continue). Each then brings her or his high moral and aes-thetic specialties to the work at hand.

One Working with Five

Sometimes Ones are confused with Fives because they are both reliable, re-strained, and disciplined. Both can make great teachers and mentors. But Ones are compulsive—they feel duty-bound to change and help others. Fives, on the other hand, are comfortable staying on the sidelines. The Five René Descartes said, "I think, therefore I am." Immanuel Kant made a One's revi-sion: "I ought to, therefore I am."

The Perfectionist and the Sage work well together when they agree on com-mon rules, boundaries, and procedures. Both respect clear guidelines and give laserlike attention to details that interest them. Together, they plan well for con-tingencies; Ones don't want to make mistakes and Fives don't want the negative attention. Ones take pride in their perfectionism, Fives in their wizardry.

Trouble arises when Five sees One's moralistic approach as intrusive or presumptuous, or One sees Five's distance as a refusal to take responsibility. Both can go overboard on details and lose the big picture, with One insisting she's right and needing to be acknowledged as such before she can move on, and Five becoming interested in some obscure fact on the theoretical margins of a problem.

When One is boss and Five is employee. Ones are happy to tell Fives how to do their work better, but Fives like to think about things in their own way. Ones like detailed progress reports, but Fives don't like to share their thinking until they are ready.

This relationship hums when the One boss give the Five employee leeway within a clearly defined private domain. In turn, get Five's contractual agree-ment in advance for reporting requirements, progress reports, and the like. Fives respond very well to objective rules as sturdy boundaries that they can use to protect themselves. If you're the Five employee, know that your insis-tence on your precious privacy feels like a wild card or self-indulgent to your boss. So get very clear on your boss's parameters and goals; Ones are very lit-eral and have no trouble stating their expectations.

Ones are conventional while Fives are not. For Ones propriety itself is a strong motivation, unlike for Fives, who may stay within the rules so their aberrations won't be noticed. One bosses generally care about office neatness and order—not usually Five concerns. If you're a Five employee, you may choose not to follow the boss's rules, but at least to make it a conscious choice.

When One is employee and Five is boss. As a gung-ho One employee, you may want more guidance and feedback than your hands-off Five manager is willing to give. You can get it if you give your boss some space. Writing or e-mail is best, so the Five can take the material to her private lair and consider it there. "Here is my understanding of the project and my position in it," you might write. "Here is my work plan. Please let me know your thoughts." Remember that Fives are sensitive to criticism and don't like being instructed. They're paranoids. Don't push. Suggest. Give reasons.

If you're the Five boss, remember that Ones are quite literal. Make a special effort to express your values and vision. It can be really helpful for Fives to get their intentions out instead of holding everything close to the vest. Most Ones are more than willing to get with the program as long as they know what it is and it doesn't violate some personal moral code.

One Working with Six

The One-Six relationship can be a real teeth clencher because both types are so critical yet hate to be criticized themselves. A Perfectionist One believes criticism calls her perfection into question, and a Troubleshooter Six will worry whether you are with him or against him. In addition, they both tend to see things in black and white and to mobilize the big guns to deal with even the smallest matters. On top of that, they both can be big procrastinators. For them to work well together, they have to share a common cause. Sixes love to fight against injustice, bad faith, and the excesses of authority, which can be similar to Ones' principled approach. Both have a sense of duty to their fellows, coupled with a willingness to delay pleasure and gratification. These are the two most tendentious types on the Enneagram; once they take a position, be prepared for them to defend it vigorously.

When One is boss and Six is employee. If you're the boss, hold off on criticism until you've made your Six employee feel a part of the team. When you do need to find fault, take pains to explain that the problem is with the work, not the person. (You yourself may find it hard to make the distinction.) Six employees do well when they understand your thinking and feel you're fair, without a hidden agenda. One's consistency is very helpful for a Six.

If you're a Six who works for a One, your attention to detail and your concern about making mistakes will please your One boss. The best way to be loyal to her is to find out what "doing it right" means for her. Personal loyalty doesn't mean as much to your boss as it does to you.

When One is employee and Six is boss. If you're a One who works for a Six, you know what's wrong with the way he does things, and you want to tell him. But even though you're just trying to help, chances are your hypersensitive boss will feel you're scolding him. This puts you in an awkward position—if you withhold your judgments and criticisms out of politeness or discretion, your resentment is bound to build up until your boss can detect it (or you explode). Sixes are masters at sensing when something is being withheld. He'll perceive your anger (almost certainly more than you do), which may make him feel that you don't support him. Convey your reservations or opinions without cauterizing the target. Don't say, "You've blown the Hofnagel account!" Say "We can really get Hofnagel and Company on our side if we act strategically in this way."

When push comes to shove, you tend to be more loyal to your conscience or to an even "higher authority" than to your boss. This is the worst thing for a Six, who needs to know that you're on *her* team. Ease her fears by showing her that standing with her against her bad guys is high on your agenda. When Six knows you're on her side, this relationship can work very well. You'll have lots more freedom.

If you're a Six boss with a One employee, rarely would the employee's criticism bespeak a hidden agenda to undermine your position. Most Ones are just critical, not only without a hidden agenda, but without even knowing they're so critical. They're just trying to help. Respond to the criticism not as a personal attack, but on its merits.

One Working with Seven

The ant and the grasshopper make the prototypical One-Seven team. The Perfectionist and the Visionary may not feel they have much in common, but they do. They're both excited by what could be. Sevens see the exciting possibilities, and Ones see the possibility of impeccable execution. Both are, in a sense, idealists. And yet both are rigid. One insists on her narrowly focused vision and is contemptuous of those who don't see it. Seven is just as rigid about following his enthusiasms and contemptuous of those stick-in-the-muds who aren't. Both are equally impractical, either with their head in the clouds (Seven) or by adhering to principle over effectiveness (One).

When One is boss and Seven is employee. If you're a Seven working for a One, your task is to stay with the program at least long enough to have an impact. Ones seethe and even explode when irresponsibility or poor attention to details or follow-through causes embarrassing mistakes. A One boss may demand details of design specifications or progress reports that you find extremely hard to supply while flying by the seat of your pants. Uncomfortable though it may be, nothing is more effective for a Seven in times of stress than to comply. (One is the salutary Stress Point for Seven.)

If you're the boss, you know from experience that Sevens are antiauthoritarian and may enjoy poking fun at you, especially if you take yourself and your role too seriously. You may be tempted to defend your position with such force that your Seven employee will think at first that you're only kidding. To you, your response seems objective, sensible, justified, even restrained. To your employee, it feels like a profoundly wounding personal attack. Cauterize with caution.

This relationship works well when the One boss is the Seven's angel: the One gives her Seven employee her wings and plenty of airspace. Seven employees need Ones to make their ideas manifest in reality: to help them stick to a project, especially a long one, and, most of all, to take themselves seriously. Although disconcerting to a One, Seven opens up possibilities that the One may not have seen. A One manager of research scientists said of his Seven employee, "I used to think that his brain was broken. I couldn't see his ideas because he was just outrageous. Now I see how he contributes to our team. I don't exactly understand the mechanism, but if I just look at his ideas, they are magical."

When One is employee and Seven is boss. Sevens lead by charging ahead with their enthusiasm. Dutiful Ones would like to oblige, but under a Seven boss the direction (and their duties) seem to keep changing, along with their department's basic premises and goals. Some Seven bosses are downright irresponsible. They may take care of the company's NBA season tickets but forget about renewing the health insurance. This is disconcerting for an overresponsible One.

A One employee and a Seven boss can work happily together when both parties are self-aware enough—and openhearted enough—to understand the contribution of the other. A One who understands that her Seven boss's flights of fancy can be inspirational as well as provocative opens herself to the possibility that she can be his most important business resource through her single-mindedness and intensity of purpose. Typically customers or other employees are charmed by the charismatic and ebullient Seven, but they count on the One for reliable information, for follow-through, and even for influencing the Seven and keeping him to his schedule and his agreements. And when a Seven honors his One employee's commitment to the job, he honors himself.

One Working with Eight

Perfectionist Ones are the great rule keepers of the Enneagram. Top Dog Eights are the natural rule breakers. For Ones, virtue is the ultimate power. For Eights, power is the ultimate virtue.

From the Eight perspective, where the focus is on exposing bullshit, One's moralizing looks like self-righteous hypocrisy. To One, Eight's intentionally provocative iconoclasm looks like self-indulgent heresy. As mirror-image solutions to the same problem (anger at frustration of will), Top Dog Eight and Perfectionist One engage each other precisely.

Both Ones and Eights want their will to prevail. Both take the initiative to see that it happens. They are angry that things are not as they should be. In trying to change what exists, they are ruthless and persistent, steamrollering over others and leaving hurt feelings, sometimes without even knowing it.

When One is boss and Eight is employee. As bosses, Ones like to set clear rules and procedures. This strict control is a precise trigger for the Eight to test the limits. Unlike Sevens, who also break One's rules but fly away if confronted, Eights freely engage in loud and very public disagreements. This can be very hard for a One boss who expects respect by virtue of his position. If you're the employee, remember that Ones don't want to be embarrassed, especially in front of other employees or customers. If you're the One boss, try to give your Eight employees their own bailiwick so that they can feel free to enjoy their expansive nature within limits.

If your boss is a One, take special note of her willingness to stand firmly on principle. Don't make the mistake of misunderstanding your boss's position as a power play. As an Eight you often imagine yourself to be standing on principle, when actually all you're doing is throwing your weight around. Your One boss can teach you the difference.

When One is employee and Eight is boss. If you're the boss, take care not to intrude on your One employee. Don't barge into his office or meddle with his areas of responsibility unless you purposely want to set him off. And don't make promises, then head off in a different direction. As with Sevens, this kind of impulsive change in direction can drive a One employee mad.

Your One employees can give you a foundation on which to build your empire. To an Eight, rules, regulations, procedures, and conventions—One's specialties—are like a red flag to a bull. They charge full speed against them, snorting. Eights can miss the subtle utility of such guideposts. Ones can help. Ones bring Eights steadiness, moderation, and restraint, just what Eights need to be effective rather than merely explosive in their work. In return, Eights infuse One with energy, boldness, and zest for living, along with a license to use it.

One Working with Nine

Perfectionist Ones try to control the flow of the river by building dams and channels. Mediator Nines control the flow by appearing to go along with it.

Both have core anger issues and can get frustrated easily with each other when they don't get their way.

Like all adjacent points on the Enneagram, One and Nine are opposites, but with these two it's particularly obvious. Ones are neat, orderly, focused, judgmental, and proactive. Nines are easygoing, diffuse, and reactive. At their best, Ones provide the order and form that Nines need to resolve their chaos, while Nines teach Ones about letting go of control and about empathy and collaboration.

Both do best when acting from impersonal goodwill so that judgments based on personal style don't get in the way. Such intention develops when both align with the enterprise, Nine with the work team as a whole and the habitual way of doing things, and One with the principles, purposes, and larger vision.

When One is boss and Nine is employee. Nines can be extremely reliable, responsible employees who are masters of cooperation. If you're the boss, they're not likely to gun aggressively for your job. They're happy for you to have the responsibility and the headaches.

However, you need to accept that your Nine employee does not define himself by his job role as you do, nor does he have the moral commitment that you do to your work. Indeed, your Nine employee may be reluctant if you ask him to do something beyond his job description. He may feel exploited, as if you want him to do more work for free. In such a situation, he may go so far as to file a grievance with the union, perhaps even without complaining directly to you.

One's normal management style—correcting exceptions—doesn't work so well with Nine employees over the long term. Nines need to feel accepted and appreciated, not because of their track record but because of who they are. The more you push and try to correct, the more Nines—the immovable objects of the Enneagram—dig in their heels. It's the rare Nine who "snaps to." Instead, Nines take time responding to an order to see if it will hold up over time as events change, or if you mean what you say, or if it's worth the trouble.

If you're the Nine employee, try turning to your One boss for help with work plan design, one of their strengths and your weakness. Ones make terrific mentors, and they're happy to do it.

When One is employee and Nine is boss. If you're the One employee, you may believe your Nine boss isn't giving you enough direction. Don't hold your breath for her to do it; give yourself direction instead. If you have to, write your own job description as well. Grab the opportunity instead of wasting time judging her for giving you too much freedom. To your boss this is collaboration, Nine's starting point.

If you're the boss, you may be offended by One's criticality, but you can really use One's critical eye. Try to enlist your One employee in tasks that make the best use of his self-discipline and decisiveness to set up systems that help you flourish. Ones are fiends for details, which Nines, who are big-picture folk, sometimes overlook.

Two Working with Two

You might think that a pair of deuces would not be a winning hand at work, each trying to out-Two the other in service. Of course, a couple of Helpers competing for the same boss's attentions could be a disaster. But professional relationships between Twos can work really well, particularly in a situation where a successful executive Two has a terrific Two assistant. They don't compete at all because they serve different masters. The Two executive is serving her boss and customers; the Two employee is serving his Two boss. Says Sandra, a Two executive, about her Two secretary, "Judith knows that I want to be a star Two to my group president and my direct reports. She wants to be a star to me." Says Judith, "We make each other look good." This relationship is about relationship.

When Two is boss. When a Two has real power, the situation has a different flavor from the Two assistant who vicariously runs the operation with the boss acting as a front. Two executives like power: they like to be relied on, they like to dispense largesse, and when their name is on the door, they are not shy about exercising power directly.

If you are a Two with a Two working for you, you already know to make sure the two of you have a special relationship. You also know to thank him for all his contributions.

When Two Is employee. If you are a Two who has a Two boss, you already know the boss cares what outsiders think and that she doesn't want to be embarrassed or surprised. This means keeping the boss well informed of your active networking, and in particular your efforts on her behalf. The not-uncommon difficulty arises when the Two employee, having acted on behalf of the boss by signing or forwarding or approving, forgets to tell the boss and the boss is caught off guard, a difficult situation for a super-together, image-conscious Two boss. All the Two employee can do is apologize profusely and explain how he learned his lesson.

Two employees usually don't need to share the public credit, but they do need to be thanked for their indispensability by the Two boss; this the Two boss is very likely to do.

Two Working with Three

A Helper and a Producer can make a hot-shot, high-performing combination. Both types want to make a good impression. Both are task oriented (Twos' tasks are often people centered) and well organized so that they can be effective. Both like getting things done and having interesting, high-level people on board. They're driven to keep proving their usefulness. But both can be single-minded, even ruthless, running over people unimportant to their goals in pursuit of what they want.

When Two is boss and Three is employee. Two executives can be really no-nonsense, contrary to Two's sweet devotee image. They make people the central part of the equation, and low-side Twos do indeed get lost in human relations. But savvy Twos know there's a business to run, and running it well is where they get their power and adulation. This relationship works very nicely because the Two does not limit the Three unless the Three forgets where her bread is buttered.

If you're the boss, remember the Three is not so motivated by relationship kudos as by opportunities for advancement, financial reward, or occasion to expand his marketability.

If you're the employee, pay the emotional piper. Two teaches Three not to run over the feelings of valuable others in pursuit of a goal. Twos will appreciate how hardworking and committed you are, but remember to make it personal; don't completely disappear in the substantive task or get lost in your blinders-on perspective. Remember, for Twos, business is about people.

When Two is employee and Three is boss. An extremely common relationship is the driven Three boss humanized by his Two assistant, who deals with supplicants, anticipates the boss's needs before he's aware of them, and remembers to send flowers with the boss's name on them.

Twos know how to obligate others by way of their own generosity. If you're the boss, your Two employee might invite you over on Saturday for a family picnic. The next week she is scheduling your personal appointments and making executive decisions on your behalf based on what she learned at the picnic. Many Three bosses are happy to play along since the Two works so hard to do a good job, handles tasks that so obviously need handling, and makes the Three feel so good in the process. Other Threes will feel smothered.

If you're a Three boss, *never* forget your Two employee needs to be acknowledged for how needed he is. That's the fuel he's running on. Don't get lost in your substantive task.

If you're the Two employee, your power and influence increases with the degree to which the boss sees you are in fact facilitating her work responsibilities. Don't expect too much cushion in the interpersonal area if you are not performing. But if the Three feels like she's getting her work done, you can be effectively running the pace, and that will be fine with her.

Two Working with Four

Helper Two and Connoisseur Four, both chrismatic and seductive, share a central orientation to the emotional life. Both are willing to break the rules for the sake of an interpersonal bond. But where Twos want you to feel their indispensability, Fours want you to be taken with their distinctiveness. Since Twos and Fours have carved out different specialities, they can collaborate nicely as colleagues.

Both, however, are looking for their sense of self-worth in others. Twos are proud and may be envious of the credit Four gets for having a unique, profound voice. Fours, who commonly feel like outsiders, are often envious of how easy life seems to be for people-pleasing, power-sensitive Twos.

The line that connects these two types on the Enneagram is about balancing appropriate emotional needs of self with those of others. Fours may judge Twos to be flighty and superficial, without an emotional center or a life of their own. Twos may think Fours unbearably self-involved. At their best, Fours are guided by their own crative flow. At their best, Twos are transcendent helpers of others. Each evolves by embracing the internal perspective of the other.

When Two is boss and Four is employee. Two managers are enthusiastic and encouraging. They really do care what their employees think of them; chronically dissatisfied Fours may be the hardest to please. Twos spend a lot of time counseling, listening, and trying to develop practical remedial actions and career pathways to address Four's complaints.

If you're the Two boss, you need to remember that Fours frequently are not really looking for the problem to be fixed (Two's speciality) but for a hook to hang their discontent upon. Don't be surprised if you feel your help is never good enough.

If you're the Four employee, your Two boss's malleability to customers and others will seem frivolous and counterfeit, since you are committed to authenticity. Twos want to help their employees; such bosses respond best to Fours who do not insist on being completely dissatisfied.

When Two is employee and Four is boss. When Fours manage a grand project or an artistic endeavor, there is frequently a Two right by their side, adoring and helpful. Fours can be very fussy about small points, and Twos know how to respond to these easily. The Four boss wants to feel appreciated for her unique taste and sensibility. Twos are the best on the Enneagram at making the Four feel personally special.

If you're the Four boss, make sure you come out of your self-absorption long enough to thank your Two employee for his contributions. If you don't appreciate him or if you take him for granted, he can become sullen and vindictive.

If you're the Two employee, be careful not to exceed your mandate. Sometimes Twos try to boss their supervisors around. This doesn't always go over well with an elitist Four, who likes putting his own touch on things. "At first, her attentions were quite flattering, but after a while she made me feel hemmed in and inept," said a Four executive of his Two assistant.

In addition, make sure you restrict your help to business-related activities. I've occasionally seen Twos sucked into covering up for tyrannical or substance-abusing Four bosses who consistently blow off important meetings and run roughshod over other people's feelings.

Two Working with Five

Helper Twos and Sage Fives look like opposites. Fives hate the idea of being dependent on others; Twos most want others dependent upon them. But in fact both Two and Five emphasize personal autonomy. Twos want to create the appearance of not having needs. Fives insist on not feeling their needs.

In a sense Twos, famous for how much they put out, are actually stingier than Fives, because Twos expect to get back what they give in full measure and more. Fives just want exceptional value for their efforts. Of course Twos (with Sevens) believe there's plenty more where that came from; Fives don't.

When Two is boss and Five is employee. If you're the boss, you need to be careful not to intrude and recreate Five's childhood drama: an intrusive parent caused many Fives to withdraw and build high walls.

Some Two bosses try to "fluff up" their Five employees and run into the high wall. But most Twos are quite good at tracking that line. Two bosses often reach out and schmooze with their Five employee, making themselves comfortable in the Five's office, an inner sanctum where nobody else goes. "If I didn't go into his office, I'd never see him," said Rosalie, a Two phone company manager, of her Five employee, Tom, a technical expert. "But I make sure not to stay too long." The best Two bosses protect their Fives and toot the Five's horn to others when appropriate. They also encourage Fives, when necessary, to take other people into account. Says Tom, "I like that she draws my attention to the people aspect of what we do, since my tendency is to avoid it. I also appreciate that she never holds me hostage to any conversation." Of course, the Two boss may also, out of habit, gush generic gratitude at the Five. Most Fives couldn't care less. Fives want to be treasured *specifically*: for how smart and clever they are, for their insight, for the arcana of which they are master.

Twos want to talk things through, back and forth, as part of an ongoing special relationship. Fives want to go off by themselves and solve their own problems by thinking about them. So it is much better to present a problem to your Five employee, be available for comments and more data, and give the Five time to think her thoughts and feel her feelings on her own.

If you're the Five employee, you typically set yourself up as the boss's technical, scientific, or academic consigliere. As the employee, you will be pulled in two opposite directions. There is the tendency to let the Two be your "ambassador to the world" so that you don't have to be troubled building and maintaining your own people network. There is the countervailing tendency (as a Five paranoid) to worry what the Two is up to and whether she has too much power and will obligate you too greatly. Either way the Five worries that he is losing his independence as the Two creates dependency. The answer is neither independence or dependence but interdependence. An interdependent Five exchanges information and expertise with the Two, neither holding too tightly to isolation nor being taken over, and also keeps direct trade routes open to colleagues, customers, and the industry.

When Two is employee and Five is boss. A Five boss is the perfect project for a Two subordinate who likes to exercise those "Two muscles" and help the Five boss interface with the world. The Two employee softens a Five's flinty edges. He is often the one person who knows how to deal with her, and how to throw her provender so that she doesn't bite.

But this relationship can sour when the Five is too difficult a case. The Two gets nary a drop of the encouragement or thanks that he needs, even though he may only need a little and only in private. If you're the Five boss, don't make the mistake of thinking there's only a finite number of *thank you*s in the world allotted to a Five. Acknowledge and thank the Two for his services on a regular basis, even if you have to get your computer to remind you.

If you're the employee, and you basically like your work, you will be getting your kudos from those who have to deal with the Five, who need paperwork or access or decisions that you can help shake loose.

Two Working with Six

The disarming Six can look very much like an ingratiating or flattering Two as he reaches out to respond to the concerns of the other. Ultimately, though, Troubleshooter Sixes are cautious and Helper Twos are impulsive. Twos will want to make a quick decision, but Six wants to think about it. Six wonders if Two can be trusted. Two wonders if there is any help for the Six.

When Two is boss and Six is employee. If you're the boss, you like to avoid getting mired in routine. You'd rather be flexible, because you feel that's the best way to get along with people. In fact, you're more than willing to bend the formal rules for the sake of goodwill and helping your friends. Your tendency to make special deals is fine with your Six employee if he benefits from the largesse, but it will seem like the worst of conspiracies if he doesn't. For a Six, hell is being screwed by an unfair authority. He wants accountability and predictability: clear roles, clear tasks, and clear lines of authority. You operate comfortably on emotion and impulse, but your Six employee does best when he has a sense that everything is on the table and that actions and decisions have a rational basis. Two can assuage the Six's concerns by communicating the ideas and understandings that are the basis for decisions.

If you're the employee, you've already seen that your boss doesn't want to do complex analyses of problems; she'd rather trust her intuition. You're in the perfect position to complement her as a reliable troubleshooter who rides shotgun and keeps his eyes open for bad guys. Six can alert the boss to difficulties arising from Two's rushing ahead without thinking, and especially with regard to the efficacy of Two's alliances. Twos have a nose for seeking out and aligning with powerful people; Sixes are the masters of checking that the boss isn't getting screwed in the process.

When Two is employee and Six is boss. If you're the Two employee, things should go well while your Six boss tends to his own domain, worrying about himself, his work, and his enemies; you can support these concerns as a sympathetic sounding board while expanding your influence and making yourself indispensable. Your boss will relish your apparent devotion to him. But be careful: Six bosses are fearful of being manipulated or taken in. If he sees your tendency to flatter him as a power play, he may become suspicious and pull back.

Decisions come easily to you, so you may get frustrated by your boss's tendency to put them off or his obsessive need to know everything that could go wrong. There's not much you can do about this aspect of the Six except to make sure you give him all the facts and enough time for the facts to register. Says a power-behind-the-scenes Two of her Six boss, "When I need a decision, I go in prepared to explore all the options without forcing a conclusion. Then I say, 'Think about it and we'll talk tomorrow.' But I really don't leave him with anything to think about because I make sure to answer all of his possible objections. The next day I get my answer."

If you're the boss, you need to understand just how much your Two employee wants to be acknowledged. This may be hard for some stiff Sixes, who do not easily express gratitude. You can keep the wind in Two's sails and yet not feel like you are out of your element by praising the Two based on a rational analysis of specific tasks she has done that have achieved a desired result. That way you won't feel swept away by emotion or fear being misunderstood or taken advantage of for your openhearted feelings. What Twos are most interested in is that they were indispensable to you or the process and that your relationship is solid, mutual, and ongoing. The specifics, important to all Sixes, matter less to Twos.

Two Working with Seven

The classic example of the Two-Seven relationship is Wendy Darling and Peter Pan. The Visionary Seven is up in the clouds; the Helper Two is enchanted but is oriented to the practical and maternal, like sewing on a shadow or remembering to grow up.

The typical presentation of this dyad has the Seven focused on his exciting projects and plans and the Two, as supporter and enabler, focused on the Seven. A cartoon shows a Two and a Seven. The thought bubble above the overly eager, dedicated Two's head reads, "Him. Him. Him." The thought bubble above the Seven says, "Me. Me. Me." The caption reads, "A relationship based on common interests."

Two and Seven are the Enneagram types most pleased with themselves. Both are optimistic, with high energy, and feel that their talents can open the world to them. Both are relatively out of touch with their shadow. There is not much tortured introspection here.

Two and Seven are the emotional and mental versions of each other. Twos are agile with (other people's) feelings and Sevens with imaginative ideas. But Twos only skim the emotional surface, and Sevens, for all their brilliance, are ingenious rather than wise. (Sevens get wise when they move to High Performance Five. Twos get profound when they move to High Performance Four.)

When Two is boss and Seven is employee. Twos, for all their emotionalism, are of a practical bent when they are dealing with others. Further, they care very much what their customers think. Sevens, who have an impractical streak, care far less ("there's plenty more customers where those came from"). If you're the Two boss, you may worry that your Seven employee will embarrass you by making promises she doesn't keep, by missing deadlines, or by being generally flaky. You may be put off by Seven's endless hypothecating.

But Twos in a power position can be charged up by the Seven's light-hearted brilliance, by their innocence, and most especially by the Seven's obvious need for the Two to adore her and create a practical forum for her to do her always-promising Seven thing. Two likes the dependence, and Seven likes to be treated as the magical child.

Reining in an untethered Seven can sometimes be a problem for Two. Low-side Twos are guilt-trippers ("I've been working hard on this project for the sake of your career! Where have you been?"), which sometimes will just kick the air out of Seven, a pathetic sight. The most sophisticated Twos keep gas in the Seven balloon: "For the next part of this project, I need all your ingenious attention. It'll be great for your career, but I need a commitment. Are you with me?" Sevens are agile mental acrobats who can throughly back up and justify Two's feeling-based decisions and plans with au courant, very hip interdisciplinary ideas and examples.

Sevens promote grand ideas and schemes; Twos are in service to particular others. Sevens think globally; Twos act locally. If you are a Seven who wishes to succeed with a Two boss, consider: Twos want specific, personal, people-oriented approaches that bring practical results.

When Two is employee and Seven is boss. Sevens love appreciation and attention, and Twos love to dish it out. Sevens may forget the other half of the Two's bargain, which is that Twos need their share of attention. If you're the boss, trouble is guaranteed when you get arrogant or patronize the Two; when you forget the Two is central, the Two will take his vengeance.

This partnership can go extremely well, especially when Seven remembers to include Two in her grand plans. Sevens are theorists. Twos humanize Seven's ideas by relating them to people. Moreover, Sevens, who may talk an egalitarian game, are basically elitists; Twos very much appreciate being the private, special, and necessary support to the great leader, but they must be acknowledged.

If you're the employee, you're a master at presenting your difficult, self-involved boss to the world. You help other employees understand your boss's intentions. Perhaps your greatest gift to paranoid, fearful-of-commitment Seven is that you press for completion so that you can make a sale and get some appreciation! But you may get into trouble taking Seven's speculations too seriously. Your boss has too many ideas for you to help him realize them all. Fortunately, you're a quick study, and you take a special pleasure in learning how to read your Seven boss so that you can figure out which of the schemes he's spinning are for real.

Two Working with Eight

Both power players, Helper Twos and Top Dog Eights frequently have a special, tight bond. Both like to take charge. Both can be predatory and overwhelm their colleagues and even each other. Both act on impulse and don't handle frustration well. Neither cares much about the rules. This can lead to a daring, effective collaboration *or* a power struggle, which either the Eight wins by brute strength or the Two wins by pulling strings and calling on favors.

Both purport to act in service to others. Twos serve their patron, while Eights serve their people and the cause of justice. Twos tend to work through others, while Eights are more blunt and direct. This relationship works well when each incorporates the perspective of the other to act genuinely in service.

When Two is Boss and Eight is employee. If you're the Two boss of an Eight, you both know you have an important ally who understands power.

Nobody manages Eights the way Twos can. Here's one reason: Eights want to bend or break the rules. Twos are fine about breaking the rules for their favorites as long as they get fealty.

But if you are an Eight who works for a Two, remember your Two boss will break the rules only so long as you are successful in your endeavor and you make absolutely sure to protect her as well. Twos care about the perceptions of others, even though you might not. Sometimes an Eight employee will say to his colleagues something like, "Don't worry about the boss. I can handle him." Don't flaunt your privileges too much to others, or your boss will rein you in.

When Two is employee and Eight is boss. Twos tend to cultivate the powerful. Eights are powerful. But Twos are far more strategic than Eights. They think about people's reactions in a way that Eights rarely do. Twos may put up with stuff they are unhappy with for far longer than Eight to get what they want.

If you're a Two who works for an Eight, you've probably already ingratiated yourself into the Eight's inner circle by working hard and being responsible, and especially by standing out as a loyal subject in your Eight's kingdom. Once in, the Eight will let you in on everything. He'll reward you with his favorite treat: power, just what you want. The most typical presentation of this dyad is when the Two acts boldly with referential power from the Eight. "This is how the boss wants it," the Two will say.

If you're the boss, know that your Two employee is far more sensitive than you are to your weaknesses and vulnerabilities. Eights are easily blindsided; they set themselves up. Your Two employee can keep you out of trouble and help you to be far more effective with people. Usually she'll be able to give you valuable insights and reports from the office front. You can be sure she will be acting in your name. Make certain she's doing what you want her to.

Two Working with Nine

Mediator Nines and Helper Twos both focus on supporting each other. They are empathic, sympatico, and work to fit in. Despite their self-effacing words, both can be very influential on the other, usually by indirection. Twos get their power by taking care of events and people and then seamlessly making policy decisions in the general course of business. Nines retain a post hoc veto by appearing to agree, or even agreeing, to a course of action but then doing things their own way regardless of the agreement.

When Two is boss and Nine is employee. If you're a Two boss, be careful about being too directive or intrusive; all Nine will do is dig in his heels. The best Two bosses use their laser-sharp empathy to see what Nine really needs and then actively collaborate to meet those needs. Often this involves helping a Nine to prioritize and encouraging a direct expression of the Nine's will.

You tend to see yourself at the center of a wheel of key people; you make and keep things personal to you and have real trouble making your operation into a project or organization with a life of its own that doesn't depend on you directly. (Two asks, "Why would I not want to be depended on?") Nines naturally understand the efficiencies of habit, and, as the business grows and the work expands beyond the capacity of a single charismatic leader, Nine can set up systems and procedures and work-flow pathways that mean the wheel does not have to be reinvented with each new endeavor.

If you're the Nine employee, don't confuse your Two boss's concern about you as an individual for a lack of interest in the bottom line. Twos are interested in both and can move quickly back and forth between the personal and the professional. Nines tend to accept "what is," but Two executives want to "force the current"; they are ambitious and they want things done, and they make things happen—their way. Nines are also willful, but they are passive-aggressive. Their will kicks in as resistance when they are being forced, however sweetly, even by a Two. This relationship works best when both view the other as cooperating. Nine needs to know that Two is not forcing. Two needs to know that Two is with the program.

When Two is employee and Nine is boss. Nines easily identify with the daily routine of the institution for which they work—perhaps too easily, because in the absence of Nine's active involvement, the place may seem to run itself.

Nines see long-term patterns and trends in large contexts and generally lack urgency. Twos are much more in the moment and want to do what they want to do right away.

If you're a Two who works for a Nine, you may be frustrated by your Nine boss's indecision. You can help by framing the choices, so that Nine can make them by eliminating one, and by "chunking," dividing up tasks and working with their discrete parts.

If you're a Nine who supervises a Two, remember that Twos are highly interventionist. Nines tend to let things take their course, which can irritate a Two. Twos like to have an impact but can get stuck in how slow it takes to make a change with a Nine boss. The aware Nine boss responds right away to Two's issues. When possible, Twos don't even let issues get framed on the Nine's desk. The Two goes about her business and the decisions seem to just happen.

When this relationship works well, the Two anticipates what the Nine wants done, and the Nine doesn't need to ask. What Nine often wants is to create merger, a sense of felt, natural, easy collaboration. This can suit the Two just fine if it serves the Two's power relationship agenda. "The bad part," said a Two of her Nine boss, "is that, if it were up to him, we could spend all afternoon having coffee."

Three Working with Three

Stand back. The glittery, high-energy, can-do pair of Producer Threes gets things done with lots of enthusiasm and commitment and without much ambivalence or many second thoughts.

When Three is boss. For the Three boss, management theory is not complicated. "My management philosophy is sink or swim. I don't like to spend money on training because people either understand what we're doing here or they don't. I expect you to figure out how to do your job. If you can't, look elsewhere; you won't last long here." Three employees thrive in such an environment. Other Threes might spend a lot on training, but it will be directed at the bottom line.

When Three is employee. Three bosses set goals. Three employees go for them. Threes crave hard work and hard-fought wins. They need the status that comes from success. Threes are motivated by the carrot-and-stick method. They want to meet their quota so they can get the trip to Hawaii, not so much to enjoy the trip but to be included as one of the winners.

Threes usually are inspired in the company of other Threes. It is common to visit a sales or marketing department at a large company, broadcast network, manufacturer, or service business and find the place populated with Threes. They are driven by competing with one another to be the most effective, the most successful, the most hardworking, the most accomplished.

But competition can get out of hand. Sometimes Three bosses will pit their Three employees against each other—the way Jack Welch won his job at

GE in a public competition with his rivals—and may the best person win. In that case Threes working together may try to gain a competitive advantage over each other by withholding information, excluding people from meetings, limiting access to higher-ups, or by straight prevaricating. Winning turns into the other guy losing. Watch out!

Three Working with Four

Poke around a Three workplace, such as the marketing department mentioned above, and you'll probably discover a beautifully decorated cubicle somewhere in the back—the home of a Four in charge of designing the marketing materials. Connoisseur Fours give class and substance to Three's achieving style. And Producer Threes know how to bring Four's artistry to market.

When Three is boss and Four is employee. The relationship between a Three boss and a Four employee works especially well when Three treats the Four employee as unique. It runs into trouble when Threes treat people as fungible. Once a task is completed, a Three boss naturally refocuses on the people who will support the next task. Fours feel abandoned by this kind of behavior. This is why Fours spend energy making a physical place for themselves; the sophisticated Three boss lets the Four know that the Four has a place and is welcome to be herself.

If you're the boss, you need to know that your Four employee may find your unadorned carrot-and-stick approach personally insulting. Unlike Threes, Fours don't find their identity in their salary or bonuses or a promotion (although they may be envious of those who have what they do not). Waving a few dollars to motivate them is a tacky mistake. Also, resist the temptation to deal head-on with Four's moodiness and tendency to become depressed. This is inviting disaster. Much better to set parameters for the Four's work and give him space for his moods. Most Fours will regain their equilibrium in due course.

If you're the employee, your Three boss may have difficulty with your moods. Your boss doesn't want your feelings to interfere with production. Fours grow as they learn to observe their feelings rather than be them.

When Three is employee and Four is boss. You'll often find a Four artist, designer, or creative leader with a Three in her employ, running the business end. The Four boss is usually delighted with the Three's attention to what the Four may consider drudgery, like the financials or the reporting.

This relationship works best when these two image-conscious points remember what the other values. Threes want to be appreciated for business achievement, Fours for uniqueness, emotional or artistic creativity, and achievement.

If you're the Three employee, you'll want to jump to closure more quickly than your Four boss. So get clear about what your boss's emotional or artistic agenda is. Then you won't press for closure before it is expected or appropriate. "Are we making a decision about the campaign at this meeting, or are we just expressing our views?" you might ask. "I'm just collecting your creative opinions" is a likely Four answer. "I want your sense of things."

Be careful not to overpromote what you can do or shade the truth or worse. Avoid your natural tendency to puffery. Fours hate phony-baloney promotion. "I mean every word of every song," said the Four Judy Garland.

If you're the Four boss, remember that your Three employee likes to know what the task is so that he can perform competently. He wants to impress you with his Three skills. Threes know about bringing the work to market. Some Fours have contempt for the commercialism in their shadow, but Three is a critical support of any Four's commercial enterprise.

Three Working with Five

Producer Threes and Sage Fives frequently make good business partners, with Three as Ms. Outside handling sales, marketing, clients, and image and Five as Mr. Inside in charge of financials, drafting contracts, analyzing documents, doing research, and perhaps managing the ongoing work of the company.

Often the Three has the initial idea and the Five knows how to realize it. For example, Ray Kroc had the idea for McDonalds. He set about franchising, creating the look, getting the right people involved, and developing the products, but he didn't figure out how to make any money out of it until the Five Harry Sonneborn developed the ingenious idea of making McDonalds into essentially a real estate leasing company.

When Three is boss and Five is employee. "Knowledge may give weight, but accomplishments give luster, and many more people see than weigh," said P. D. Stanhope. In many large high-tech firms, a Three boss runs the research and development department filled with Five engineers. This allows Threes to get ahead and Fives to concentrate on interesting technical concerns.

If you're a Three supervising a Five, you know that he resists being swept away by your enthusiasm and is suspicious of being manipulated. Although you're a natural motivator, your style most easily excites other Threes. You'll find this relationship works best when you give your Five employee time and space to think and plan. When Five feels secure, he can provide you with thoughtful, comprehensive analyses of the issues.

If you're a Five working for a Three, you can help your Three by letting her know you're present and on the team. "I have a tough time with Fives," said a Three manager at an aerospace company. "I don't know what they're thinking. It's hard to have a give-and-take." Try couching your arguments and proposals in terms of your boss's goals or the corporation's goals instead of just proffering a neat, objective analysis.

When Three is employee and Five is boss. Fives, although they can seem to be philosophers or absent-minded professors, are secretly concerned with being masters of their universe. This makes them very specific about how things get done.

If you are a Three working with a Five boss, you'll win points by slowing down and giving your boss the sense that you have carefully reviewed a particular situation and are not foolishly rushing ahead. Read carefully those long, detailed memos that issue forth from behind his closed door. This may not come easily to you. You want to get going, and surprises don't throw you; you're willing to fix what needs fixing after you get going. Not so your boss, who wants to lock up the details in advance so that there will be no surprises.

If you're the Five boss, do you park your Three employee outside your door to act as a buffer? You probably see the power and influence your buffer person wields as an acceptable tradeoff in return for insulating you from unpredictable confrontations with subordinates and outsiders. In many cases, though, it keeps you stuck in your isolationist habits. Try making periodic fact-finding tours into the jungle.

Three Working with Six

The Enneagram line that connects Producer Three with Troubleshooter Six is about balancing the urge to push ahead (Three) with the need for prudence (Six). Threes who move ahead too quickly can overlook important problems. But Sixes can be a drag on a fast-moving entrepreneurial enterprise that needs to make deals now and fix problems later. When appropriate "go" is balanced with appropriate "whoa," this dyad can really fly.

Threes feel successful partly because they ignore failure messages. But failure messages are not necessarily bad. The Six specialties—reflecting, doubting, chewing things over—deepen and give meaning to the Three's experience. In turn, the Three's zest for action gives Six the opportunities and experiences upon which to reflect.

When Three is boss and Six is employee. If you're a Three boss with a Six employee on board, your Six may be a terrific troubleshooter who can name potential problems and point to what you are overlooking. But the Six tendency is to blow the problems out of proportion until they paralyze him. As the boss, you can help by encouraging the Six to take action when it's clearly appropriate.

If you're the Six employee, state clearly your concerns about problems or conspiracies or what the Three is up to directly, clearly, and forthrightly. Subtlety and indirection don't get far with a Three boss. Don't forget recommendations for action. Sometimes Sixes think that naming the trouble is enough.

When Three is employee and Six is boss. Sixes always have issues about exercising their own authority. A fast talkin', fast walkin' Three will make a Six boss fear that things are out of control. If you're the Three employee, your boss's ambivalence and procrastination are sure to be frustrating for you, but you will be able to move ahead smoothly only if you slow down enough to respond point by point to his concerns. See this as a part of your job rather than as an inexpedient obstacle. Once your boss knows that you understand and respect the need for caution, she will back you up. If you get caught in the Three tendency to inflate, exaggerate, or lie, your boss will lose trust.

Part of you is a premier packager who can promote your boss's ideas to the outside world. Your willingness to be highly visible and take the credit may be both a boon and a bone of contention for your boss, who, even though she naturally seeks a low profile, will not want to be overlooked. Give credit where credit is due.

If you're the Six boss, make sure your Three employee knows that part of his task is to cover the potential downside and let you know about it. You need to be explicit with the Three not to get ahead of the game. Sometimes Six bosses are not clear what the parameters are for doing a good job. They like to keep their own rules secret so they can change them as circumstances change. Put performance appraisal standards in writing.

Three employees need to be "publicly" acknowledged and credited. Many (not all) Sixes are far too cautious about spreading the credit around for fear it will make them somehow vulnerable or diminish them.

Three Working with Seven

This is the relationship between marketing (Seven) and sales (Three). Producer Three and Visionary Seven look alike from one perspective. Both are high-energy, optimistic, can-do types. But where Threes are willing to hunker down and do the work, Sevens need a constant infusion of exciting ideas and possibilities. Sevens rely on inspiration, Threes on perspiration. Both these optimists blow past people and avoid working through interpersonal problems for fear they may get bogged down.

The two points differ in their cognitive styles. Threes are continuous thinkers. Their universe is linear. "If I do this, then that will happen. If I work hard, then I will be successful." Sevens are discontinuous, nonlinear thinkers: "If I do this, then *anything* could happen!" Sevens may find

Three's carrot-and-stick approach pedestrian. Threes may find Seven's "magical grab-bag approach" incomprehensible and irresponsible.

Threes like to get on a road toward a goal and stay on it. But Sevens are driving off-road vehicles. Threes may find the velocity with which Sevens change their minds disconcerting. Sevens may be startled with how quickly Threes bring ideas into action. Indeed, for Threes there's no time like the present; for Sevens there's no time like the future.

When this relationship works well, Three and Seven cover each others' blind spots as they approach a problem from opposite pathways. Threes build towers from the bottom up. Sevens build towers from the top down.

When Three is boss and Seven is employee. Seven employees are motivated not so much by goals as by enthusiasms. Sevens in that sense are amateurs (they "do it for love"); Threes are professionals who grind it out whether they are in the mood or not. So if you're a Three boss, motivate your Seven employee through the excitement of ideas, possibilities, and fun—not your natural triggers of duty, status, and accomplishment.

For Threes a commitment to completion of a particular project is liberating; it puts them on track. For Sevens, it's prison. The same goes for deadlines: where they turn you on, they turn your Seven employee off. Sevens are actually frightened of a deadline's finality. When it's feasible, assure the Seven he'll have the opportunity to revisit the question in the future, and he'll lighten up right away.

If you're a Seven employee of a Three boss, you have the opportunity to take yourself seriously with her as a model. Approach meetings with the boss with a sense of purpose—targeting a decision, getting the go-ahead, or seeking advice—rather than just thinking you'll enjoy the experience and see what happens.

When Three is employee and Seven is boss. Seven can be the perfect boss for a drudge Three. Seven, through ebullience and verve, can give Three just the magic he needs, much the way the Wizard of Oz, a Seven snake oil salesman, gave the Tin Man, a Three, a heart (or reminded him he already had one). Threes in turn can be godsends to Seven bosses. They flesh out and concretize projects. They make outlines and action plans. When the Seven gives the go-ahead, they go ahead. Things get done.

If you're the Seven boss, you'd do well to set clear markers along the way for your Three employee. Just being in on the endless Seven "experience" won't be enough without specific goals and wins that are acknowledged and celebrated.

If you're the Three employee, you may find your Seven boss's reluctance to finalize anything frustrating. Negotiate with her to get as much leeway as possible to close deals, and remind her that there will always be other deals down the line. And try not to splash cold water in Seven's face. "I could hardly get an idea out and she would be picking it apart," said a Seven of his Three deputy. If you're a Three, see if you can do your excellent, practical work without bringing your Seven boss down.

Three Working with Eight

Producer Threes and Top Dog Eights are the most proactive, go-for-it types on the Enneagram and the most common types that I see at workplace seminars. Neither is shy about taking responsibility and having an impact. Often a crusty old Eight tough guy founds a business, then his young, super-busy Three M.B.A.s take over, doing the planning and the financials, providing the structure, and squaring the business with the markets.

Eights want raw power; Threes want to be efficient and competent as a predicate to accomplishment. In a sense, Eights are more committed to their way of doing things: exercising power and enjoying it. Threes are much more committed to their results and will shape the process with the goal in mind.

Both Threes and Eights can be interpersonally oblivious when they are on task. Threes may seem like they have ice water in their veins. Eights have fire.

Threes are practical types who tend not to hold a grudge. They have no time to go back and take revenge because they're going full speed ahead. Anyway, a quick industry realignment could put your former enemy on your side. Eights, on the other hand, take offenses personally and will not rest until appropriate revenge settles the score.

When Three is boss and Eight is employee. Eights must have their own bailiwick to run. If you are a Three who has an Eight working for you, the secret is to establish firm, justifiable boundaries and to make the goals clear. Then the Eight can feel free within those boundaries to run his shop his way to reach the target goals. Just be forewarned that Eights find pressing these limits fun, often justifying it as a legitimate test of what will hold up.

If you are an Eight working for a Three, your boss will want to know that you don't think you are self-employed. Sometimes Eights give the message that they are more interested in power for themselves than success for the group. Use those natural but sometimes neglected Eight talents for protecting and nurturing (High Performance Two).

When Three is employee and Eight is boss. Eights tend to make up and then revise the hurdles and requirements as they wish. Threes are very flexible, but they need a pretty clear idea of what winning means. If you're an Eight boss, give your Three employees clear achievement points along the way. Low-side Eights forget that Threes are playing a success game. Don't get sucked into thinking that being a loyal subject of your Eight kingdom is the whole point of the exercise.

If you are a Three who works for an Eight boss, don't lock horns with her, but don't fade away, either. Eights like it when their colleagues "stand their ground," so that the Eight can see "where they stand." But be exceedingly careful not to lapse into self-promotion or overpromotion. Eights, whose mission is to expose bullshit, will charge at what they perceive as a lightweight Three conning them.

Three Working with Nine

Producer Threes are competitive and want to shine. Mediator Nines are rarely overtly competitive and are oriented to alliances with the group as a whole. Threes are proactive; Nines are reactive. The Enneagram line connecting Three and Nine is about finding the balance between direct, responsible action (at Three) and letting go to trust the system, the process, and your colleagues (at Nine). This relationship works well when the Nine grants the Three the freedom to act and the Three grants Nine the freedom to react within the context of the Nine's broad perspective.

When Three is boss and Nine is employee. Threes walk and talk faster than most. Nines are slower and more long-winded than most. Three bosses (and employees) may find themselves finishing Nine's sentences out of frustration. Many Threes experience the Nine's passivity to be as intentional as their own behavior. So it may seem to the Three that the Nine is spiteful. Since Nines are usually not motivated by the Three's cheerleading to a goal, managing Nines can be very frustrating for Three, like pushing on a rope.

But Three bosses—representing Nine's High Performance Point—can really help Nine employees get moving, which is when Nines do best. Help your Nine employees prioritize and stay on deadline. Make them feel accepted and part of the team. Nines delight in a sense of collaboration and mutuality. Perhaps most important, Threes can help enormously to counter Nine's tendency to obsessively revisit decisions by keeping questions that are closed, closed.

If you're a Nine employee, to work well with a Three boss you need to be cogent. Say what you have to say, be ready to decide, and, once decided, stand enthusiastically behind your position and implement it right away. Pare down your peripheral vision for your Three boss. Threes can't tolerate that much context.

When Three is employee and Nine is boss. If you're the boss, your Three employee may feel dragged down by what appears to be your lack of direction and focus. Threes like to make quick decisions. Nines like decisions to emerge after processing and letting nature take its course. Instead of stringing your employee along, be as specific as possible about what it would take for you to be comfortable making a decision. "I'm prepared to make this decision after you talk to X, Y, and Z and review the technical literature," you might say. And then stick to it.

If you're the Three employee, take care that your Nine boss does not feel unduly pushed or crowded. Threes are naturally relentless. You won't have a problem when you want to get something done and your boss agrees. But woe unto the Three who thinks he can pressure a Nine boss who disagrees. Nine will usually outlast the Three.

Four Working with Four

Double Fours, whether they get along or not, always work from a sense of aesthetic purpose: they're trying to do something beautiful or meaningful. As with the double Ones, the key question is whether their visions are congruent.

If they are, each may at first feel, "Oh, at last I'm understood." But because Connoisseur Fours are invested in not being understood, don't be surprised if down the line there's a parting of the ways over some misunderstanding or disappointment. This may start out as a competition to be the most original or the most profound. Four's competitiveness—as strong as Three's—often appears as envy.

If you are a Four who works with a Four, to keep the relationship well oiled remember to ask how the other Four is doing before you go off on an emotional tear of your own.

When Four is boss. To be sure, Four bosses want to know that you appreciate their aesthetic and their vision, and that you take pleasure in sharing their special world. But they also want to know that you bring passion to your work. The more you see your job as a calling or mission, the better.

When Four is employee. Four employees flower when their private sense of aesthetic calling can be matched up with the organization's purposes. The fit is rarely perfect (Four's dissatisfaction again), but comfort is not the Four game: exquisite production under difficult circumstances is (like an oyster experiencing the discomfort of a grain of sand in order to make a pearl).

Four Working with Five

For all their apparent differences, Connoisseur Fours and Sage Fives have far more in common than not. Both tend to introversion. Four and Five invariably create a magical private workspace that is both a defense against the hoi polloi and a personal touchstone.

But where Fours are emotional and take things super-personally, Fives are mental and impersonal. Fours are most comfortable when filled with intense feelings; Fives avoid feelings and are excited by the life of the mind.

Fours are often attracted to Fives because they are emotionally unavailable, a big Four trigger. Fives are taken by Four's bold willingness to engage feelings and people.

When Four is boss and Five is employee. Fours can intrude on others: they assume they know what's best and that you are sure to agree. If you're a Five employee with a Four boss, you need to delineate your boundaries, both emotional and physical. If you're the Four boss of a Five, you would do well to honor your employee's special wisdom and protect his private space.

One of my clients is a firm, run by a Four, that does specialized architecture and engineering. Fours and Fives work side by side in this company on projects located all around the world. Fours and Fives can be very jealous of each other, and so it is here. The Fives envy the Fours' grace and depth of feeling. The Fours envy the Fives' coolness and brilliance. All the Five employees are put off that only the two senior executives have private offices. Everyone else works on drafting tables in a crowded, skylit loft.

For the Fives, there is too much interaction and not enough privacy, so they have learned to set their own psychoemotional boundaries. "No," said one Five engineer to the Four boss, "I cannot leave for Brunei tomorrow. I need more time to plan such a trip." The engineer told me later, "I would never have been able to do that when I first came here. But when all you have is crisis after crisis, then nothing is really so critical anymore."

When Four is employee and Five is boss. If you're a Four employee, you want to make things special. You want the five-color brochure. You prefer to have a business meeting at that nice cafe on the corner. But your Five boss is afraid that you will trap her in commitments of time, energy, or money that she will regret later on.

Be as creative as you can be without committing the boss or stretching the budget. Let the boss know you care about her concern that you not be profligate. At the same time, watch your boundaries. Be especially careful not to burden your boss with your melancholia or your insistence that every project be meaningful, which Five will find onerous. Justify your plans and decisions in terms of logic and the hard evidence, even though you made have made them based on feeling and intuition.

If you're the Five boss, you may have contempt for your Four employee's impulsiveness and lack of emotional mastery. Be careful: Fours are sensitive to this judgment, and anyway, it probably says more about you. Four may judge you as unresponsive and withholding. This configuration works best when

Five allows Four to prime his shadow emotionally and Four can let Five teach him patience and the necessity of passionately dispassionate observation.

Four Working with Six

With all their focus on what's missing, Connoisseur Fours can luxuriate in their delicious anticipation of events, only to find that the actual event is rarely as good. Troubleshooter Sixes are the opposite. They worry about what will happen, but once it does, things are rarely as bad as expected.

Both Fours and Sixes have suffered trauma and are a bit world-weary. Both are looking for the real deal, the hidden meaning or unexpressed truth. But it's facts (Six) versus feelings (Four). Sixes look with their eyes and brain for clues, for leaks of information, for incongruencies. They repress powerful emotions in a misguided effort to keep their thinking logical. Fours trust their deep, powerful feelings and use them as a guide, but sometimes they act wildly and impulsively, driven by their moods.

This relationship works really well when Four, so afraid of abandonment, perceives Six as steadfast and loyal, and Six, so afraid of being done in, perceives Four as steady, authentic, and true.

When Four is boss and Six is employee. If you're a Four boss, you need to feel special, but your Six employee needs to feel safe. Treating a Six as special may make her think she's being set up. Sixes like predictability, logical thinking, and emotional transparency, but these are not your strong points. Moodiness and unpredictable, impulsive decision making, the low side of Four, upsets the Six, who may misinterpret your feelings as a judgment of her or perhaps evidence of a plot against her.

If you're the employee, Four bosses often find themselves in a position where their depth, creative vision, and passion is misunderstood by the outside world. Loyal, logical Six is a comforting, confident ally in fighting the heathens and infidels.

When Four is employee and Six is boss. If you're the Four employee, you and your boss may seem to be temperamental opposites: while you're waiting for the action to begin, she's waiting for it to stop. And while you have strong opinions and know what you like, your Six boss struggles with decisions. Here's the key to working with a Six boss: go ahead and base your decisions on your exquisite taste and special insights, but understand that your boss will want marketing research and logical reasons to move ahead.

You both can be pretty gloomy at times. Your boss may blame her employees. You tend to blame yourself. It may be tempting to accept her blame on top of your own. Better to build esteem by staying with the work in spite of the emotional ups and downs. When the going gets tough, you'll do well to rely on standard operating procedures and routine ways of doing things, even though it's not your habitual style.

If you're the Six boss, you will note that your Four employee is sensitive to things that you are not, for example, subtleties of presentation and emotional tone. You will no doubt find this intelligence useful, but remember that Fours need to be expressly appreciated for their gifts.

Four Working with Seven

Emotional melancholy (Connoisseur Four) versus intellectual optimism (Visionary Seven): what an exceptional polarity! Inspirational Sevens have spirit, but they lack interiority—the sense of the soulful self, where melancholic Fours live. Sevens live the unexamined life of which Socrates spoke, but Fours lead the overexamined life.

Yet there are similarities. Sevens are pied pipers. Fours are seductive sirens. They both delight in seeing magic in the ordinary, and they can promote each other's special talents to the world. This relationship hums when each esteems the other's uncommon touch. Things break down when Four shows contempt for the Seven's surface skimming and Seven feels like Four wants to bring her down.

When Four is boss and Seven is employee. Four bosses can be charmed by the Seven's unbounded imagination. But where Fours take their projects seriously and work hard to realize them (even though the final result may be a letdown), Sevens don't make that kind of emotional commitment and instead float on to the next project. Fours correctly perceive that when everything is magic, as it is for a Seven, then nothing is special.

If you are a Four who has a Seven working for you, try to let her fly and set her up with an air traffic controller (someone to help with follow-through) when she has to land. Take advantage of the fact that she bubbles over with ideas.

If you are a Seven who works for a Four, learn how to stay with a knotty problem past the inspiration stage and work it through. Don't be a lightweight. Use your Four boss's depth as a resource. It's easy to dismiss a Four as a heavy who takes himself too seriously, but Sevens desperately need Four's *gravitas*.

When Four is employee and Seven is boss. This configuration works well when a Seven boss picks a Four employee out of a crowd, seeing her special possibilities, and personally encourages her, just as Cinderella Four has hoped. Four gives substance and weight to Seven's imagination. As Seven generates idea magic, Four can make manifest the feeling magic that goes with it.

If you are a Seven boss, your attentions can charm the Four out of his self-absorption. But be careful: when your attention moves on to other projects, as it inevitably will, your Four employee may feel abandoned.

If you're a Four who works for a Seven, watch the tendency to be fussy, critical, or overbearing. Sevens don't tolerate criticism well, and advice and reports are best given in an upbeat, slightly detached manner, not with the urgency and fervor you ordinarily favor.

Four Working with Eight

A Connoisseur Four with a Top Dog Eight represents one of the great "opposites attract" pairings on the Enneagram. Eight and Four are perhaps the two most intense of the nine types: big, difficult, imperious, each wanting his or her way. This frequently encountered relationship often works well because each is intrigued by the other and can match the other's energy.

As with Two and Eight, Four and Eight have a special bond; the rules and conventions do not apply. Eights are fearless people who live in the moment with few, if any, regrets. Fours live in the romantic past and future. Fortunately, Eights can jar Fours into the material world, while Fours can inspire Eights to look past what is right in front of them to a truer reality inside themselves.

When Four is boss and Eight is employee. Four bosses can be quite practical and knowledgeable managers, but problems arise when difficult, hard-headed Eight employees can't take a hint or even a direct message. If you're a Four with an Eight employee, you need to stand your ground so the Eight knows your limits mean something. You don't need to escalate the conflict; just stand by your clear vision of how things should be (Four's strength).

This relationship works well when the Four boss does not get lost in self-pity or wimpy victimhood. Eights can understand Four's sense of having been "done wrong to," but when Eights feel screwed, they like to "go get the bastards!" Eight can be your best champion.

If you're the Eight employee of a Four boss, the boss almost always has a grand vision. Your skills power the vision in the real world, defending the Four against outside attack and particularly internal implosion. If you are stirred or put off by the Four's emotionalism, consider: Fours always remind Eights to look inward to their real power; it's up to the Eight to get the message.

When Four is employee and Eight is boss. If you're the Eight boss, pressuring, bullying, or overcontrolling your Four employee is a mistake. He'll feel further isolated and misunderstood—his basic defense—and may sink deeper into himself. Find ways for the Four to put his personal stamp on what he does. Fours need to be the boss of their own creativity. And where you might take a hard stand, take a cue from Four's subtlety and emotional deftness, which might show you where an intractable situation can be elegantly turned.

If you're the Four employee, know that your Eight boss's attention is on using her power in the world. An unevolved Eight may interfere with the creative process. Eights come to play; she's just making sure that you acknowledge her power and influence. If you do, her interference will typically wane as she moves to conquering new worlds. If you engage her, you will have an epic Eight battle on your hands.

The best Eights want their power to be effective. They may want to set the creative parameters, but they expect you to boldly flesh out their vision. Eight bosses need and will usually appreciate what you have to offer and will defend the collaboration against the rest of the world.

Four Working with Nine

A pairing of Connoisseur Four with Mediator Nine is another excellent match of opposites. Nines need most of all to learn to want what they want, which is Four's specialty; Fours most of all need to learn equanimity, the Nine sine qua non.

When Four is boss and Nine is employee. Four bosses have a clear vision and a clear agenda. They know how it should be. Nines are usually happy to go along. But Fours can be self-involved, which means that a Nine employee can feel neglected or peripheral to the action, recreating Nine's childhood drama of being overlooked. This sets the stage for Nine to be passive-aggressive.

Your tendency to be highly judgmental can feel like pressure to your Nine employee. Nines need time and space to offer up their valuable opinions and connections. They can provide information that you, with your more narrow focus, might have missed, but they need to be asked; they won't offer it up if you're arrogantly pursuing your own course.

If you're the Nine employee, you can be a sturdy anchor for your Four boss. Nine has the advantage of being able to enter Four's subjective reality and also speak from an objective place. Nine does best for herself by reacting to Four's strong vision to see where she agrees and does not agree and thereby finding her own position.

When Four is employee and Nine is boss. If you're the Nine boss, you want to have a congenial, conflict-free work team. You like to treat everybody equally. But Fours like special treatment. The most empathic Nine bosses treat people the way they want to be treated.

If you're the Four employee, know that Nines tend to be reactive, even as bosses. They wait for problems, and also possibilities, to show themselves. For creative types like Fours, a highside, equanimous, live-and-let-live Nine environment can encourage individual initiative and risk taking. (Lowside Nine discourages initiative.) Cover your bases with your relevant colleagues in advance so that your projects seem to emerge out of the general course of business without so much Sturm und Drang, just the way Nine likes it.

Five Working with Five

You'll often find double Fives working together on a problem-solving assignment. Likely to be conscientious and mutually deferential, these Sages share a sense that energy, money, and time are limited and need to be tightly managed. Energy is inner directed whether personally or within the group. This may mean that when a team of Fives needs to publicize or coordinate what they have done, such efforts won't come easily. It's hard to crack an insular Five dyad. It may be hard to find out what they are up to or how far along they are.

For all their emotional "coolness," double Fives are quite sensitive to each other. Often they seem to know intuitively each other's habits, preferences, lunch times, and secrets without having talked much to each other.

When Five is boss. A Five boss offers Five employees just the sort of respect for boundaries and space that they want for themselves. I know a Five engineer whose boss is a Five. "She never wastes my time with pleasantries or other distractions," he says admiringly. "She lets me get right down to work."

When Five is employee. Fives employees typically don't need much direction. They know what needs to be done and they do it. But they may not be terribly concerned about what the fellow in the next cubicle is doing. A Five researcher told me, "I feel closer to the people in my academic area whom I have never met than to the fellow who works right next to me."

Five Working with Six

Both Five and Six understand caution and the need for privacy. Sage Five is the guru who has special expertise, and Troubleshooter Six is the player who parries the outside world. Together they're a private cabal of two, like George Bush, a Six, who had a special relationship with his Five wise man and confidante, National Security Adviser Brent Scowcroft. Six knows he can trust Five with his private thoughts—very important for a Six—and Five likes to have a single patron to whom to feed information.

When Five is boss and Six is employee. Five's behind-closed-door style and stone face can trigger Six's paranoia. It also doesn't help that Fives tend to hoard information and to have hushed one-on-one meetings. If you're the Five boss, share as much of your office's "inner workings" as you can, even though this goes against your grain. Remember that most Sixes like the psychic glue that comes from feeling part of a team. If you're too isolated, you may end up being the object of blame and suspicion. Better to be on the same side.

If you're the Six employee, check things out when you need to, but also give your Five boss as much space as you can. Sixes can be real worrywarts, sometimes very emotional and agitated, which is irritating to a Five who is trying to keep fears and emotions under wraps..

Sixes like to argue for the good guys against the bad guys, but your Five boss will trust you most when she feels that you're objective, when you don't have an ax to grind or a secret agenda and when you don't seem too agitated. Don't ruin your presentation with your preoccupations.

When Five is employee and Six is boss. Sixes love to be spoon-fed data by a knowledgeable and trustworthy Five. They want to know what things cost, what the employees' corporate politics are, and who's aligned with whom. Fives are excellent at spotting these and objectively reporting them back to Six. A Five employee working for a Six boss is often a reliable sidekick without an agenda of his own, someone who does not get out in front or push the boss too far.

If you're the Six boss, you probably admire your Five employee's emotional detachment. But you may not like the way she keeps you in the dark about her work. Set up an easy but formal reporting structure, even though it may go against her grain. A written, long-term work plan will make it very clear what you expect, with *built-in* reporting procedures. That way your employee can go off and do her work on her own without feeling you're looking over her shoulder all the time.

If you're the Five employee, you already have the knack of advising your Six boss from a cool, logical place, just the way he likes it. But watch out. You have a powerful streak of reticence and willfulness. Difficulties arise when you are not forthcoming about what you are working on or if you feel drained by the boss's intense reporting demands and react by clamming up. Your boss is already insecure enough about his authority and probably your allegiances without your silently and diffidently going back into your cubbyhole without even lip service to his instructions. Take the time to write up the work plan suggested above. When impersonal structures are in place and followed, you'll both feel better.

Five Working with Seven

The combination of a Sage Five and a Visionary Seven can feel like mixing oil and water. Fives like to nail ideas down; Sevens like to float them. Fives like precision; Sevens thrive on ambiguity. Fives are linear thinkers who extrapolate from a clear understanding of specifics to a general theory. Sevens conceive a grand theory and then test it on specifics. But both of these mental types understand and are excited about grand intellectual schemes and complex ideas. For both, a good idea is as valuable as a good deed.

This is the relationship between research or engineering and marketing. Dilbert, the Scott Adams cartoon character who is a Five engineer, is sent on assignment to marketing, generally a Seven function. The entrance to the marketing department is bounded by Roman columns holding a sign that says, "Marketing—Two-Drink Minimum." Inside, one can make out a bacchanal. This is the Five's view of Seven.

When Five is boss and Seven is employee. Fives tend to keep everything close to the vest. Sevens tend to be freewheeling and may feel oppressed by Five controlling too much. If you're the Five boss, you may find that your Seven employee floats a great many imaginative ideas—so many that you become exhausted and disaffected. (Five takes ideas seriously in a way that Seven does not.) Learn to take Seven seriously without having to take each Seven idea seriously.

You can help by pinning your Seven down. A Seven doesn't necessarily want to realize every new idea she has, as she has so many of them. Help her decide which ones to pursue. Help Seven with a process for really making the idea happen rather than just thinking it through.

If you're the Seven employee, your Five boss needs to know that you take your job seriously. Follow-through helps. Take the time to add thorough, comprehensive appendixes and references to your reports.

When Five is employee and Seven is boss. If you're the employee, your enthusiasm will sell your Seven boss on a project as much as will the project's merit. Five employees of Sevens do well when they are enthusiastic about the boss's ideas or at least about their own. Fives usually are very enthusiastic about their own ideas but not so as anyone might know.

If you are a Seven boss, you are likely very bright, but you may be emotionally casual in a way that can come out hurtful or cruel, especially with sensitive Fives. Consider the impact of your emotional self. And although you're a natural performer who may find a ready audience in your employees, remember that the Five does his real work in private.

Five Working with Eight

Top Dog Eight is the most explosive type on the Enneagram. Sage Five is the most implosive, shepherding what feels like a finite amount of energy. The more space Eight takes up, the more Five becomes invisible. But Fives are not weak; they have the toughest, most impenetrable boundaries on the Enneagram.

Perhaps because of their differences, Five and Eight often have a terrific collaboration in the workplace. They rarely compete over turf, and they're able to see each other's strengths. The best Fives finds Eight's willingness to engage others and marketplace transforming. Sophisticated Eights understand the power in dispassion. And like Eight in the interpersonal arena, Five can be quite the bully in the intellectual arena. It's useful for Fives to see how Eights give way for experts among their employees who have data, advice, or wisdom that fortifies the Eight's empire. Similarly, it's useful for Eights to see how Five's quiet, reserved persona belies a ferocious approach to business.

When Five is boss and Eight is employee. If you're the Five boss, you already know that your Eight employee sometimes needs a strong leash. Eights like to test boundaries; as employees, they may press against your rules or space or authority. But you can handle your Eight—after all, your boundaries are mighty. And at his best, your employee can provide the muscle and enthusiasm to make your ideas happen as well as his own.

If you're the employee, don't make the mistake of seeing your Five boss as a pushover. It's true that sometimes she may get overwhelmed, but you won't find her caving in to your pressure. Fives can dig in their heels with the best of them. Better to make private or written appeals to logic on the boss's terms.

When Five is employee and Eight is boss. If you're a Five who works for an Eight, your boss likes to have everything exposed and on the table. Fives, of course, like to shield as much as they can. Give the boss the sense that everything's in sight. Eights don't need all the details, just the sense of dominion and that things are being handled. If you've got a problem with something at work, don't brush it under your mouse pad; come out with it. "I expect my managers to tell me when they don't agree," says one Eight boss. It won't hurt for you to learn to be a little more direct, to risk a bold encounter. You can plan it in advance. This lets your Eight boss know she can trust you.

Eight bosses at their worst can be bullies who run over their Five employees, but at their best they rely on their Fives to tell them when they've gone too far or to provide a cool workout of the numbers after they've completed their tirade. Sometimes, just for fun, Eights will push Fives hard just to see what happens. Some Fives flee out of habit. The best Fives stand their ground.

If you're an Eight with a Five in your employ, be careful not to lose his potentially crucial contributions by insisting on your high-energy, confrontational mode of communication. Let him write reports or e-mail, with summaries to you or to your assistant.

Five Working with Nine

Sage Fives are the most highly bounded on the Enneagram. Mediator Nines are the most boundaryless. Nines are social and conventional, concerned with avoiding conflict and disapproval. Fives are not particularly social (although they may pretend to be) and are unconventional within their private world. Fives are cogent and focused. Nines bring a broad perspective. Both can feel a certain hopelessness, a tendency to despair or to give up too soon. This often translates into being unable or unwilling to enjoy the fruits of one's labors for oneself. Yet this relationship can work well because Nines are accepting creatures of habit and Fives don't like surprises.

When Five is boss and Nine is employee. How can you as a Nine get on with your Five boss? Your boss wants the facts, cold and direct. Encounters must not be draining. He gets nervous when he sees you start to talk and it's obvious you're settling in for the long haul. Stop. Spit it out and get to the point. State your position and emphasize your contribution (both hard for a Nine). State the decision points for the Five. Then go.

How can you as a Five get on with your Nine employee? You know what you want, but you're not inclined to nurse others along if it takes too much effort. Fives are self-starters, but Nines need a jump. One way to enlist the Nine is to get her involved in collaborative or group activities, which hold out a particular appeal. Nines call their best mediating skills into action when the Nine is an intergroup boundary spanner, someone who communicates between work teams or projects. Fives often forget to fill up these intergroup or interproject spaces, leaving the people in such enterprises isolated and unaware of the connections they can and should be making. Fives learn when Nines make connections to persons and groups. You may not be particularly interested in commingling, but your Nine employee likes to feel connected.

One final bit of advice: Don't necessarily be impatient or cut your Nine employee off when she starts to talk. Highside Nines have an extraordinarily broad and balanced view—they have plenty of "random access memory"—and can help you to usefully expand your vision beyond your precious intellectual concerns, if you let them.

When Five is employee and Nine is boss. If you're the Nine boss, you like your people to be part of a team; your Five employee likes to hold himself apart. However, your Five employee will be interested in how his work fits into the grand plan. Fives can team up with ideas if not with good vibes. Fives might feel flooded with such feelings but not with information they need. Make your assignments clear and discrete for the Five.

If you're the Five employee, you might find a Nine boss ideal. Fives are the least open on the Enneagram to demands being made on them. Nines are the least likely to make demands. Some types may feel unmoored, but you know exactly what to do with this kind of freedom. Memo the Nine as appropriate.

Six Working with Six

Sixes were betrayed as children, so they look for signs of perfidy in their colleagues. This hyperalertness actually creates suspicion in others. When Troubleshooter Sixes work together, they both suspect there is more going on than meets the eye. But rather than simply asking, both prefer to figure out what the other is up to. Misunderstandings and mixed signals abound.

Authority and trust are always the central issues between Sixes. "What authority do you have over me? Can I trust you?" each Six silently asks the other. Interactions between Sixes, however sympathetic and warm, may avoid spontaneity and dwell on the negative, with accomplishments getting short shrift. Movement to action may be a long time in coming.

But this dyad works well when the Sixes are on the same side and when the issue is vanquishing the competition, forestalling disaster, or crusading for just causes. They can be terrifically perceptive about others outside the dyad. They will thoroughly discuss and analyze ideas and hash them out.

When Six is boss. Six bosses have to learn to be authorities. But because authority issues are so close to a Six's heart, the best Six bosses are the most thoughtful and considered about being a boss.

If you're the boss, don't be accusatory when you're feeling mistrustful. Sit down with your Six employee, air your concerns, and ask her to air hers. The more Sixes let each other know what they're thinking, the better. If your Six employee feels you don't trust her, explain that for you trust is built brick by brick. You can explain that specific actions will help build trust, like meeting internal deadlines and interim performance goals.

When Six is employee. If you're the employee, in order to get rid of any doubt, you may find yourself idealizing your boss as a strong protector, or you may cast yourself as the devil's advocate, the person who gives the boss the hardest time. Don't worry. Your skeptical boss won't trust either. The issues between you and your boss are about trusting each other and trusting yourselves. You have to learn to work under an authority without losing yourself in the process.

Since your habits of mind are similar, this relationship can work extremely well if both of you agree on who the bad guys are: the government, the suits in the front office, the competition. But if you can't agree on who the enemy is, it may turn out to be each other.

If your boss does something that makes you feel uncomfortable, check things out. Ask directly. Ask about purposes and intentions. Reveal your own self-interests. To be trusted by your Six boss, be trustworthy, transparent (even in your dissatisfaction), responsible, and a team player.

Six Working with Seven

The pairing of a Troubleshooter Six with a Visionary Seven looks like a relationship of opposites. For Sixes, nothing is certain. For Sevens, everything is possible. Pollyanna Sevens believe the hopeless mess in front of them will magically turn out all right. Sixes suspect that, even though everything seems all right, it will shortly turn to manure. Sixes are serious and often fearful. Sevens rarely seem either fearful or serious.

When Six is boss and Seven is employee. If you're the Six boss, you probably wonder whether you can trust your Seven employee, who so obviously embellishes and may not follow through. But take some time with this clever fellow. He'll open your horizons to possibilities that you dismiss, and with his chutzpah he can go a long way to making them happen. The trick with this trickster is to take the time to put agreements and assignments in writing, with clear deadlines and obvious consequences. Give yourself a cushion, though, because Seven is bound to miss the first deadline. Setting a deadline only to extend it may seem like a silly game, but try to be nice about it. Sevens just don't respond well to reprimands. You will need to hold firm to the second deadline so that your Seven employee knows to get the work done.

Sevens have as much problem with authority as Sixes. Sevens typically try to equalize authority when they are the employee. "We're all just people here," says the Seven employee, "even though I'm a little more imaginative."

If you're the Seven employee, your boss wants a predictable course of action she can rely on. You have a pocketful of plans, all constantly in flux and adjustable according to your circumstances and your mood. This is guaranteed to make your Six boss frustrated and nervous. Moreover, since you disdain hierarchy, believing it only inhibits your creativity and fun, your tendency to treat your Six boss like a colleague offends her, since she relies on her place in the hierarchy for identity, even when her power is understated or implied.

Although you have a strong temptation to move on to new projects as your initial enthusiasm fades, your Six boss strongly prefers that you finish what's on your plate. The keys to Sevens carving out a place for themselves with a Six boss are completion, regularity, and predictability, and keeping your word, all of which are a stretch for a Seven, and all of which are central to the Seven's own growth.

When Six is employee and Seven is boss. If you're the Six employee, know that your constant naysaying and worrywarting is likely to make your Seven boss unhappy. Why are you raining on his parade? Sevens want good vibes. Ask questions not as a cynic or skeptic but as a fellow enthusiast. Get the Seven going with brainstorming, and let him help you: "How can we handle this?"

If you're a Seven boss, your Six employee is looking for an authority she can trust. She has been since she was a kid. When Sevens are the boss, authority often seems casual and diffuse. Help your Six feel safe by answering her inquiries directly and responsibly instead of with dismissive or patronizing comments that reflect your own insecurity as an authority. Take your own inspirational leadership seriously, always central guidance for a Seven but especially when there are Sixes around.

Six Working with Eight

Top Dog Eights are not ambivalent about exercising power. Lacking guile, they plow straight ahead. Troubleshooter Sixes, on the other hand, are far more strategic and circumspect. Sixes are by nature worriers, whether it shows or not.

Yet both Six and Eight consider themselves tough-minded realists. Both share an interest in righting unjust wrongs, particularly the abuses of authority, and in defending the underdog. Both agree that there are a lot of fools at work and that the business world is a jungle where you have to watch out for yourself.

When Six is boss and Eight is employee. If you're the Six boss, the world where you live—in your head, pondering hidden motives and meanings—is not your Eight employee's natural playground. The powerful concerns that loom so large to you (about the pitfalls in a project or the vulnerabilities in a negotiation, for example) do not generally register with much intensity for Eights. You may have to megaphone these concerns to your Eight employee.

You find direct confrontation not only difficult but unwise. But your Eight employee thrives on it. She's tempted to test you constantly. (Are you a wimp? Do you mean what you say?) You're not likely to stop her from doing this, but you don't have to rise to the bait. Your strong sense of your own authority—all the best Sixes have it—will save you. (*You're* not a wimp!)

Eights are among the most loyal types on the Enneagram. A smart Six boss will give her loyal Eight employee a fiefdom the Eight can run more or less independently. Then you both can fight the entrenched bureaucracy, while supporting worthy underdogs and avenging those foolish enough to try to take advantage of you.

If you're the Eight employee, your boss wants to know that you're not a loose cannon on deck and that you will yield to his authority as boss. The Six boss's world is like film noir: what's going on may not be completely clear—there are a lot of shadows and a lot of whispering—but it's sure to be ominous. The Six boss's strategy is to keep a close watch on what's happening. You, on the other hand, don't look that carefully. Something bothers you and you charge ahead, more like a bull in a china shop. This can be terrifying for your Six boss, who feels that the only legitimate approach is to be careful.

As an Eight, you like to do things your own way, and you value your independence as a leader and manager. But your Six boss will be reluctant to give you that much power unless you have shown a cool head and loyalty and fealty for some time and indicate that you will do so in the future. Once you apply your extraordinary confidence and energy to being your boss's ally and defender, your boss will give you considerable latitude.

When Six is employee and Eight is boss. Eights have little or no ambivalence about telling people what to do and no regrets about reprimanding them or keeping them in line. Sixes are always afraid the authority might annihilate them. If you're a Six employee of an Eight boss, you might be looking for hidden agendas or subtle clues about what your boss is up to where none exist. What you see is what you get. And, as a Six, you may want to keep the ball at least partially hidden for your own, or the project's, safety. Your boss is likely to find this sneaky and infuriating. Eight wants everything on the table.

If you're the Eight boss of a Six, you have your in-house counsel. If you blow off Six's concerns as weak or pointless in the way that some Eights do, you stand a good chance of missing something important. The situation at hand may call for Six's subtler strengths: insight, commitment, consensus building, and strategizing.

Six Working with Nine

Mediator Nines handle problems by fuzzing over conflicting positions. Troubleshooter Sixes are precisely the opposite, bringing the adversary into sharp relief. "Are you with us or agin' us?" asks the Six of Nine, but the Nine is, to some extent, both. This relationship can be immensely successful and particularly stable over the long term when each includes the perspective of the other. Six takes the blinders off to a wider perspective at Nine, seeing connections previously ignored; Nine hunkers down, taking a focused personal position at last, at Six. When both are oriented to getting work done—the Three position—the Enneagram's sturdy inner triangle is complete.

When Six is boss and Nine is employee. Six is looking for evidence that she can trust her Nine employees. Nine's easygoingness can seem sloppy and untrustworthy to an ever-vigilant, tightly wound Six. But Nine's regular habits go a long way toward establishing confidence. If you're a Nine who works for a Six, be on time. Pay attention to details. Don't say yes when you mean to say no. Do what you have agreed to do instead of justifying noncompliance because you want to avoid confrontation. Respond to your Six boss's concerns with concern rather than mediating them away or overcontexting them.

If you're a Six boss of a Nine, remember that Nines have to feel accepted before they can shine. Your native criticality and suspiciousness obviate against that. Instead, ask the Nine to flesh out decisions for action—to consider alternatives, interpretations, consequences, and affected parties that you may have missed but that the Nine naturally senses.

When Six is employee and Nine is boss. Nines are mellow, calm in the belief that the organization can run itself. Sixes are concerned. Six employees are looking for a similar sense of concern from the boss that their issues are being taken seriously. But Nines believe everything will come out all right in time—and probably sooner if you leave it alone. Nines are focused on good feeling, mutuality, and connectedness. They'd rather experience harmony than deal with unpleasant facts that cause dissension. Six's specialty is attention to unpleasant facts.

If you're a Six who works for a Nine, express your concerns without also implying that the sky is falling (unless it is). Nine is always helped when you don't exaggerate and when you don't dump the problem in his lap without having thought through some possible solutions.

Moreover, as a Six you are likely to ascribe intention to your boss's actions that he does not have. Nines simply are not coy or strategic like Sixes. Sixes have a need to create enemies and allies. Nines don't. Nines create "us-ness." Be wary, as a Six, of making attacks on those whom the Nine tends to include, especially co-workers.

If you're the Nine who is the boss of a Six, your insistence on pleasant relations may feel like a threat or subterfuge. Instead, lay out the rational basis and underlying motivators for running things in a certain way. Don't paper over the problems. Sixes like problems. Dealing with them helps them feel safe and aligned with you.

Seven Working with Seven

Bright and facile Visionary Sevens can make a terrifically imaginative pair. Enthusiasm is the glue. They're not bogged down by history or the way things have always been done. They're actively open-minded. But the rules of their game, their plans, and their priorities change quickly, so colleagues and assistants need to check in regularly as they move forward or make commitments on behalf of any given project.

Of course, Sevens can be narcissistic—it's their *own* grand plans they're interested in—and so in a work group with other Sevens they may find themselves competing for the position of Top Seven. It can be hard for them to collaborate, especially with other Sevens, because they tend to see things only from their own point of view. Unlike groups of Nines, who usually merge together easily, Sevens irritate one another as they see their own Seven predicament right in front of them: ideas that had so much romance yesterday die of neglect as everyone moves on to the next set of ideas and schemes.

When Seven is boss. Sevens as bosses, for all their hogging of the agenda, still give the appearance of being antiauthoritarian. However, when their own ox is being gored and they go to Stress Point One, they can bark out a fusillade of corrections or instructions that would make any One proud.

The best Seven bosses are inspiring leaders who borrow from a range of disciplines to forge new pathways. Seven bosses are terrific at pulling together all the disparate elements to make a project come together. On the low side, they can be irresponsible, changing directions when the impulsive wind blows and confusing their followers. They may wake up in the morning having in mind Microsoft's question (meant to illustrate the unbounded imagination): "Where do you want to go today?" But with Sevens the imagination can be too unbounded.

When Seven is employee. Sevens as employees can be problematic because they are antiauthoritarian without owning it. They are easily distracted, they don't naturally follow through, and they seem to think they work for themselves even though you pay their salary. They need to be frequently reinspired, and they frequently reinspire themselves and all those around them.

Seven Working with Eight

Eight and Seven are the physical and mental versions of each other. Sevens are conceptualists who fly in the air. Eights are concretists who roam the earth. Both are very confident within their domains. Both like to create excitement, to poke at the establishment, and to question conventional wisdom. Both also tend to overdo, gamble, and stir things up, often to the point of muddying the waters.

When Seven is boss and Eight is employee. If you're the boss, your Eight employee may be frustrated by frivolous changes in direction or disappointed that you don't seem to back him up. What a waste of good fight-power! Eights, though, are just the ticket to back up a Seven. They can be sturdy and responsible, and they offer Seven the ability to power things through to completion in the real world. Help your Eight employee help you by unleashing him on a specific project with a mandate to get the job done.

If you're the employee, your Seven boss may strike you as insubstantial, as fearful of commitment, and as all talk and not really wanting to make an impact. But Seven has just what Eight needs: the view from above. This takes Eight out of "my way" into systems thinking, into imagination, into considering his impacts and effects. Eights are in high performance when they are conscious of their impact on other people.

When Seven is employee and Eight is boss. Eight bosses have a strong hand and are firm leaders. But if you are an Eight boss, setting out to put your Seven right may yield you only a handful of air: rationalizations, excuses, and a flashy smile. You may feel you can't rely on your Seven, who seems like a lightweight dilettante. Sevens work very well as members of a fast-moving interdisciplinary team. Don't put your Seven in a box just so you can control him. Instead, smooth his path by making him *responsible* for results, and give him the power to actualize them.

Eight bosses may seem earthbound and heavy to free-spirited Sevens. If you're the Seven employee, your task is to lighten the Eight, not with foolishness, but by opening her up to possibility, flexibility, and imagination. Eights, who plow straight ahead, can get blindsided because they miss important premises or the premises have changed. Sevens rarely miss a changing premise.

Eights need to feel that the Seven is backing them up, that the Seven is not distracted or seduced by other interests, and that the Seven will be there if push comes to shove. For Seven, it is a question of sober commitment.

Seven Working with Nine

Nines may stay with one company over a career: they like comfortable, long-term relationships where they are known for who they are without having to sell themselves. Mediator Nines are conservative—not necessarily politically—but in terms of their interest in and ability to tolerate change. Visionary Sevens, on the other hand, are master innovators; they need to move on, to be energized by new opportunities. Along the way they may drop commitments and people.

From their different places, both Seven and Nine strive to eliminate conflict, disharmony, and bad vibes. Sevens want things to stay upbeat, and Nines don't like interpersonal turmoil. So they may avoid hashing things out when that's just what the collaboration needs. Nine's collusion against dealing with difficulties means that the enterprise could suddenly come crashing down unless there are fail-safe processes and procedures that force red flags to be acknowledged.

When Seven is boss and Nine is employee. If you're the Seven boss, you probably have a font of ideas about how to energize and help your Nine subordinates. Your employees, though, will feel overwhelmed unless you give them time to assimilate your suggestions.

Nines are real workhorses, a boon to Sevens, who hate drudgery. Your Nine employees will be generally happy to do your routine work so long as they can stay on a course and in a groove. Change your plans whimsically, and you effectively pull the rug out from under them. I have seen Nine employees sink into despair because by the time they were halfway though a project it was no longer central or interesting to their Seven boss. Much worse for the Nine is the disruptive chaos that Seven generates simply because it feels exciting—like assigning work or having meetings at odd hours or taking sudden trips or rushing to make crazy deadlines. The best Seven bosses give Nine employees a sense of continuity despite the fact that it goes entirely against their grain. Seven bosses can encourage Nines to be the responsible backstop during their frequent flights of fancy. For Nines, taking a position is a major task involving a large mobilization of energy. For Sevens, experimenting with a position is just an experiment, no big deal. Seven bosses can encourage Nines to so experiment.

If you are a Nine employee and your boss is a Seven, the boss's frequent and inevitable changes in direction can lead to resignation. Nines, however, often came on board originally because they liked the boss's enthusiasm. Problems invariable arise when Nines rely on the Seven for their energy fix instead of sourcing themselves and their own lives.

When Seven is employee and Nine is boss. If you're the Nine boss, you like things done consistently, the same way over and over. You perceive the chameleon Seven's rejection of the established routine as annoying and too time consuming. You much prefer for people to fit in with the group. But your Seven employee wants to be seen as special and needs a steady diet of enthusiasm and new ideas. Make a comfortable (for the group) place for Seven to experiment, share her vision, and hypothesize without due consequence. The imaginative Seven can help you create it.

If you're the Seven employee, for your own advantage, notice your unspoken contempt for what you see as the Nine's stodginess. You may be only vaguely aware of it, but Nine is very sensitive to that kind of lack of acceptance. It comes back to you as a tighter tether and a lack of encouragement. Instead of your intellectual pretension, why not see what the boss's needs really are?—

always helpful for a Nine. This requires you to settle in for an ongoing give-and-take. Nines like to talk things through and let the conclusions emerge. Don't take silence—or in the case of Nine, even yes—for agreement or an answer. Once the direction is clear, Nines like you to keep in close touch ("merger") so that what needs to be revised can be by collaboration.

Eight Working with Eight

When two Top Dogs come together, worlds collide. Eights are driven by what Alfred Adler called "the will to dominate." A double Eight partnership, whether as colleagues or as boss and employee, is bound to be a power struggle of a kind, even though it may be hearty and warm, as well. Eights can be powerful allies, willing to channel their power for the good of the company or their mutual benefit, but the relationship can degenerate into a vindictive, ruthless, and bloody war.

Although Eights are easily offended by a perceived trespass upon their prerogatives, they are relatively thick skinned vis-à-vis the subtle emotional states or evanescent motives and desires of others. Nor do they have easy access to the fine points of their own inner landscape or to such feelings as guilt and remorse. The consequence is that while Eights can bond tightly with each other (and with other types) and the relationship can be exciting and especially productive, the feeling tone is typically painted in primary colors.

When Eight is boss. As bosses, Eights are strong leaders who expect absolute fealty, which they magnanimously repay with money and perks and authority. The positions of others may seem puny and distant compared to the clear course charted by the Eight's own will. "There's only one general in this army and that's me," said an Eight to his Eight employee. As an Eight boss, see if you can structure situations that don't simply crush the aspirations of your Eight employee, because the employee will have little choice but to take revenge. Bullying or threatening only recreates the Eight childhood dilemma. Instead, carve out an area in which your employee can be the Eight in charge. The very best situation for a double Eight is where the company or the job is ever expanding, just as Eight has an expanding appetite for power. Otherwise the Eight employee will soon be crowding his boss.

When Eight is employee. As the Eight employee of an Eight, what will surely seem like a fight for respect and a just result for you and your people will seem like a threat to your boss. Her response won't be complicated. Like any self-respecting Eight, she'll escalate the situation until she gets what she wants. No need to wimp out. Instead, show your true strength. Hang tough, but don't engage in battle. Yield where it makes sense to yield. If you do threaten the boss with a power struggle, you'd better be sure you can win it all, or you will be out.

Eight Working with Nine

Top Dog Eight and Mediator Nine are both creatures of will. Both are very stubborn. Eights get their way by powering ahead. Nines get their way by yielding or by appearing to yield and outlasting their opponent.

Eight and Nine together can be a great pair. More than anything, Eight is looking for "the peaceable kingdom," which Ally Nine represents. Nine is stuck, unable to express his repressed shadow, which is enormous rage at having been forced to give up his will; Eight's blunt directness primes the Nine to express his own position directly.

When Eight is boss and Nine is employee. Eight is a potentate who leads by decree. If you're a Nine creature of habit, you'll be upset that procedures seem to change according to your Eight boss's whim. Eights like to know that the people in the foxhole with them can be counted on in battle, so they create turmoil to see how everyone acts under battle conditions. Your habitual distractedness, conciliatory tendencies, apparent lack of ardor, and, most of all, your abiding ability to see the other side may make your boss wary.

Your biggest problem point may be that you ruminate too much. Your Eight boss wants to move ahead as quickly as possible. Getting it right, or getting it balanced, is far less critical to her than getting it. In fact, seeing all sides seems to her like a failure of will. Make choices deliberately; if it's complex, as it often is to a Nine, keep it simple and "just do it."

If you're the Eight boss, you'll quickly learn that Nines don't respond well to being bullied. It recreates the battle of the chamber pot, Nine's central issue. Instead, welcome your Nine employees as part of the operation. They don't need to be in a central decision-making role, they just need to feel like they belong.

Don't overlook the fact that Nine can be a terrific help to an Eight boss, especially one who is locked into a public position. Nines are outgoing, easy, and friendly, and they can renegotiate an agreement for the boss after the fact without anyone quite realizing what has happened.

When Eight is employee and Nine is boss. If you're the Eight employee, you probably feel frustrated by your boss's tendency to move ahead at a snail's pace and by his tortured ambivalence about decisions. But you can't force or bully. Nine just digs in and becomes steadfast. A power tip: don't understimate the power of Nine. Lao Tzu said that in the war between Nine (yin) and Eight (yang), Nine wins inevitably over time.

Most Nine bosses are willing to cede considerable field command to Eights as long as things go smoothly. Nines don't want to deal with added conflict or make decisions they don't need to. Think of Patton, an audacious Eight who usually got his own way. But when he went to excess, the Nine Eisenhower was quick to put him in his place.

If you're the Nine boss of an Eight, delegate. What do you need to make the decision? A trial run? A problem resolved? A division restructured? Some employees told what for? Let the Eight handle it. But clearly state the limits to her authority. Eights just naturally want to expand their bailiwick, and Nine is strongly advised not to compromise. Nines like give-and-take, but with an Eight it's much better to set strict limits and enforce them with certainty.

Nine Working with Nine

Nines prefer to respond and react, so who goes first? Who prioritizes? A pair of Nines may struggle to find direction or change direction.

At their best, Nines act within their role, with the power and authority of their role, supporting each other as necessary. When they're stuck, both may sell out in order to avoid conflict. This is the appearance of harmony, not the real thing.

Decision making is a killer for this pair. Nines have an agenda, but it is usually clarified in response to another. The trick is to act existentially. Do something that creates a position. Then the other Nines can react to it and use their exceptional skills at collaboration to eliminate the least desirable alternatives in sequence.

When Nine is boss. Nines can be terrific bosses capable of creating a collegial, cooperative atmosphere and bringing out a wide range of opinions in their diverse employees. They're the best on the Enneagram at honoring the natural, organic life of the organization. Nine leaders want the workplace to hum by itself, which can be either the most callous form of neglect or the highest form of leadership.

If you are the Nine boss of a Nine employee, you *must* claim your vision, prioritize, and make choices. Procedures need to be established so that your employees (not just the Nines) feel comfortably on track. You may see yourself as a major delegator, but unless a task and its goals are crystal clear, your Nine employee will see you as passing the buck. Give your employee an established position to respond to. But take care: excessive willfulness on the part of the boss can lead to passive-aggressiveness by the employee.

When Nine is employee. If you are the Nine employee of a Nine, you face the danger of being lost in the Land of the Lotus Eaters. Here's a way out: use your Nine skills to help your Nine boss set an agenda for you and your work. Let it fit into the natural flow of the work that is already being done, but let it match your goals that you have determined for yourself. Nine bosses prefer to react and respond as much as Nine employees. Put your views in the context of collaboration and consensus. Be proactive but don't push.

Making the Numbers Work for You

Even the most ancient and esoteric practitioners of the Enneagram meant this eminently pragmatic system to be put to good practical use. So go forth and type.

But be careful out there.

Because, if the truth be known, there are no Enneagram *types*—there are only people, people who have habitual patterns of thinking and seeing and feeling, patterns of being in relationship, of leading or following or deciding. Getting a handle on these habits and the forces that create and drive them can make a person accessible and understandable, especially if that person happens to be you. More than anything else, the Enneagram is a tool for compassion.

Still, there are those who will take the Procrustean approach. Procrustes ran an early discount motel on the road from Megara to Athens. When tall travelers were too long for the bed, he lopped off their feet to make them fit. When travelers were too short, he stretched them to make them fit. Many people use a similar torture with the Enneagram. "Oh, you argue just like a Six! You're such a blamer!" one student berated her poor husband, until they discovered he was really a Four. He didn't even know what had hit him (except that it was tragic). He had been . . . *Enneagrammed*.

Perhaps Enneagram "masochists" do even more damage. These are the people who limit themselves to the perceived boundaries of their type. "I don't relate well to others; I'm a Five," says one such self-torturer, convincing himself and others, and putting himself in an Enneagram prison of his own making.

Such people, by rigidly hiding behind their type, can turn the Enneagram into a vicious circle. They use their style as an excuse to hold tighter to their own patterns rather than as an opportunity for letting go. "I am an Eight. I tell it like it is. You'd better learn to deal with it," says someone unwilling to look at how supple the Enneagram system really is.

The truth is that in the Enneagram all of the types are connected. All of the types are available to each of us. Once you know where you are on the map, you can always "get there from here." The Enneagram is about flow, as each type becomes its opposite. It is about balance as we appreciate our essential polarities. The Enneagram is not about constructing a series of boxes; rather, it is a tool for exploding them.

The Enneagram teaches us to look beyond behavior to deep intent. When we see the world as others see it, from their own frames of reference, we can more accurately hear and understand—and be more clearly heard and understood. By knowing your own frame you can get out of your own way, call on your natural skills and gifts with authority and without reservation, work effectively with heart and power, and bring spirit into the world. That is what the guardians of the system intended. Godspeed.

ABOUT THE ENNEAGRAM

The Enneagram styles are very old. Homer (ca. 750 B.C.E.) knew the nine basic themes essentially as they are today. Odysseus travels through each of the Enneagram domains in *exact reverse numerical order.* Here is his itinerary:

2. Calypso, the Two nymph who offers Odysseus every worldly good and even immortality if he will but stay with her.
1. The Phaeacians, perfect Martha Stewart One hosts, where honor, respect, fair play, and courtliness count most, along with beautifully prepared meals.
9. The Land of the Lotus Eaters, dreamy, forgetful Nines.
8. The Cyclops, powerful, vengeful giant Eights; "Each one dwells in his own mountain cave, dealing out rough justice to wife and child, indifferent to what others do."[1]
7. Aeolia, a Seven island that floats whimsically on the sea, relocating with the wind, where the Seven residents feast and party.
6. The paranoid Laestrygonians, Sixes who attack Odysseus without provocation.
5. The solitary Circe, the cunning Five sorceress.
4. The visit to Hades, the psychic underworld. The Sirens, Fours who bewitch passing mariners to tragedy with melodious song.
3. Scylla and Charybdis, a monster and a whirlpool, a rock and a hard place, where skillful sailing full speed ahead is the only way through.

Homer must have known something of the relationships among the Enneagram types as well, because he knew the critical order. He was likely associated with long-established civilizations to the east, the Chaldeans, and the Persians, who had developed elaborate cosmologies. Centuries later, Pythagoras (ca. 550 B.C.E.) traveled east and studied these ancient traditions and perhaps the Babylonian Hebrew as well. As philosopher Oscar Ichazo has noted, the Enneagram symbol itself is one of the geometric "seals" Pythagoras, and later the Platonists, used to show the special qualities and relationships among numbers.

With the extraordinary spread of Neoplatonism, the material entered the Catholic and Orthodox churches through the early church fathers and eventually traveled east into Sufism and west to reconnect with the Jewish Kabbalah in France and Spain.

The basic themes of the Enneagram—including the balancing of a formal series of opposites as a pathway to development—came to a full flower in Kabbalah, the central works of Jewish mysticism.

George Gurdjieff (d. 1949), an Armenian-Russian teacher, used the Enneagram extensively as a mystical tool, although not as a personality system. For Gurdjieff, the Enneagram was "the fundamental hieroglyph of a universal language," and he said that for those who knew how to use it, the Enneagram made libraries useless.

The father of the ideas of the Enneagram of personality as it is taught today is Oscar Ichazo, a philosopher and teacher initially from Bolivia. Ichazo's original work elaborated the psychology of each type as part of his larger philosophical system in the 1950s and '60s in Bolivia and Chile. He used the Enneagram symbol to describe the habitual, cyclical nature of the Enneagram styles, the importance of the various pulls on them, and their paths of development. Perhaps most important, he emphasized that all of the styles are available to each of us, so that his ingenious version of the Enneagram is far more than a collection of personality types.

Ichazo's student Claudio Naranjo, a psychiatrist, first taught the system in the United States in 1971, elaborating the types in the light of modern personality theory. From these teachings come a broad array of Enneagram applications to leadership, communication, relationships, and personal development.

1. Homer, *The Odyssey*, trans. Robert Fitzgerald (New York: Vintage, 1961), 148.

ACKNOWLEDGMENTS

This book evolved out of years of teaching and consulting. Hundreds of people participated on panels of examples of Enneagram type over the years. Thanks particularly to Diana Brennan, Sheri Cark, Lee Christian, Katherine Cole, Sue Colin, Becky Crusoe, Carole Cunningham, John Davis, Cathy Flanigan, Sam Fraser, Fritz Furrip, Annika Gruenn, Hans Gruenn, John Hornick, Margaret Kerry-Wilcox, Helene Hancock, Lowell Hancock, Bill Heiser, Linda Heiser, Carol Houst, Mary Ellen Knowles, Peggy Ogata, Peggy Painton, Jamie Persky, Liza Perksy, John Phillips, Judy Phillips, Margaret Prietto, Kristin Pugliese, Rick Rodriguez, Thomas Rodriguez, Judith Searle, Richard Seraile, Sophia Sharpe, Don Speuhler, Jane Speuhler, Laura Sullivan, Suzanne Taylor, Katherine Welds, Phyllis Zatzick, Tommie Jo Zimmerman, and special thanks to the Rousseaus — Kathy, Ann, Cindy, Julie, and Mary — who appeared at far-flung seminars.

Many busy executives and professionals took time to be interviewed for this book. Thanks to Jessica Andrews, Laurie Biscaro, Rich Byrne, Jeannie Fields, Jim Goodwin, Doug Grue, Kristin Harrison, Jane Ingalls, Doug Ingoldsby, Peter Jay, Michael Kaplan, Joan Matyas, Alice Moore, Darlene Mumm, Ron Ogulnick, Peter Oldfield, Peggy Painton, Mike Perna, Peg Pinard, Roger Pugliese, Mark Rasmussen, Gary Robinson, Bobbie Rose, Elsie Rubin, Kevin Schultz, Carl Scott, Barney Sofro, Tim Spiegel, Alynne Wilkinson, Marjorie Yasueda, and Howard Zelefsky.

Rhonda Spiegel, vice president of St. Francis Medical Center in Santa Barbara, and surely the best Two executive that ever was, has been the guardian angel of this book. Much thanks to St. Francis's president, Ron Biscaro, and CFO, Dave Glyer, for making me so welcome and to the department heads who sat for interviews: Cathy Arnold, Robyn Basiago, Patrick Connor, Michael Cruse, Tom Fisher, Ed Jones, Melody O'Shock, Andrea Portner, and Leslie Willingham. And special kudos to Julie Smith who made it all happen with grace and style.

Some great friends read the manuscript and had invaluable comments: Michael Abrahams, Louise Cann, Darlene Chandler, Karen Donahue, Carl Elkins, Steve Levitt, and Susan White. My Enneagram colleagues were very helpful: Mona Coates, Robert Evans, Susan Forster, Michelle Indiana, Dale Knutsen, Sandhya McCracken, Mary Mortz, John Richards, Maggie Saucier, Linda Trudeau, and Stuart Sovatsky. The magnificent Johanna Putnoi has been my Enneagram co-conspirator, and I'm much indebted to our ongoing conversation. No one has been more central in my thinking about Enneagram theory than my friends David Rapkin and Monica Leith. Thanks.

At Strategic Decisions Group, thanks for the time and encouragement from Steve Barreger, Don Creswell, Sam Holtzman, Bruce Judd, Konrad Knell, Joyce Mattea, Carl Spetzer, Leitha Spetzer, and Yesh Subramanian.

Thanks to the wonderful Enneagram gang in the Iowa heartland: Joni Baker, Ann Chase, Marianne Fons, Ernestine Griswold, Kristie Hirschman, Myron Hirschman, Peggy Huppert, and Cordell Svengalis. And special thanks to Jan Arkeny, who teaches the Enneagram course at the University of Iowa. Thanks to the core group in San Diego: Tracy Carr, Tracy Lenda, David Riley, Alice Rogow, Sue Volkman, and, at the center, Patrick Fagenstrom.

Betsy Amster, my literary and publishing high shaman, offered much essential sage wisdom. At HarperCollins, John Loudon and Karen Levine could not have been more engaged, encouraging, and committed to this project. Mimi Kusch managed the production of this book with extraordinary elegance and panache. They magically made what needed to happen, happen. Judith Searle and Garrett Soden were assiduous line editors. Dr. Rose McDermott was an amazing researcher.

Anyone who works with the Enneagram owes a substantial score to the extraordinary ideas of Oscar Ichazo. I thank him for our excellent discussions. (I don't pretend to represent Oscar's complex ideas herein, and I refer interested readers to his original works.) Claudio Naranjo's scholarly exposition of the nine types in light of modern personology has been a beacon for all.

I thank my stellar, savvy literary agents, Angela Miller and Betsy Amster, whose ceaseless enthusiasm and encouragement made the writing and publishing of this book great fun.

For seminar and consulting information, contact:

Michael J. Goldberg
Goldberg Consulting
32 West Anapamu Street
Santa Barbara, CA 93101
(310) 288–1114
e-mail: enneawork@aol.com